IMAGES
of America

ALAMEDA COUNTY FAIR

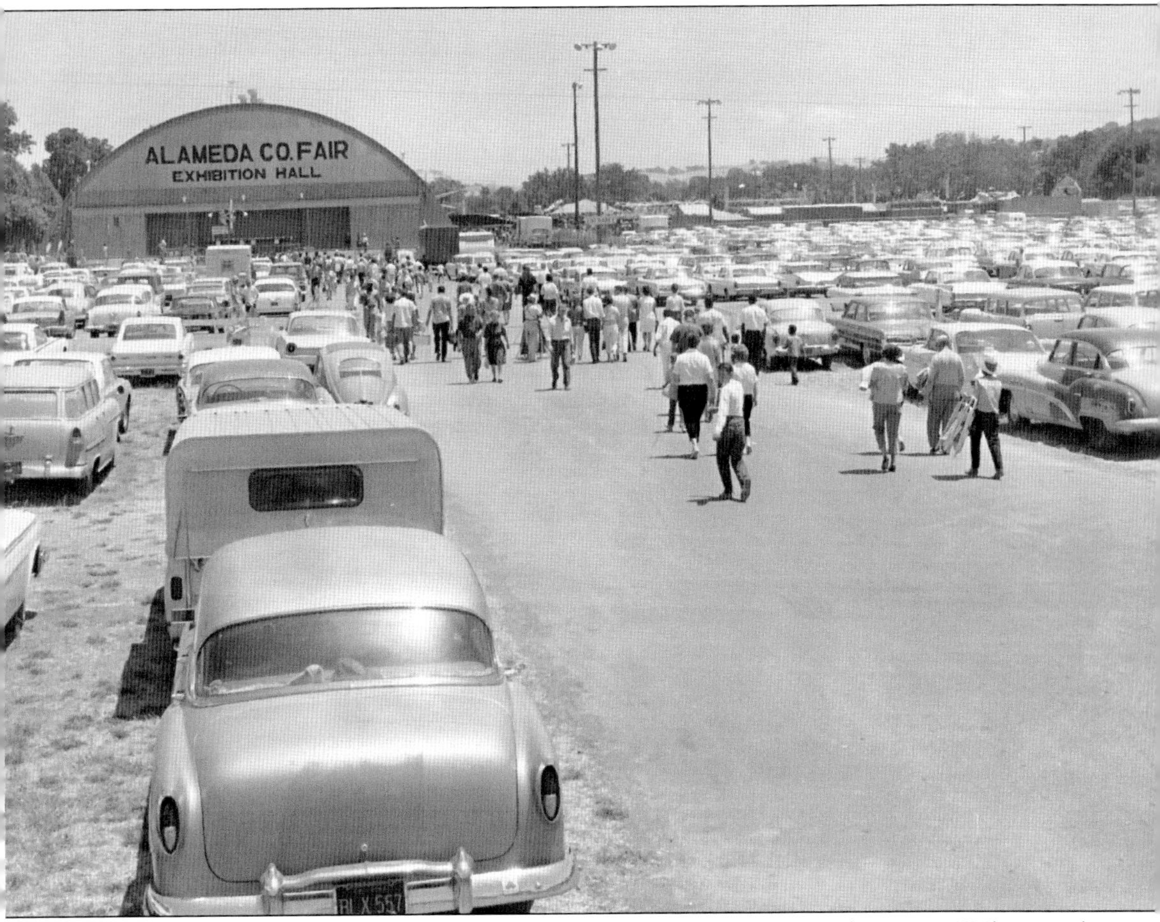

In 1948, Pleasanton mayor Earl Trimingham made the following proclamation: "Whereas, the Alameda County Agricultural Fair Association has designated one day during its 1948 county fair as Pleasanton and Livermore Day; and Whereas, the holding of the Alameda County Fair in the town of Pleasanton is of particular benefit to the town and gives it much favorable publicity, and is deserving of the support and cooperation of the community; Now, therefore, as Mayor of the town of Pleasanton, and pursuant to the authorization and by the direction of the council of the town of Pleasanton, I do hereby proclaim Thursday, July 15, 1948, as a day on which the town should participate to the fullest extent in the Alameda County Fair, and to that end I request that on that day all places of business in the town close between the hours of 12 noon and 6 p.m." (Courtesy of Alameda County Fair.)

On the Cover: This 1962 parade float celebrates Alameda County Fair's 50th anniversary and features the Maid of Alameda County and her court. Pictured from left to right are Karen (Kamp) MacDonough, Linda Haskell, Sue Hannsman, Carolyn Wing, and queen Sandy Black. (Courtesy of Alameda County Fair.)

IMAGES
of America

ALAMEDA COUNTY FAIR

Victoria Christian

ARCADIA
PUBLISHING

ISBN 978-0-7385-8193-4

Published by Arcadia Publishing
Charleston, South Carolina

Printed in the United States of America

Library of Congress Control Number: 2010934472

For all general information, please contact Arcadia Publishing:
Telephone 843-853-2070
Fax 843-853-0044
E-mail sales@arcadiapublishing.com
For customer service and orders:
Toll-Free 1-888-313-2665

Visit us on the Internet at www.arcadiapublishing.com

To my parents, Joyce and Ario Ysit, and to my daughter,
Jessica Christian, who will always be my inspiration

Contents

ACKNOWLEDGMENTS

As those early settlers who founded the first Alameda County Agricultural Fair Association worked hard to provide a safe and wholesome place for residents to enjoy a day of fun, the current leaders strive to maintain the fair's historical significance and are committed to making the fair one of the best in the state. To the Alameda County Fair Board of Directors, who effortlessly volunteer their time and talent, I give thanks. Without you and those who served before you, the fair would not be the gem that it is today. I would also like to thank Rick Pickering, chief executive officer; April Mitchell, marketing manager; Peter Bailey, former fair manager; Bonnie Bruton; Katheren Morris; Ken MacLennan, curator at Museum on Main; Bob and Pat Lane for their wonderful book *Celebrating Family Fun at the County Fair*; and my many friends and family for being so supportive and patient with me while I was working on this book. All of the photographs presented in this book are courtesy of the Alameda County Agricultural Fair Association's archives unless otherwise noted.

INTRODUCTION

In 1839, California governor Juan Alvarado allocated to the four children of Jose Bernal and Maria Sanchez a land grant of Rancho el Valle de San Jose, which is located 40 miles east of San Francisco. Early Spanish settlers were known for their horsemanship, and the Bernals enthusiastically embraced the sport of horse racing. The family built the state's first racetrack just east of their Pleasanton adobe in 1860.

Meanwhile, a board meeting was held in San Leandro, the former county seat, to form an agricultural society on July 24, 1858. Held in Oakland in June 1859, the fair offered horse racing, livestock and farm equipment, and flower, fruit, and vegetable exhibits. The fair was held in Oakland semiannually until the event was moved to Hayward in 1866.

After changing ownership several times, Canadian businessman Rodney G. Mackenzie purchased the racetrack in 1911 and offered the surrounding property to Alameda County on the condition that an annual county fair be held. The first meeting of the Alameda County Fair Association was held in a Pleasanton warehouse on June 29, 1912. Fifteen officers were elected from the towns of Fremont, Livermore, Pleasanton, Hayward, Dublin, and San Ramon.

The fair was held sporadically over the years, and in 1939, the first modern fair was held. It included three days of horse racing and 360 stabled horses, a carnival with four rides and 20 games, a temporary racing grandstand that could hold 250 patrons, and vaudeville performances between races. After a successful second start of the Alameda County Fair, board members agreed to continue holding the fair annually, though the fair was forced to be cancelled from 1942 to 1944 due to World War II. Horse racing–related activities continued during the war.

The business leaders who revived the fair in 1939 convinced Alameda County to purchase the land on which the fair resided for $40,000 from the fair trust fund, and under the supervision of the county board of supervisors, a 16-day fair was held in October 1945.

The future of the Alameda County Fair looks bright. Attendance grows every year, buildings are upgraded, improvements are made, and horse racing continues to be successful. In fact, the fair recently celebrated its 150th year of horse racing and boasts being the oldest continuous racing venue in the state.

The fair attracts residents from all over the county and beyond. Summer vacations are planned around fair time, and parents bring their children (and grandchildren) year after year. Memories are made and traditions are kept as the fair begins to celebrate its 100th anniversary in 2012.

The Alameda County Agricultural Fair Association's mission statement is "to assure the long-term viability of the Alameda County Fairgrounds, present an exceptional Annual Fair which celebrates the heritage and diversity of Alameda County, and provide year-round opportunities for facility usage."

One

History in the Making

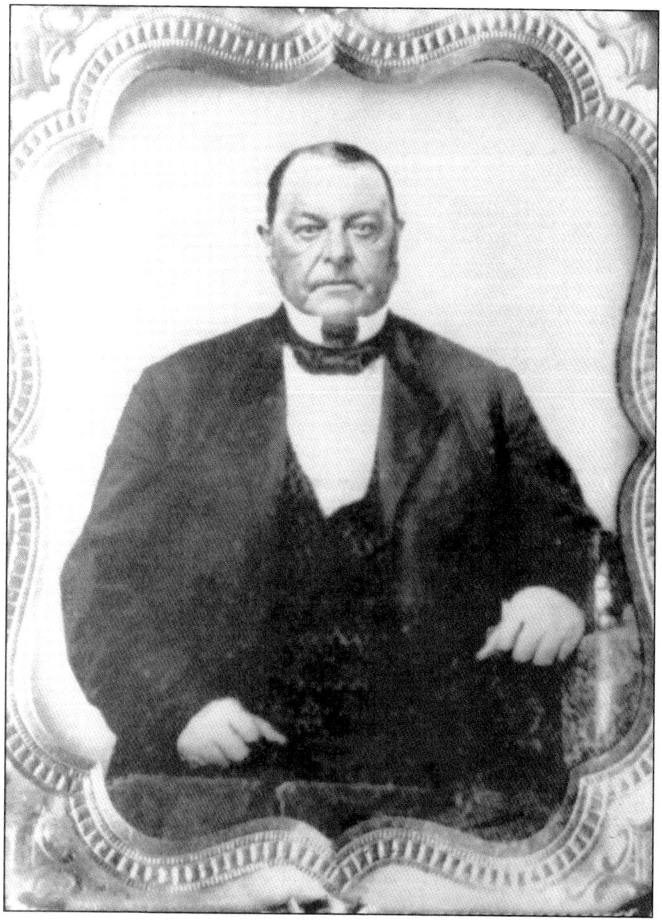

Jose Bernal and Maria Sanchez Bernal's eldest son, Augustin Bernal (pictured), was enlisted in the San Francisco Company of the Spanish military when he discovered Pleasanton, then known as Alisal. Bernal resigned from the military, settled in San Jose, and built his Foothill Road adobe home in 1848 before moving his large family to Pleasanton in 1850. Augustin's son Frederick managed the family racetrack after his father's death. (Courtesy of Amador Livermore Valley Historical Society.)

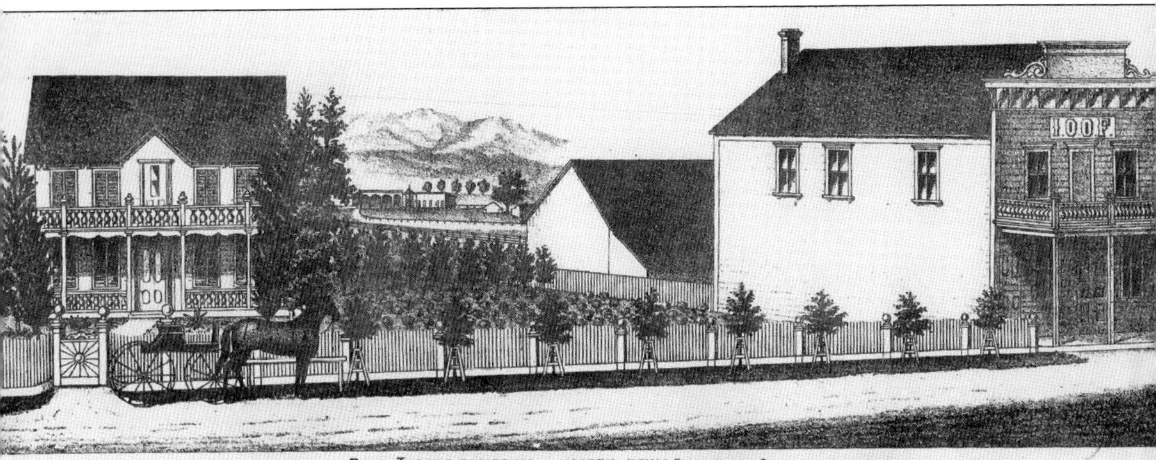

RACE-TRACK & RESIDENCE OF JOSEPH NEVIS, PLEASANTON, CALIFORNIA.

Augustin Bernal's widow, Maria Bernal, married Joseph Nevis, who purchased the track from Bernal's sons in 1876. He then sold the track to Australian businessman Monroe Salisbury for $25,000 in 1883. Salisbury successfully made the track famous for its excellent horse training facility, and by 1898, the track, now referred to as Pleasanton Stock Farm, was drawing large crowds. The track was subsequently sold to Pleasanton businessmen Tom Keating and Lew Crellin, who then sold it to Tom Ronan, who in turn sold the track to Oregon lumberman Henry Armstrong. Armstrong then sold it to Ferdinand Reese. (Courtesy of Thompson and West Atlas.)

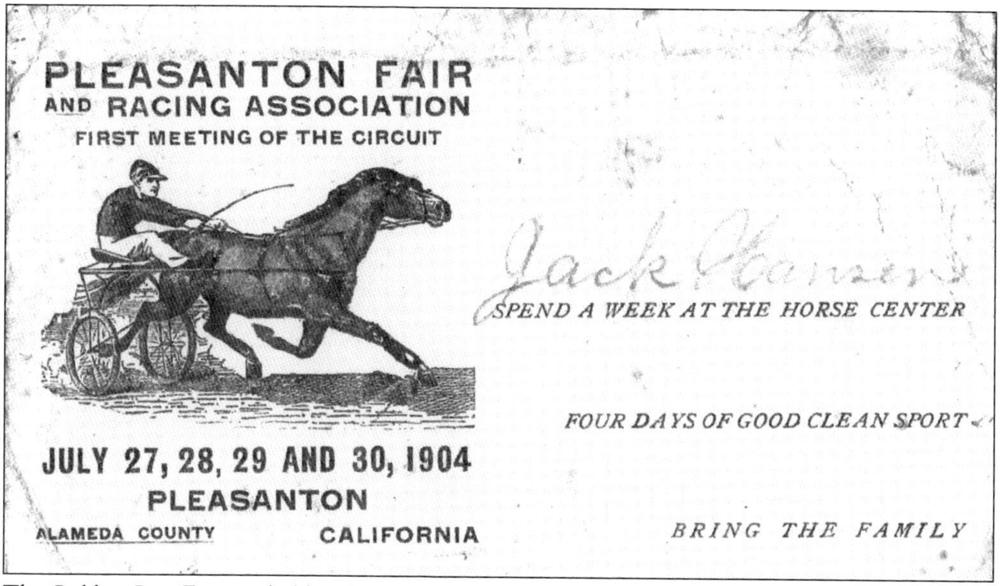

The Golden Gate Fair was held at the track site in Pleasanton from August 26, 1902, through August 30, 1902, and the Pleasanton Fair and Racing Association's races were held July 27–30, 1904, at the track and on nearby Main Street. (Courtesy of Amador Livermore Valley Historical Society.)

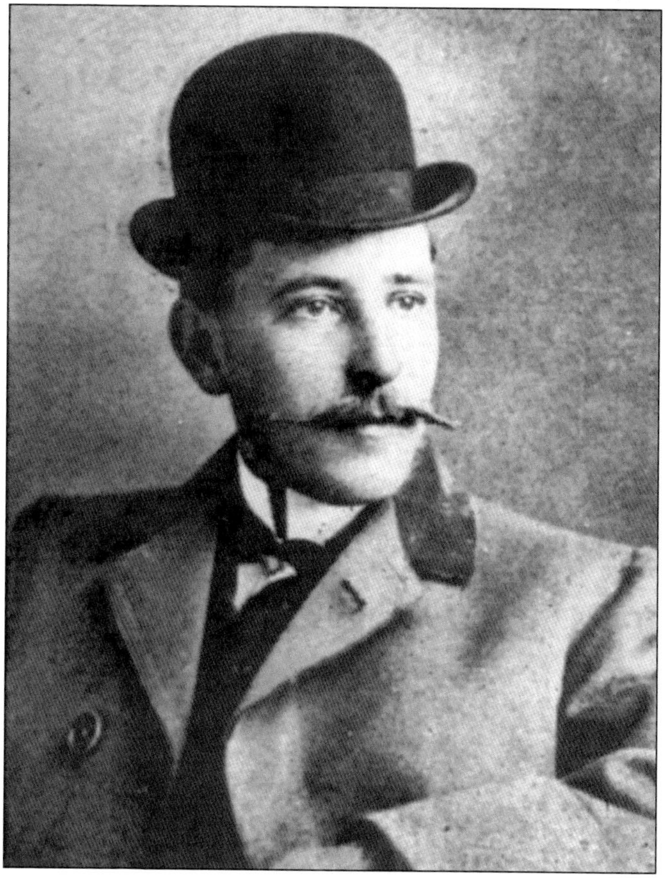

A corporation led by H.F. Anderson purchased the track in the early 1900s. The name of the facility was changed to the Pleasanton Training Track Association, and 200 new horse stalls were built. Anderson also made the track into the regulation one-mile distance and improved the track so there was proper pitch at the turns. The track was finally getting recognized for its mild climate and perfect alluvial soil. (Courtesy of Amador Livermore Valley Historical Society.)

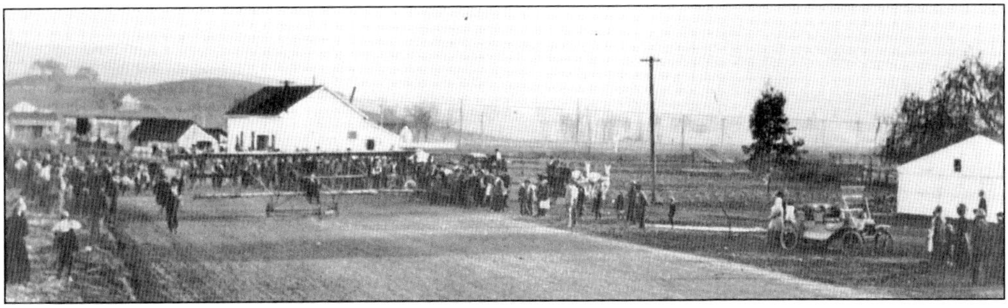

Canadian Rodney G. Mackenzie purchased the track in 1911. Mackenzie encouraged local businessmen to form a county fair on his property and offered financial assistance with a stipulation: as long as the fair continued, the association would own all the newly erected buildings, but if the fair ceased, the buildings would belong to Mackenzie. Horse racing took a small decline in popularity due to the invention of the automobile. Airplane and automobile trials were held in 1910, and motorcycle racing was held in 1912.

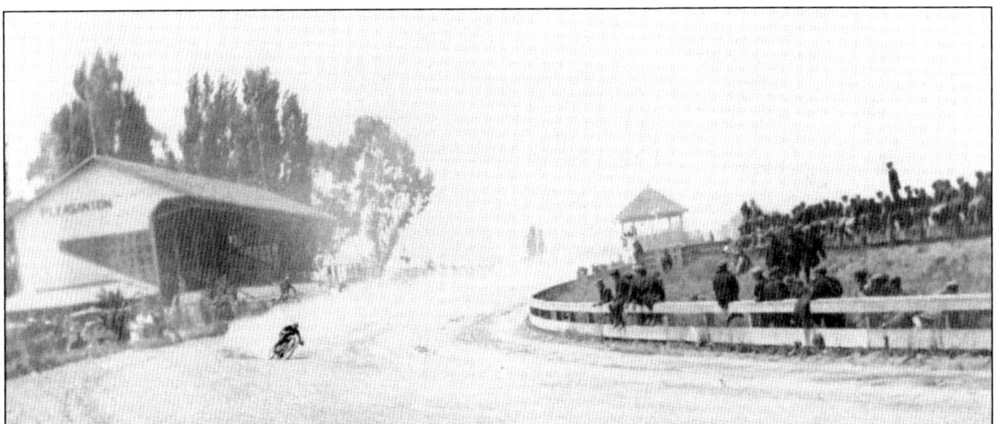

The Alameda County Fair Association first met in a warehouse owned by E.E. Hall on June 29, 1912. The association's officers were Pres. E.E Hall, Vice President I.B Parsons, Secretary T.H. Silver, and Treasurer H.P. Mohr. By August 1912, the fair's buildings were quickly sprouting up in anticipation of the October opening.

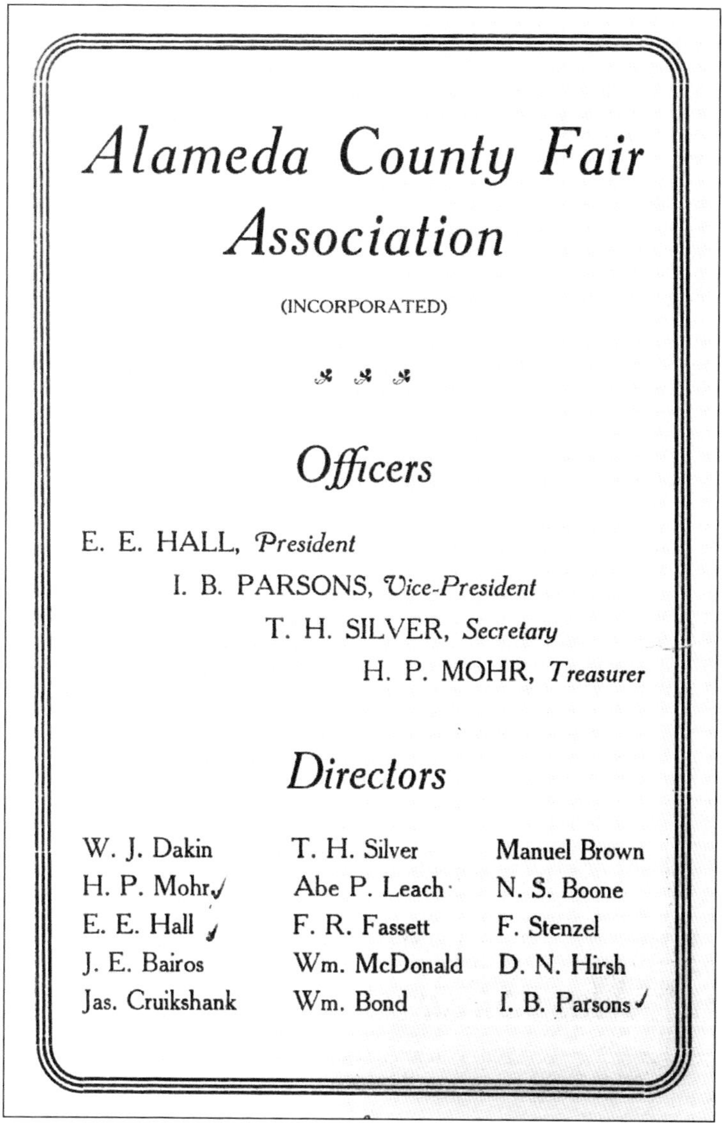

Alameda County Fair Association

(INCORPORATED)

Officers

E. E. HALL, *President*

I. B. PARSONS, *Vice-President*

T. H. SILVER, *Secretary*

H. P. MOHR, *Treasurer*

Directors

W. J. Dakin	T. H. Silver	Manuel Brown
H. P. Mohr	Abe P. Leach	N. S. Boone
E. E. Hall	F. R. Fassett	F. Stenzel
J. E. Bairos	Wm. McDonald	D. N. Hirsh
Jas. Cruikshank	Wm. Bond	I. B. Parsons

The main exhibition hall, built by contractor brothers Percy and Dan Madsen, was framed, and the cement floor was poured. Its octagon shape was 100 feet in diameter. Attached to the exhibit hall is the 80-foot poultry building. The early planning stages were secured by various committees focused on exhibitor prizes and awards.

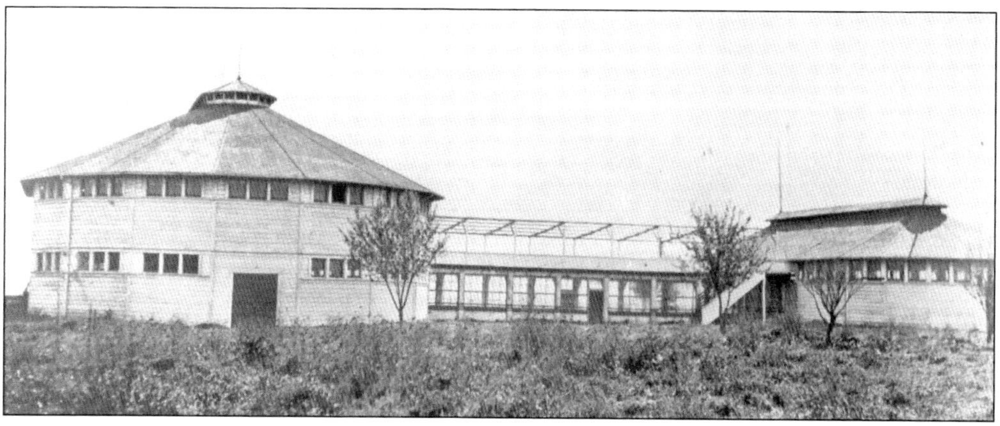

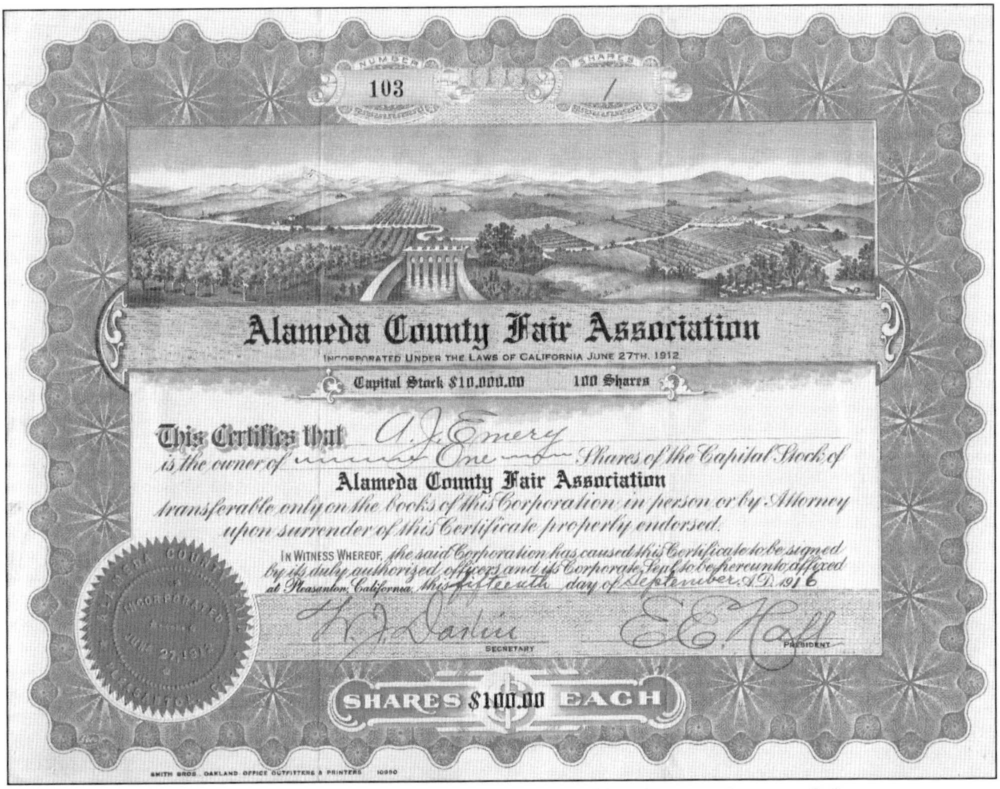

NUMBER 103 SHARES 1

Alameda County Fair Association

INCORPORATED UNDER THE LAWS OF CALIFORNIA JUNE 27TH. 1912

Capital Stock $10,000.00 100 Shares

This Certifies that A. J. Emery is the owner of One Shares of the Capital Stock of Alameda County Fair Association transferable only on the books of this Corporation in person or by Attorney upon surrender of this Certificate properly endorsed.

IN WITNESS WHEREOF, the said Corporation has caused this Certificate to be signed by its duly authorized officers and its Corporate Seal to be hereunto affixed at Pleasanton, California this fifteenth day of September A.D. 1916

SECRETARY PRESIDENT

SHARES $100.00 EACH

SMITH BROS. OAKLAND OFFICE OUTFITTERS & PRINTERS 10090

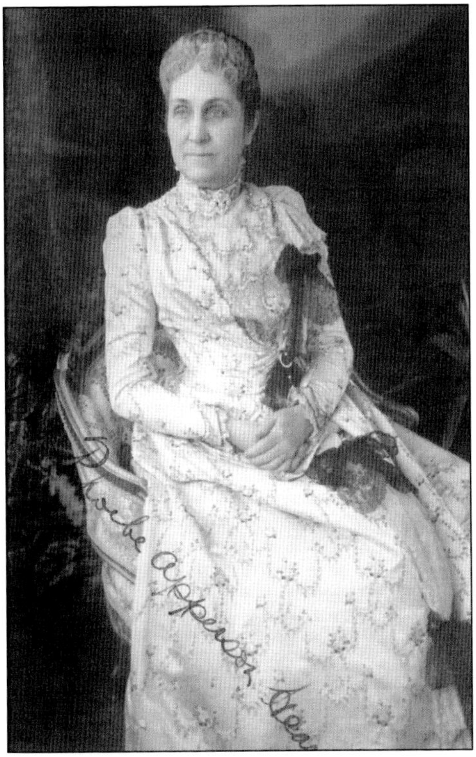

Stock sold at $100 a share and donations were accepted, but volunteers performed most of the work. No county or state funds were used to finance the fair. The fair's premium book stated, "We propose to make this one of the most popular fairs in California and we are paying higher premiums than almost any other fair in the State. We are providing for entertainment for every evening as well as harness races, running races, ball games and motorcycle racing."

Nearby resident Phoebe Apperson Hearst, mother of William Randolph Hearst, contributed by loaning plants and her gardeners. Advertisement for the fair consisted of pulling a wagon through the streets of larger cities a few days before the opening. Thousands of out-of-town visitors arrived twice daily by train and were greeted by bands playing music. The *Oakland Tribune* reported that the town of Pleasanton had been transformed: "The town has been fittingly decorated with flags and bunting for the occasion and presents a scene of unusual brilliance." (Courtesy of Amador Livermore Valley Historical Society.)

According to a newspaper article published on August 7, 1912, "The fair is one of the most important local undertakings of recent years in its possible beneficial effects upon our county. Its benefits, like other good things, will depend upon the enthusiasm with which each man and woman of Alameda County lends it his support."

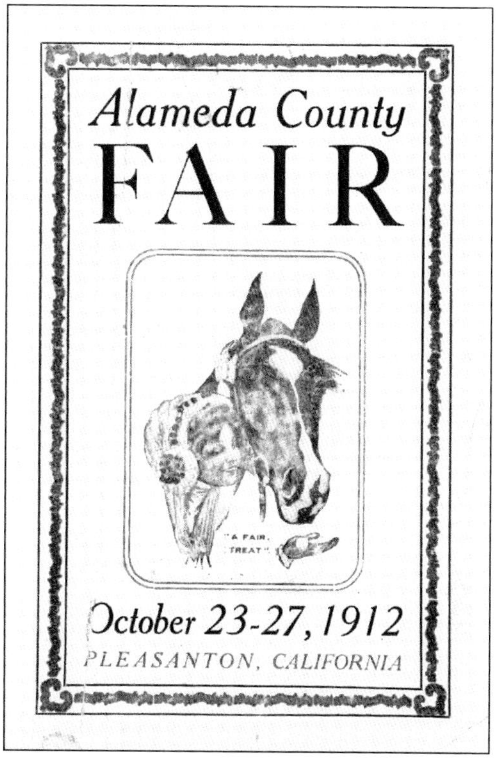

The very first Alameda County Fair opened on Wednesday, October 23, 1912, and ran through Sunday, October 27, 1912. Contests included a spelling bee, relay races, chariot races, bronco busting, donkey riding, and ball games. The fair's exhibits included a special women's department, which featured needlework, quilting, rug making, and baking.

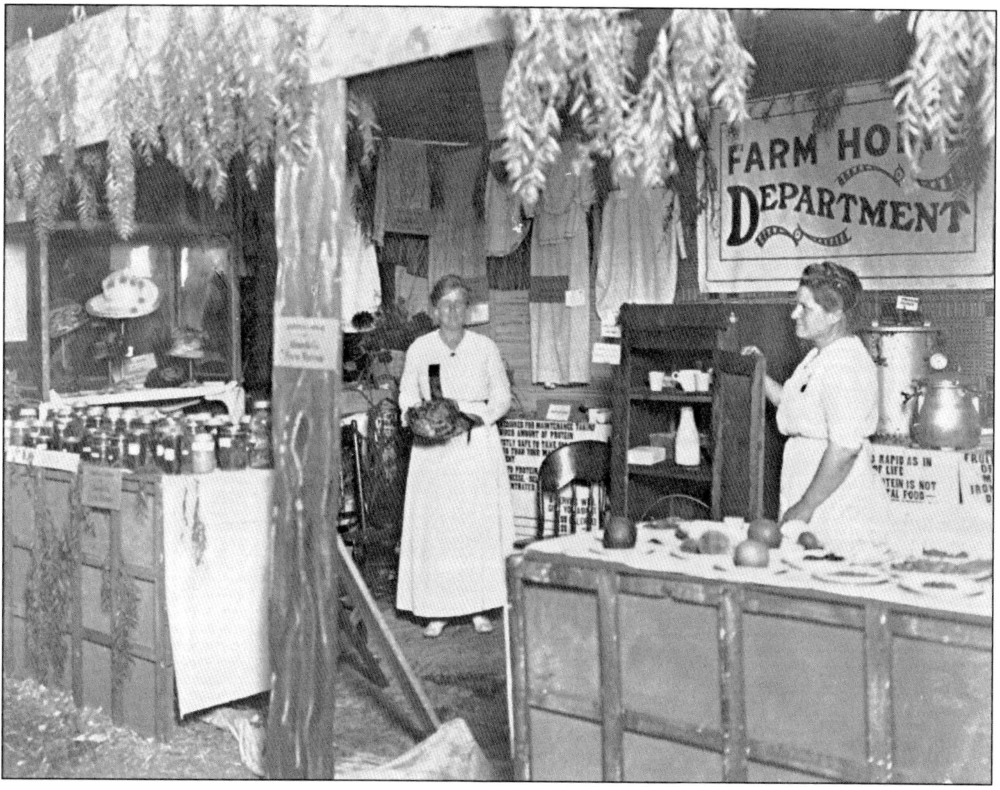

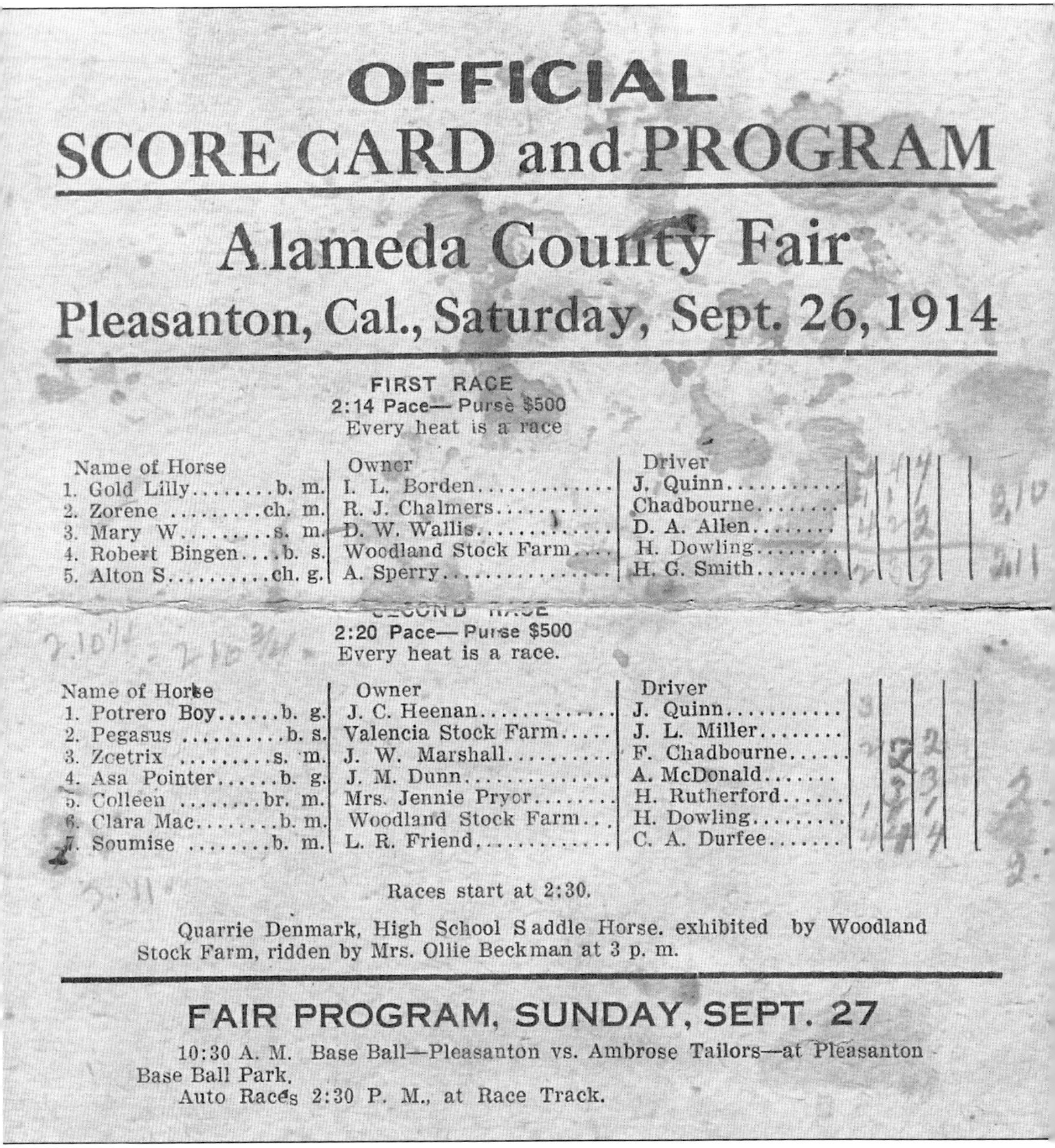

OFFICIAL
SCORE CARD and PROGRAM
Alameda County Fair
Pleasanton, Cal., Saturday, Sept. 26, 1914

FIRST RACE
2:14 Pace— Purse $500
Every heat is a race

Name of Horse	Owner	Driver
1. Gold Lilly........b. m.	I. L. Borden............	J. Quinn..........
2. Zorene ....ch. m.	R. J. Chalmers..........	Chadbourne........
3. Mary W.........s. m.	D. W. Wallis............	D. A. Allen........
4. Robert Bingen....b. s.	Woodland Stock Farm....	H. Dowling........
5. Alton S..........ch. g.	A. Sperry..............	H. G. Smith........

SECOND RACE
2:20 Pace— Purse $500
Every heat is a race.

Name of Horse	Owner	Driver
1. Potrero Boy......b. g.	J. C. Heenan............	J. Quinn..........
2. Pegasus ....b. s.	Valencia Stock Farm.....	J. L. Miller........
3. Zcetrix ....s. m.	J. W. Marshall..........	F. Chadbourne......
4. Asa Pointer......b. g.	J. M. Dunn..............	A. McDonald.......
5. Colleen ....br. m.	Mrs. Jennie Pryor........	H. Rutherford......
6. Clara Mac........b. m.	Woodland Stock Farm...	H. Dowling.........
7. Soumise ....b. m.	L. R. Friend............	C. A. Durfee.......

Races start at 2:30.

Quarrie Denmark, High School Saddle Horse, exhibited by Woodland Stock Farm, ridden by Mrs. Ollie Beckman at 3 p. m.

FAIR PROGRAM, SUNDAY, SEPT. 27

10:30 A. M. Base Ball—Pleasanton vs. Ambrose Tailors—at Pleasanton Base Ball Park.

Auto Races 2:30 P. M., at Race Track.

The fair of 1914 proved to be a financial bust, and due to the 1915 Panama Pacific International Exposition being held nearby in San Francisco, it was decided that the next year's fair would be cancelled. The fair continued to be cancelled for several years due to World War I, and the track was leased to various persons for training purposes only. The grounds were neglected, and the grandstand burned down.

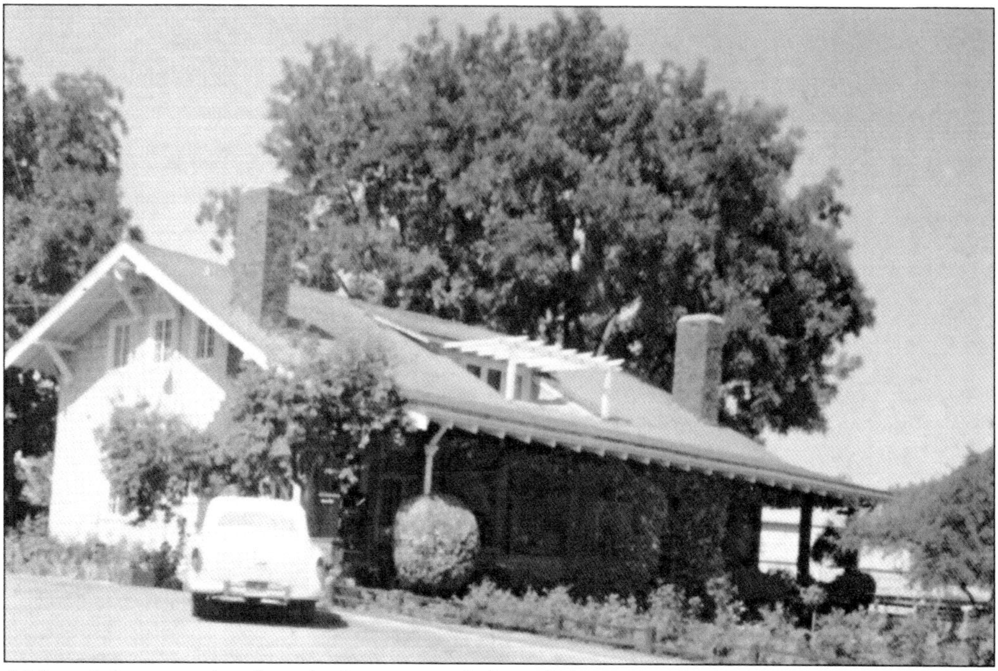

Although he never lived in the house, it is believed that it was built during Mackenzie's reign between 1911 and 1914. The California bungalow–style home was listed on the National Register of Historic Places in 1991. Several of Mackenzie's employees resided in the home until it was remodeled in 1939. The home's first floor was the location of the fair offices, and in 1941, the first fair manager, Wray Bergstrom, lived on the second floor. The fair's newly constructed administration building was built in 1967, thereby making room in the house for the Amador Valley Historical Society to use until it moved to a new location on Main Street in 1985. The historical home remained empty until renovations in 1990, when the building was used as special fair offices, the fair museum, and the office of Alameda County supervisor Ed Campbell. Presently, the home is primarily used as offices for Alameda County supervisor Scott Haggerty. Below is a current image of the home, which is located near the center of the fairgrounds.

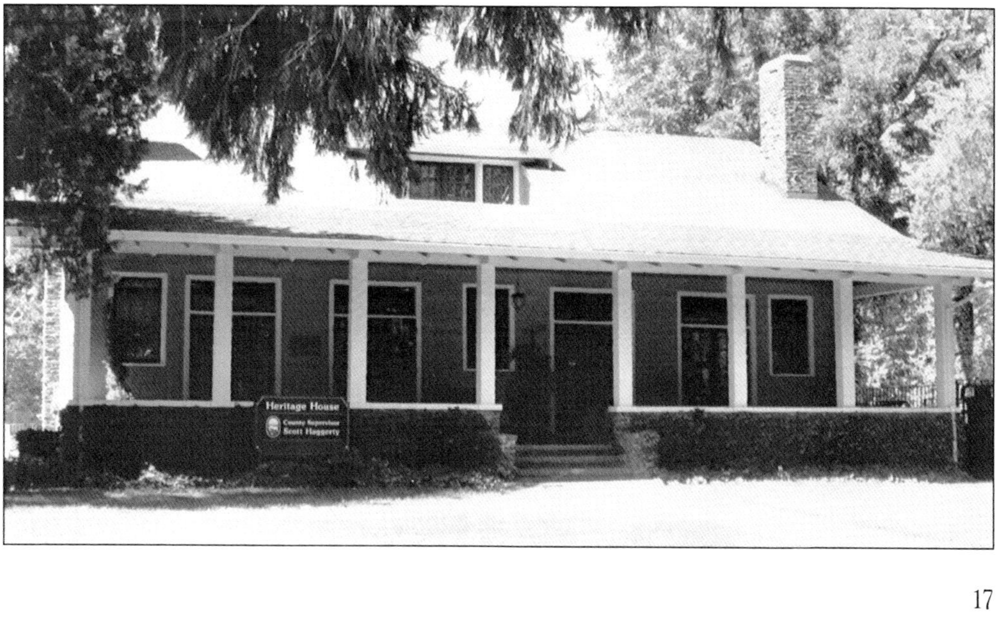

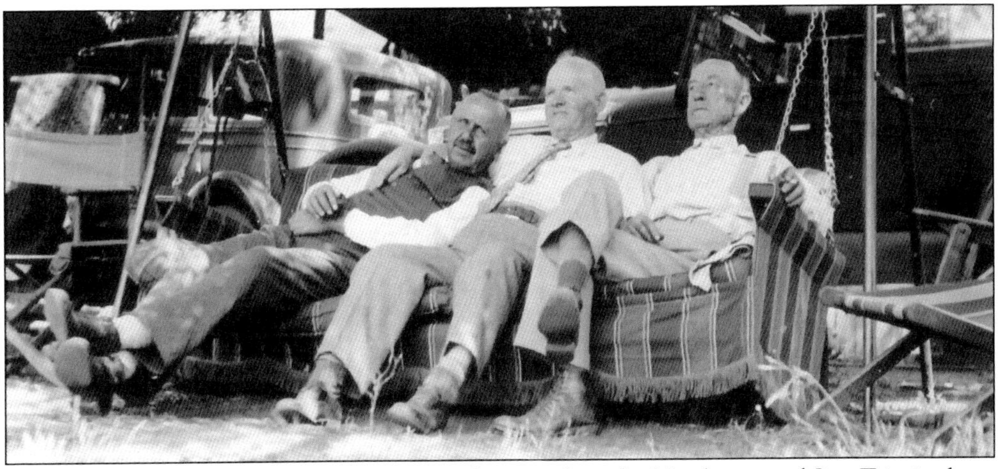

In 1936, Pleasanton businessmen Ernest Schween, Crawford Letham, and Jim Trimingham suggested reviving the fair to bring revenue to the town by using their own funds. In 1938, county supervisors approved funds for the fair, and the Alameda County Agriculture Fair Association was founded on February 25, 1939. There were 82 fair board members that year, and all of the employees at the fair were volunteers, except for the manager, who was paid a small salary. In the photograph above are, from left to right, Letham, Schween, and Crellin. Pictured below in 1956 are former fair board director Sam Whiting (left) and former fair secretary-manager James Trimingham. (Courtesy of Amador Livermore Valley Historical Society.)

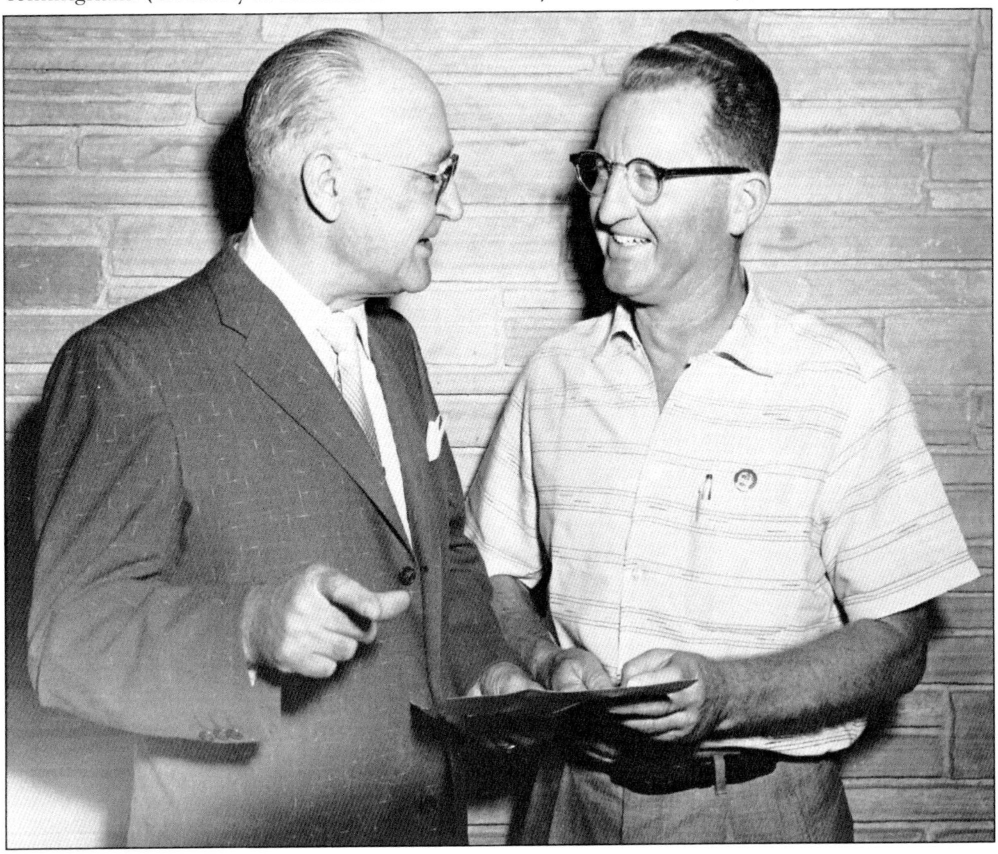

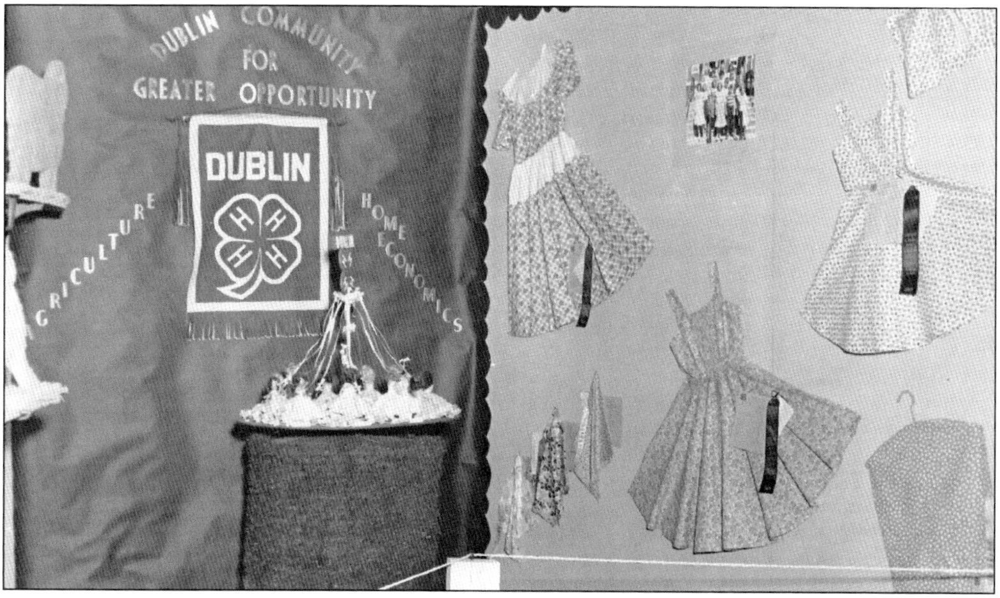

The 1939 fair had a few exhibits featuring homemaking, fruits, vegetables, farming equipment, and livestock.

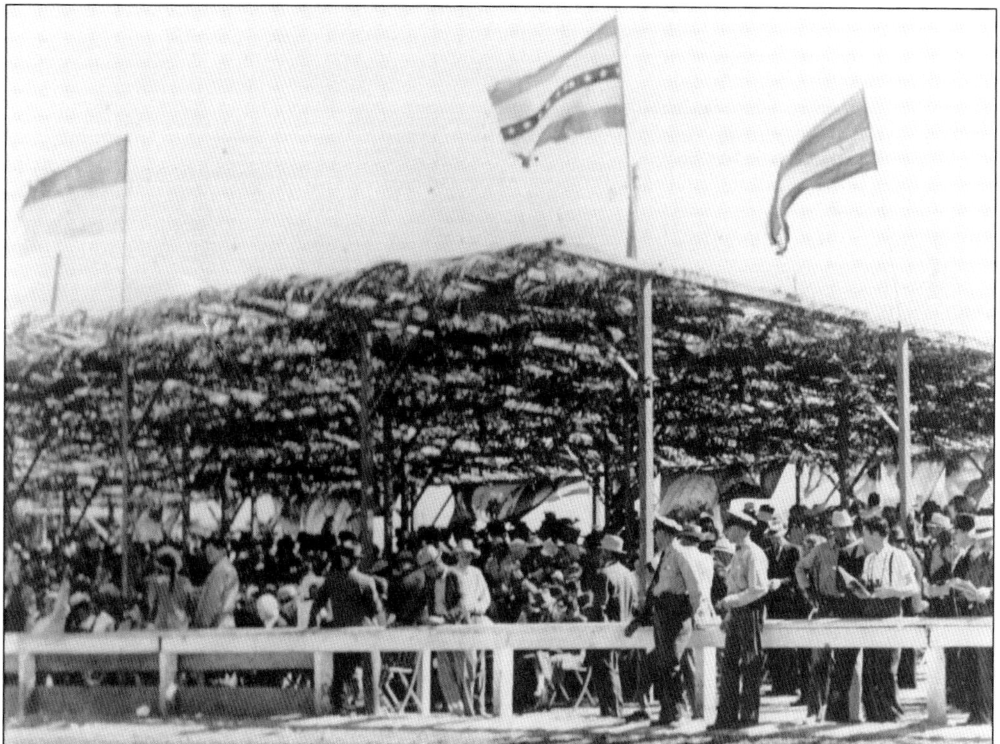

The fair only ran for four days, from August 10 to August 13, 1939, but netted a profit of $78. A temporary grandstand was constructed of donated lumber and palm fronds. The horse races were the main draw at the fair, which brought a pari-mutuel handle of $19,800.

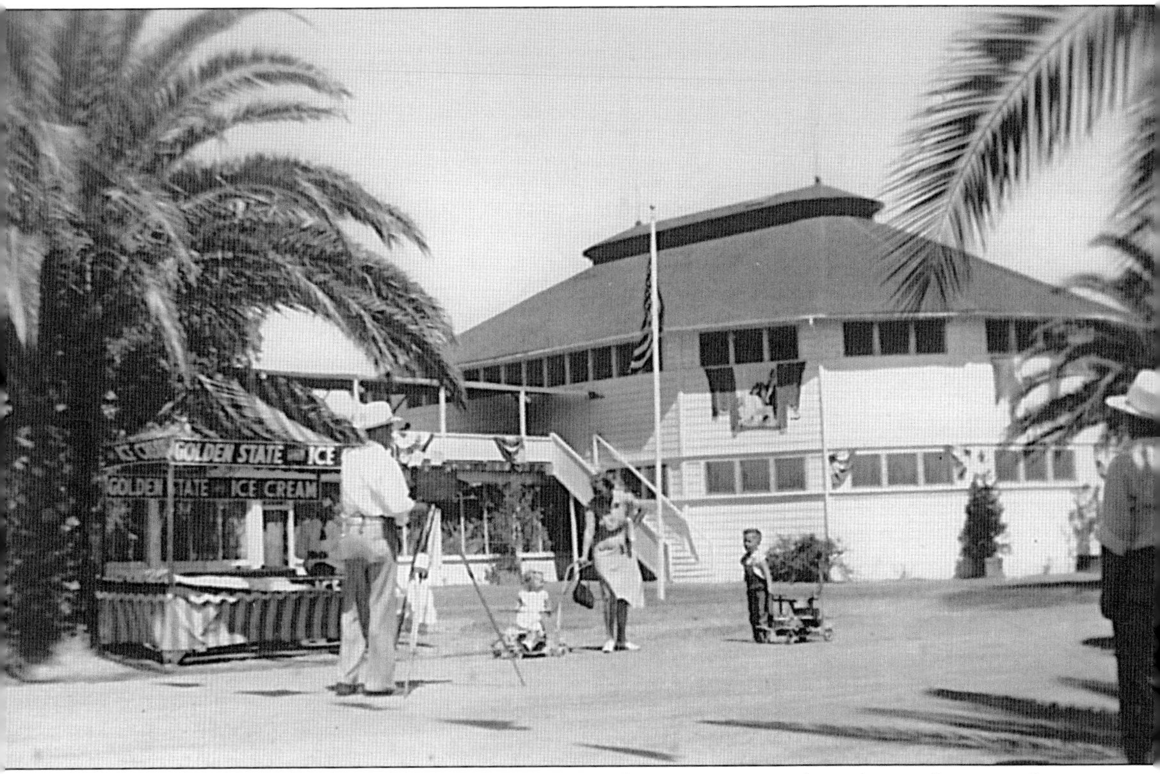

In 1939, the fair's stated purpose was "to promote and encourage agriculture, horticulture, mechanics, manufacturers, stock raising and general domestic industry; to advertise and give publicity to Alameda County as a desirable, prosperous and advantageous place in which to live and settle; to promote the general welfare of the people of Alameda County; and to hold annually, or at such other intervals or times as the members may designate, a county or agriculture fair for the purposes herein before mentioned." (Courtesy of Amador Livermore Valley Historical Society.)

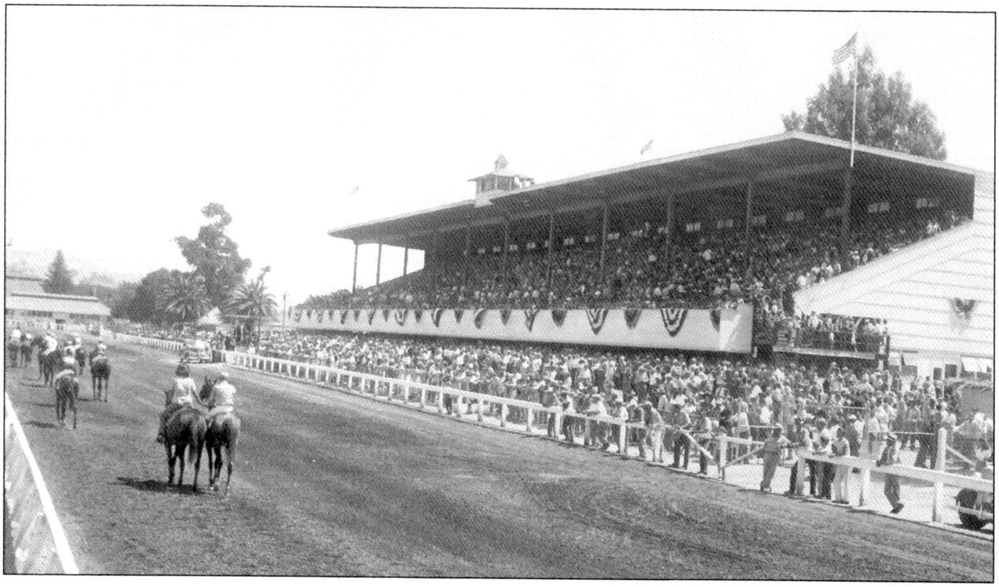

In 1941, the fair association worked with Alameda County to purchase 100 acres from Mackenzie's heirs, including the racetrack for $40,000. A new grandstand that held 5,000 was also built at a cost of $69,000. The 10-day fair in 1941 was regarded as the largest county fair in Northern California. It was this year that the movie *It Ain't Hay*, starring Abbott and Costello, was filmed on the fairgrounds. Unfortunately, the fair was cancelled in 1942 due to World War II.

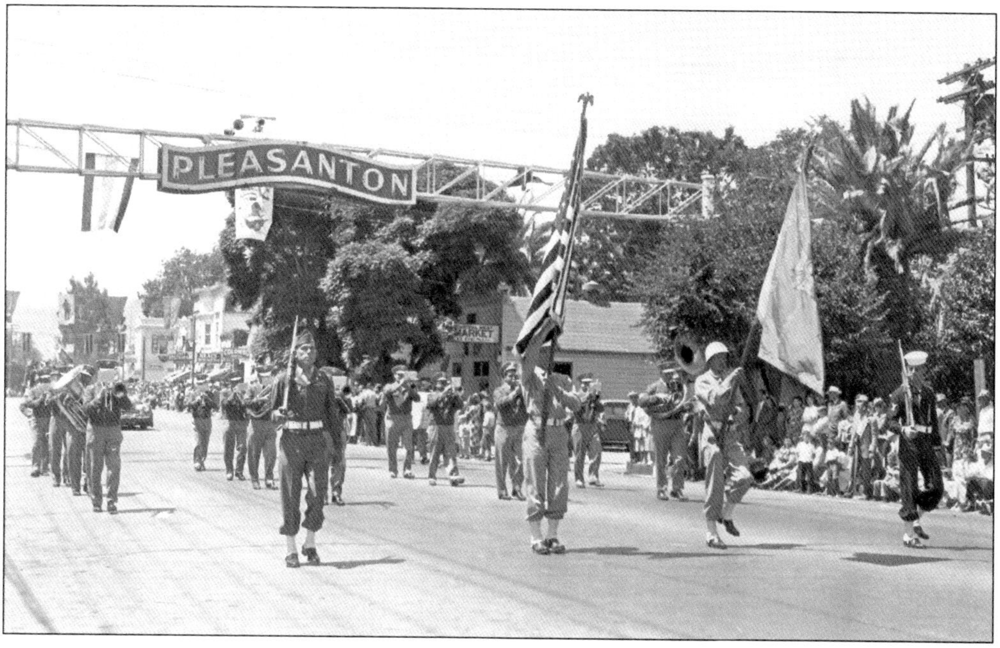

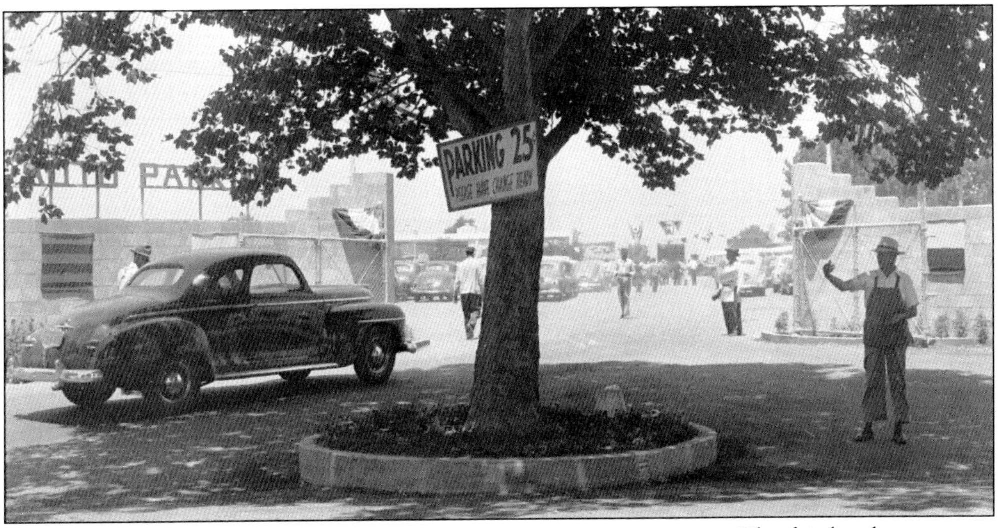

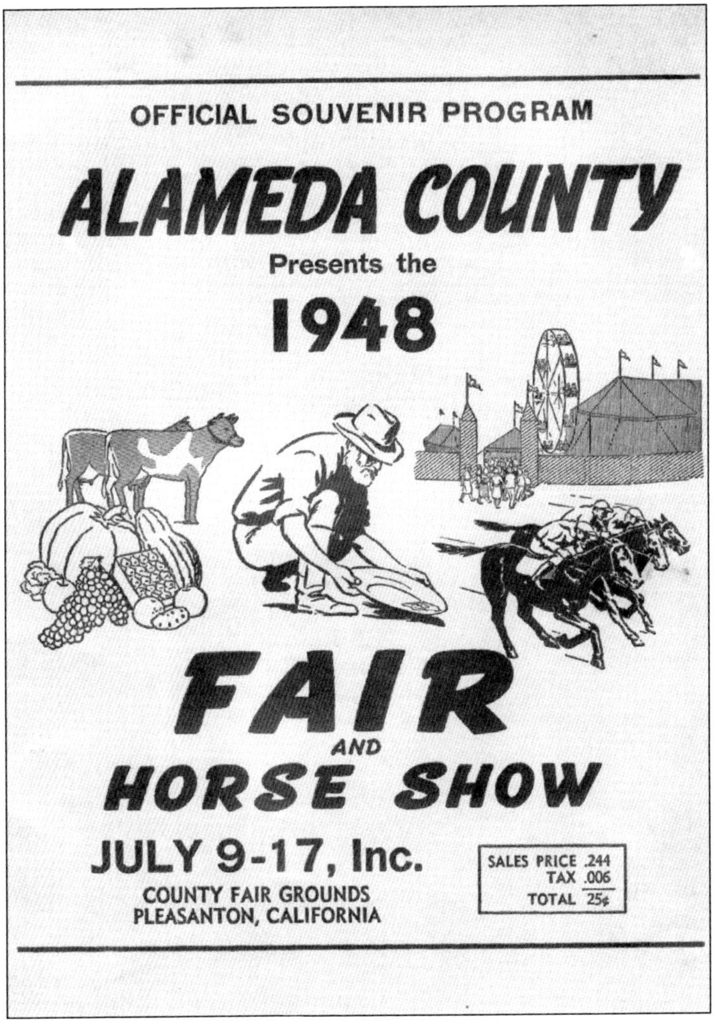

The fair has been running annually since 1945. That year during the October fair, there was no entrance fee, and the only cost besides a parking fee was grandstand admission. Also in 1945, the Jackson and Perkins Company donated 1,000 rosebushes.

Opening day on July 9, 1948, attracted more than 10,000 fairgoers. In 1948, Alameda County's population was 735,000, and the fair's total attendance was 133,000.

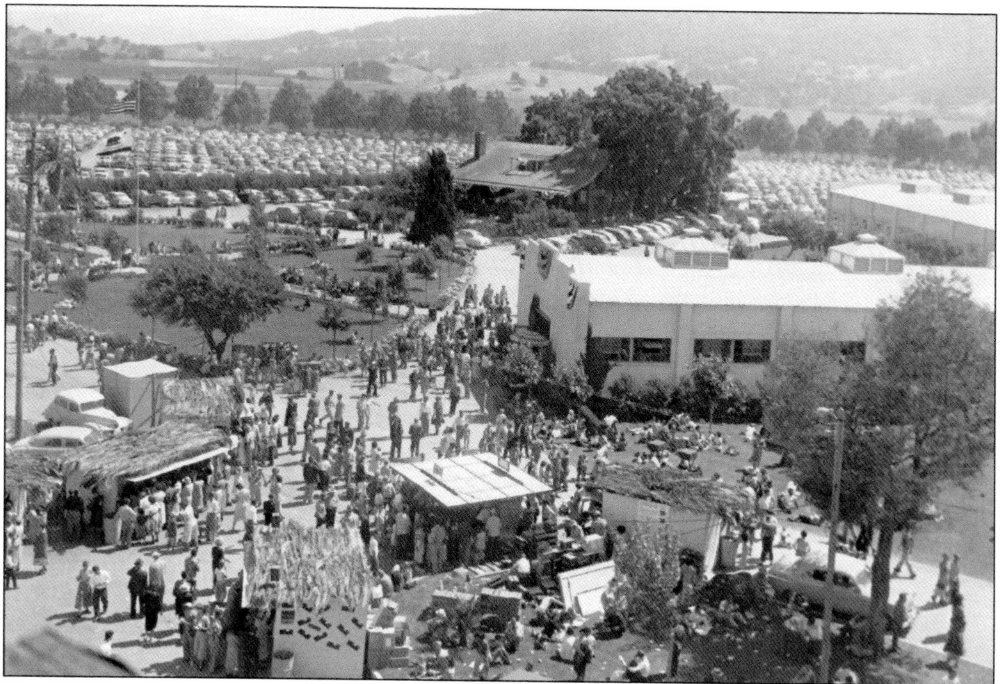

The nine-day fair in 1948 boasted a new, spacious exhibit building as well as harness and Thoroughbred racing. Fireworks featured in 1948 only cost $500. Daily events included harness racing, exhibit judging, amateur camera exhibits, a fashion show, the crowning of the Farm Bureau queen, and Navy Reserve aircraft maneuvers above the fairgrounds.

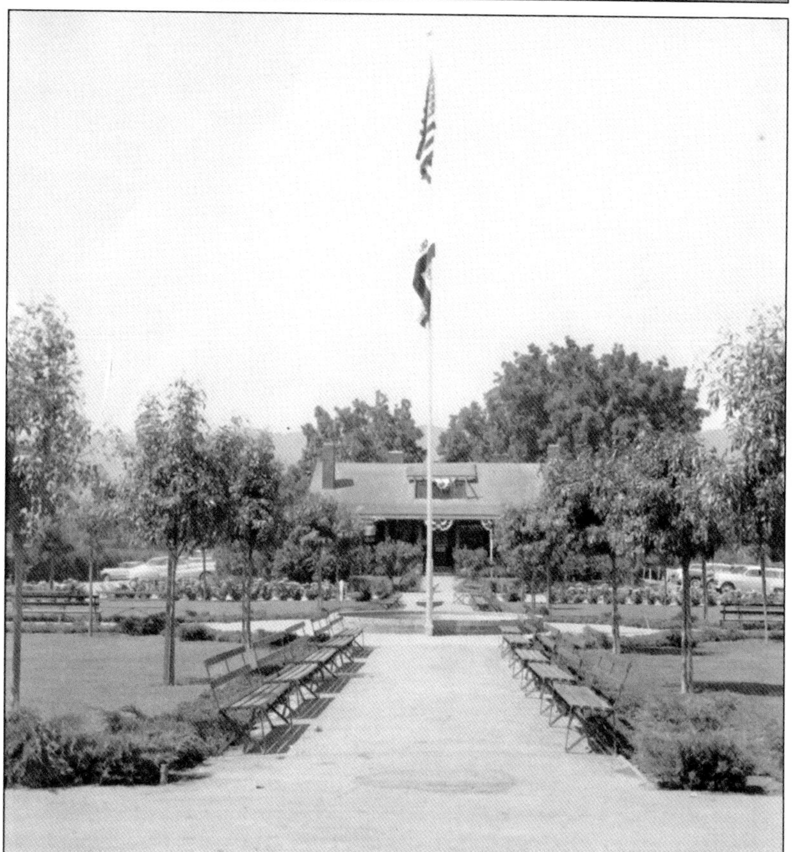

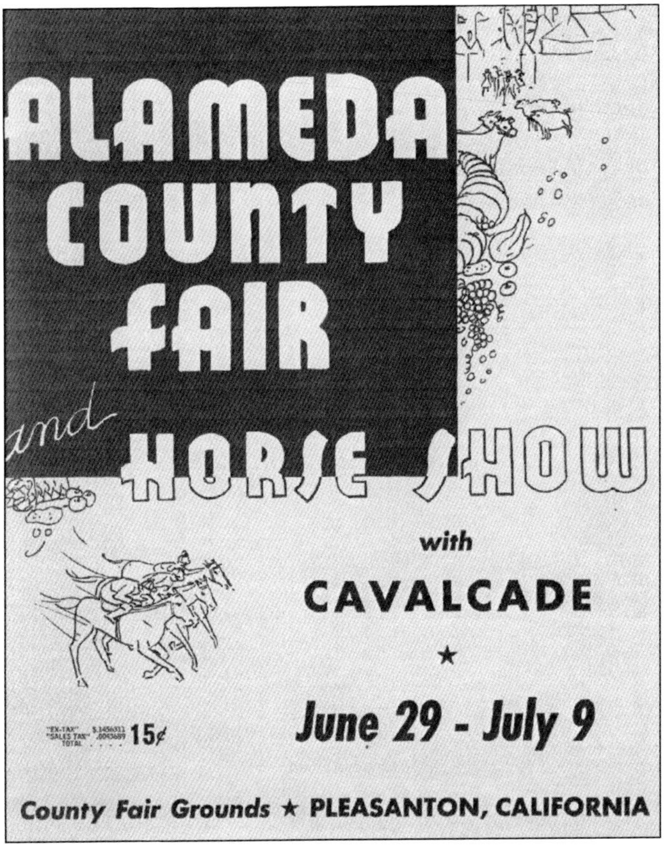

The 1949 Alameda County Fair and Horse Show featured several events during its 11-day run, including a parade, a beauty pageant, a horse show, four fireworks shows, and an evening cavalcade.

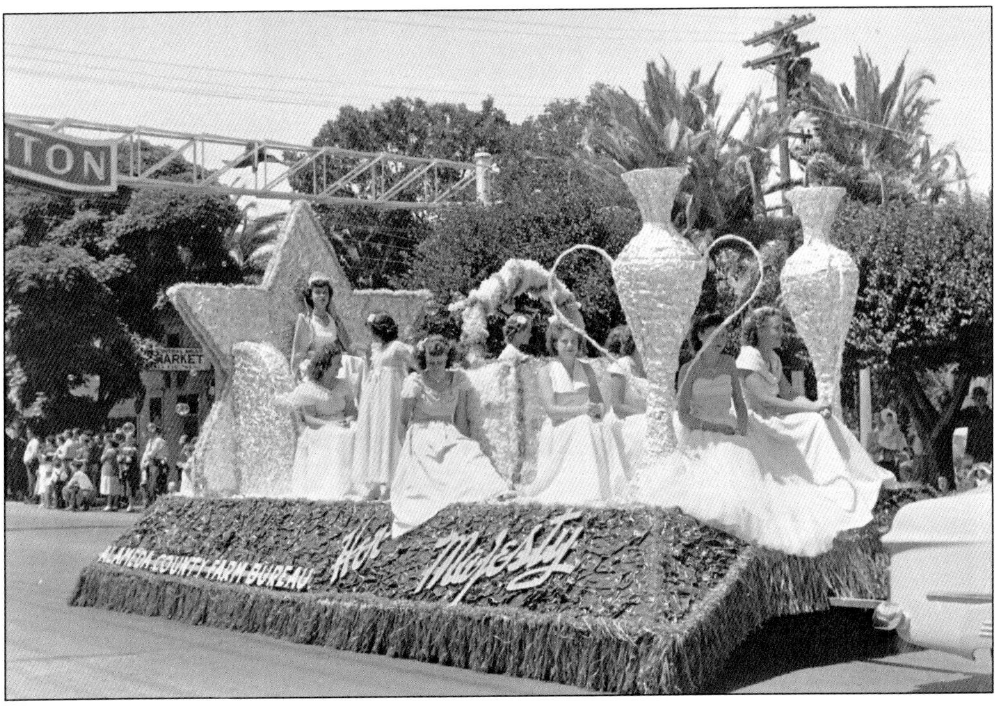

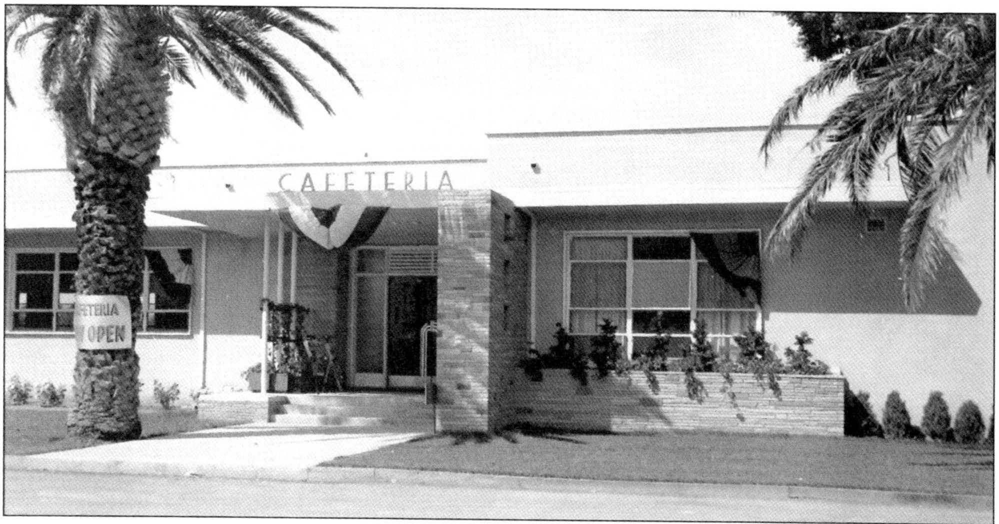

The new cafeteria building was constructed in 1952 for $127,500. New art exhibits were added, and more than 1,400 additional rosebushes were planted.

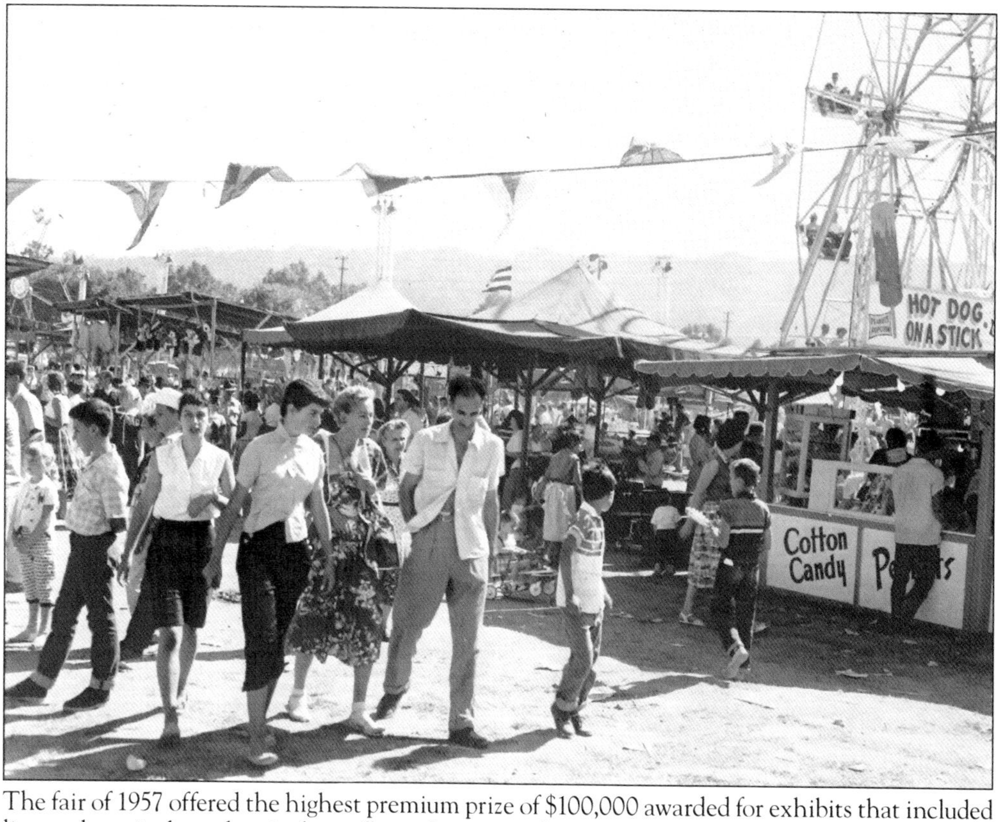

The fair of 1957 offered the highest premium prize of $100,000 awarded for exhibits that included livestock, agriculture, horticulture, floriculture, art, photography, wine, home economics, mining, mineral, poultry, FFA, and 4-H.

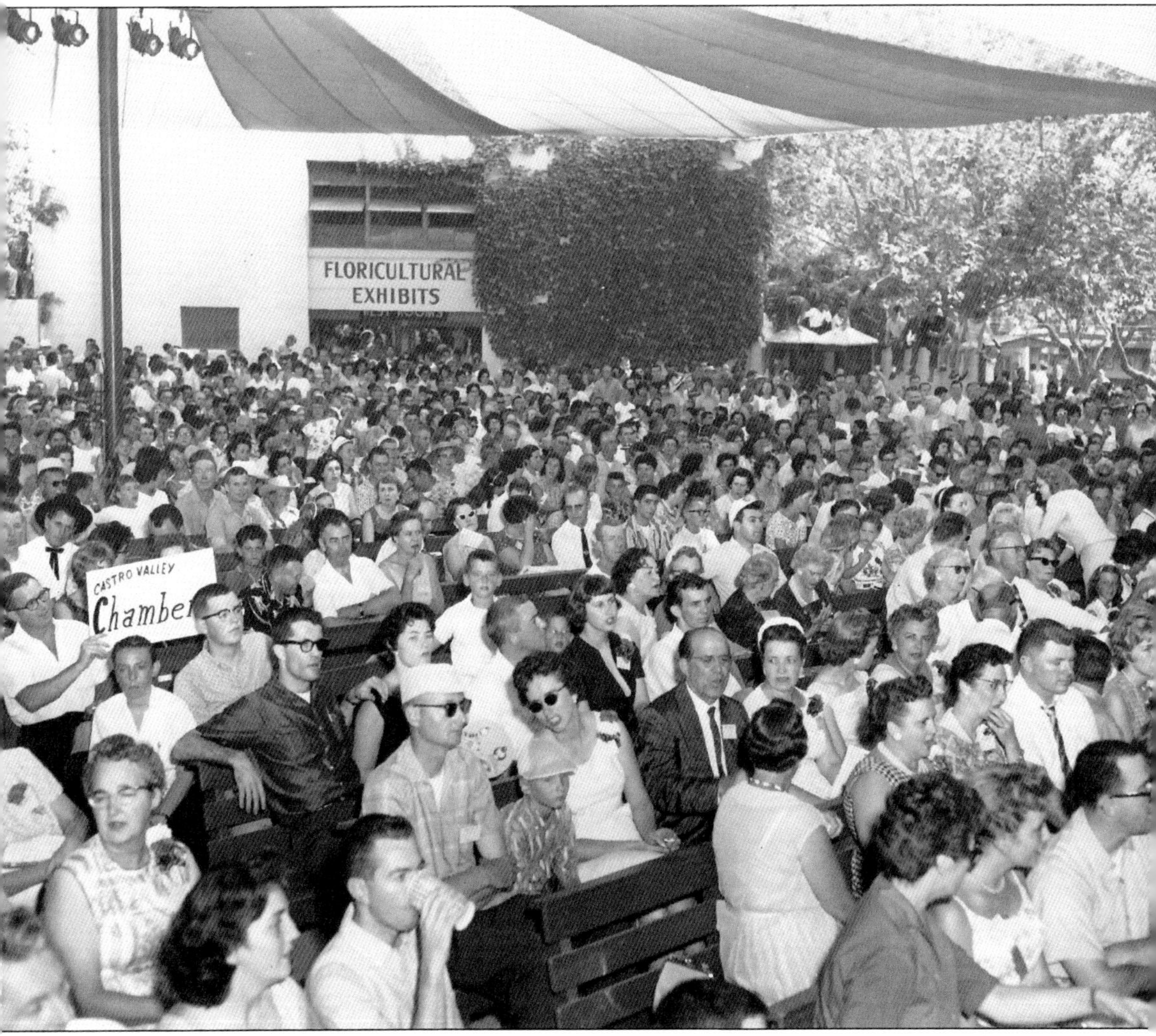

The fair proved profitable during the Golden Jubilee 50th Anniversary in 1962, when several records were set. The record pari-mutuel handle was up 9.3 percent, admission increased by 18,000 guests, and a record 4,000 pounds of hot dogs were consumed.

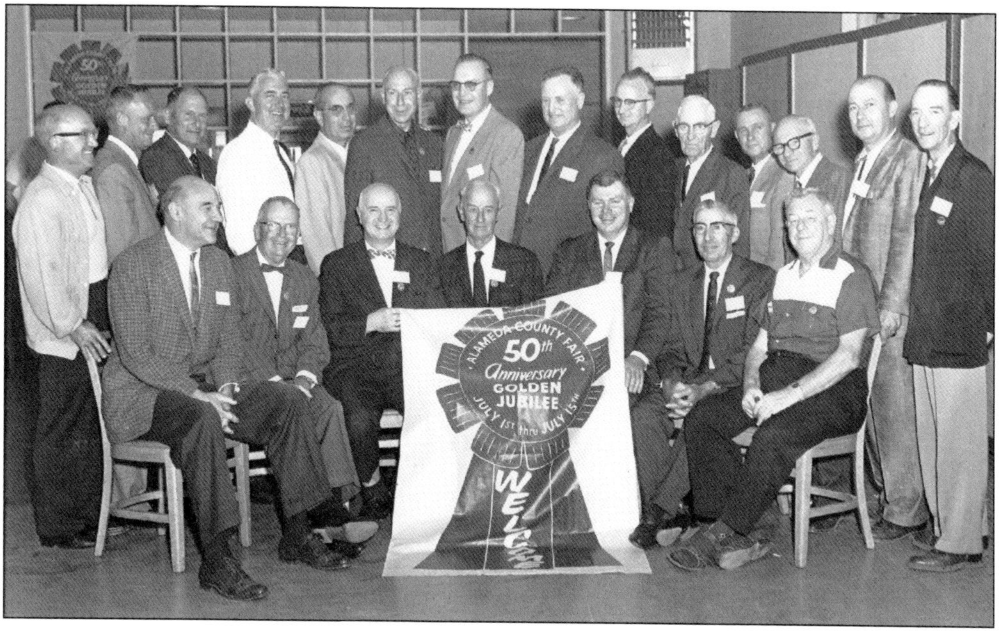

Pictured above is the board of directors celebrating the fair's Golden Jubilee 50th Anniversary in 1962, and below is the ceremonial birthday cake cutting.

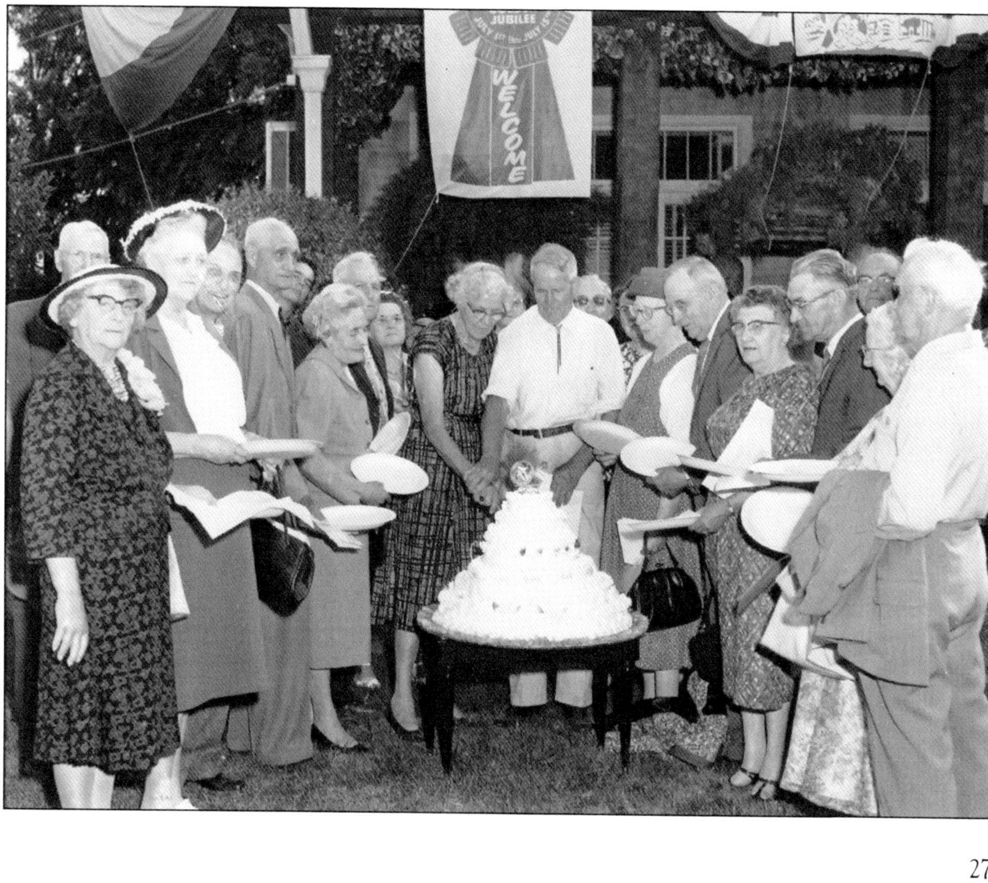

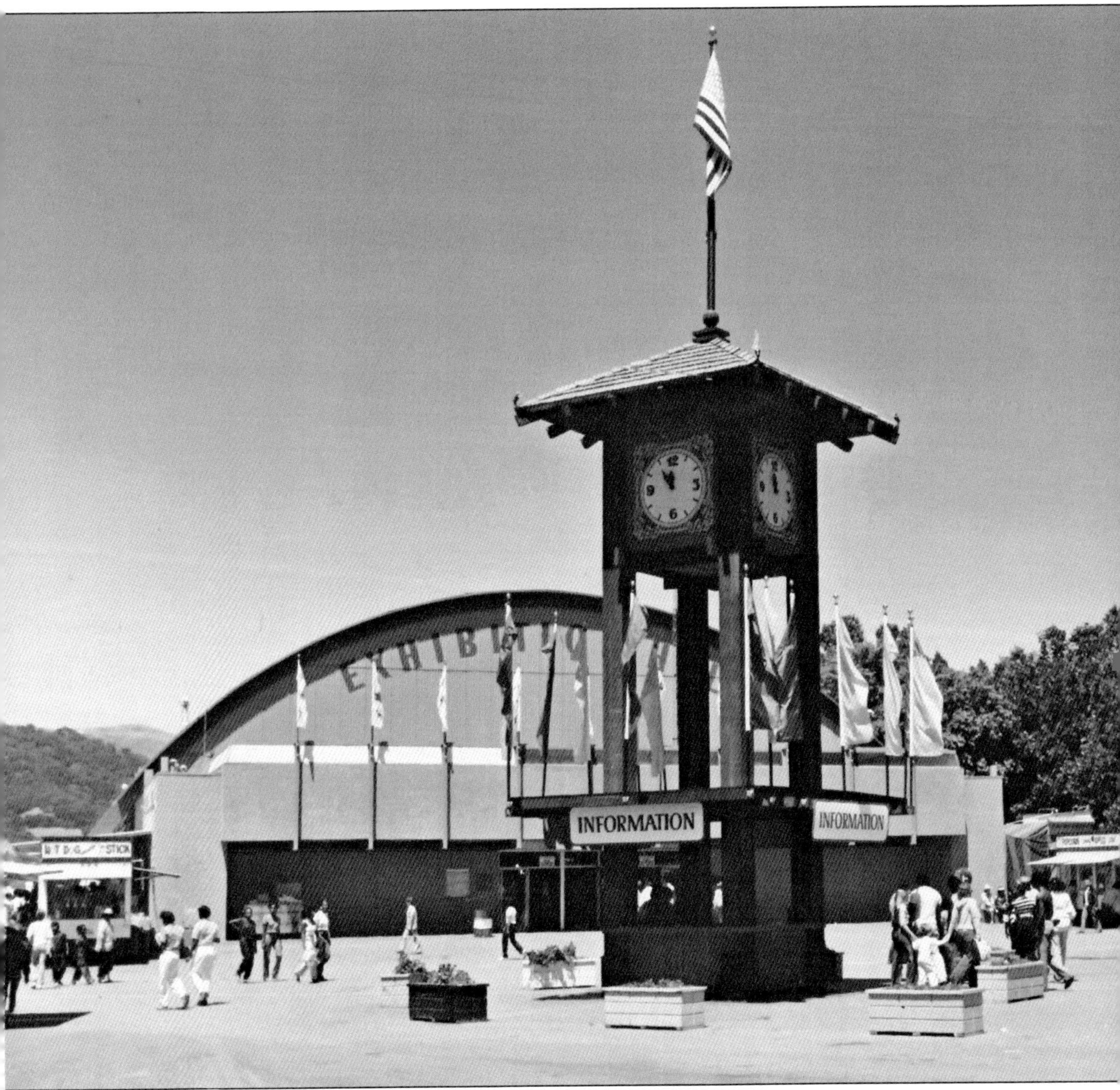

The clock tower, which also doubles as the information booth, was built in 1979. The 30-foot-tall wooden structure topped by a 16-foot flagpole serves as a focal point at the fair. Although the original tower remains the same, it has slightly changed in appearance due to the addition of decorations and, more recently, a marquee naming the entertainers in the amphitheater.

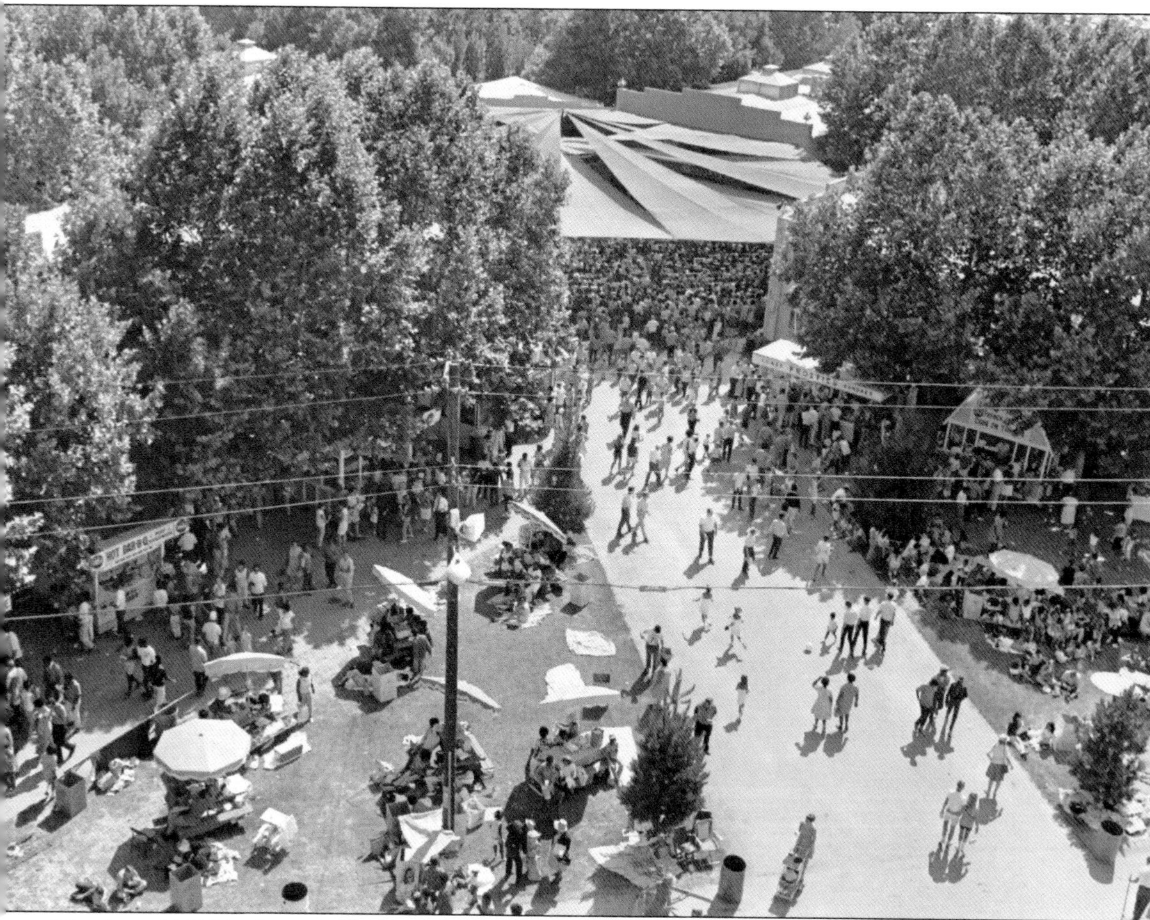

The fair of 1985 broke records with an astonishing 470,643 in attendance during its 16-day run, making it the fifth consecutive year the fair surpassed 400,000 guests. It was suggested that the increase in attendance was due to the popular free entertainment in the amphitheater.

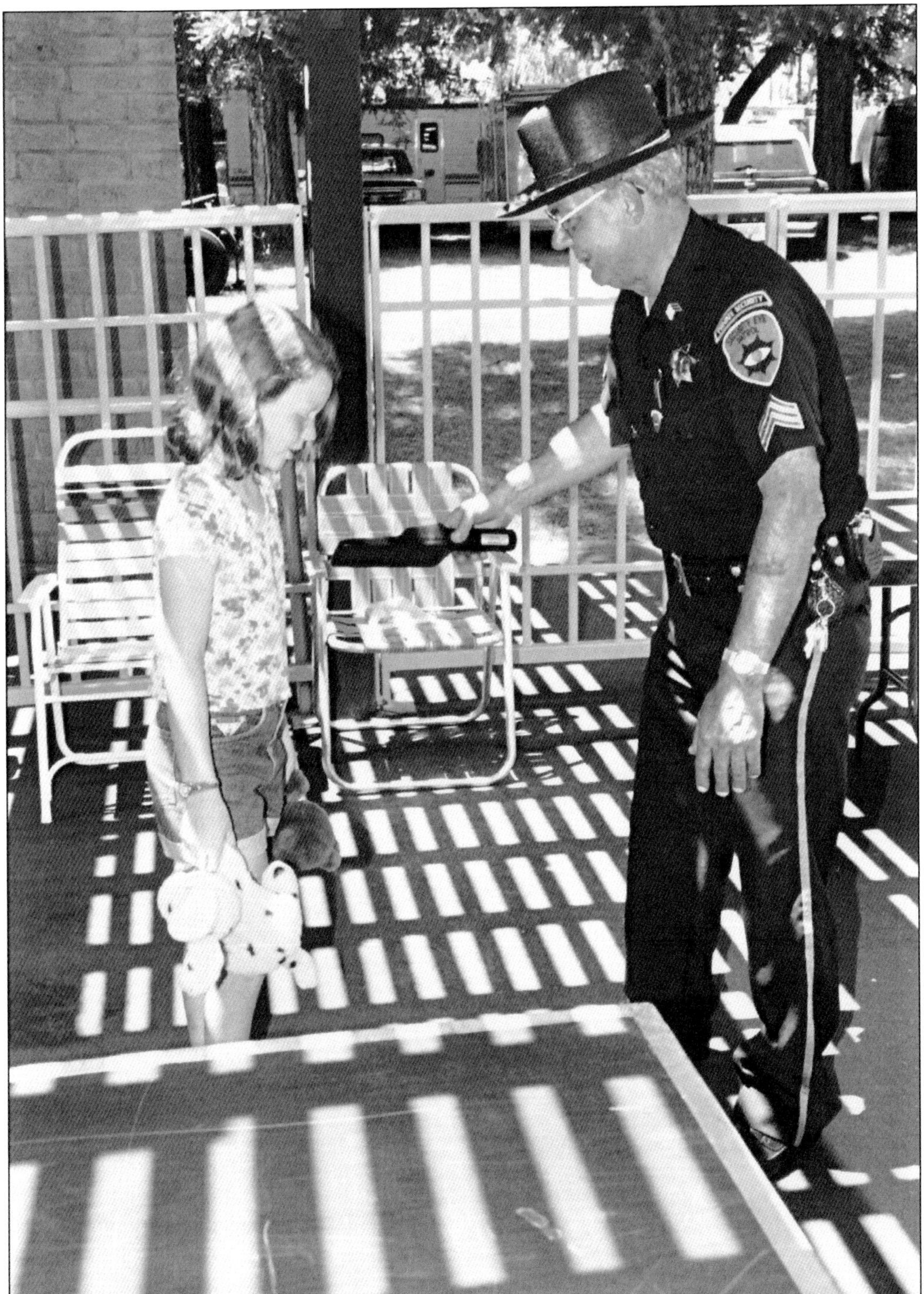

Several major changes were made at the fairgrounds during the 1990s. The oldest exhibit building was refurbished, electrical work was completed, concession stands were improved, and the small animal area was upgraded. Security was increased with the implementation of metal detectors and scanning devices installed at all entrance gates. Pictured above is security person Dave Rezendes.

Two

An Agriculture Adventure

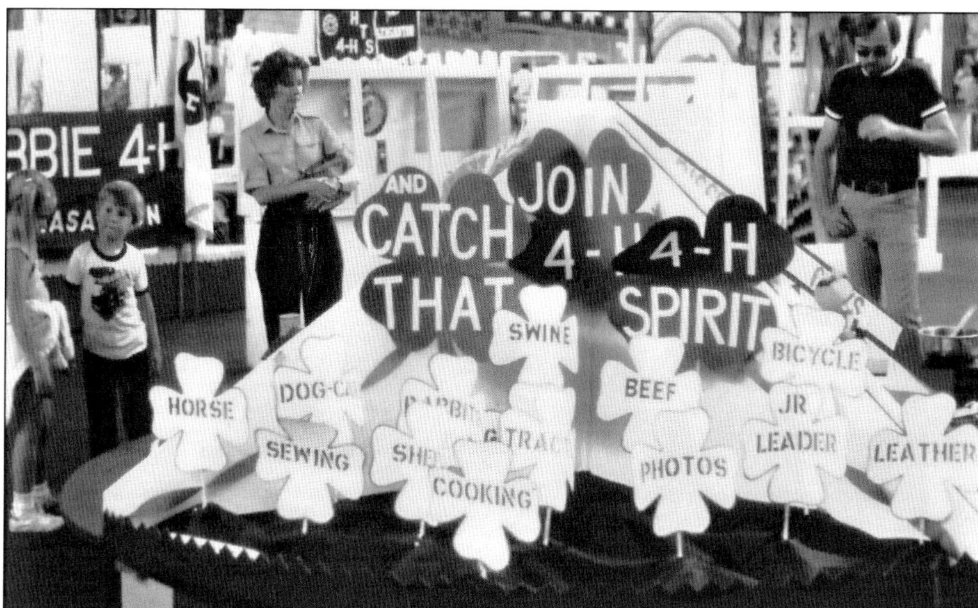

Formed in 1902, the 4-H group is a national organization for youth to develop good citizenship, leadership, and skills through learning programs that include science, technology, cooking, animal husbandry, photography, and public speaking, among others. The 4-H symbol is the four-leaf clover and the four Hs represent head, heart, hands, and health. (Courtesy of Peter Bailey.)

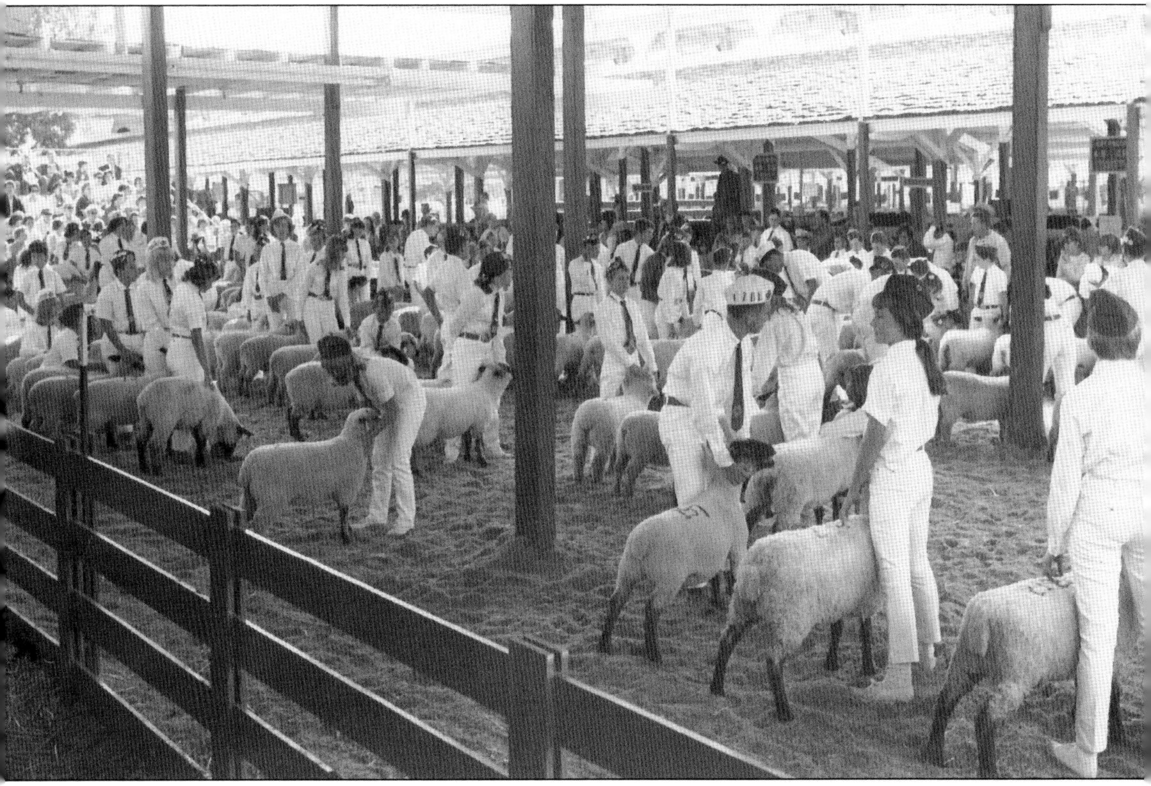

There are approximately 1,000 youths in Alameda County involved in 4-H and almost 400 adult volunteers who lead its various programs. In 2010, the local community 4-H clubs represented at the fair were Montclair (Berkeley/Oakland), Palomares and Redwood (Castro Valley), Dublin, Bayside (Fremont), East Hills (San Leandro), Crane Ridge, Del Arroyo and Valley Vista (Livermore), Mountain House, Abbie and Tassajara Valley (Pleasanton), and Sunol.

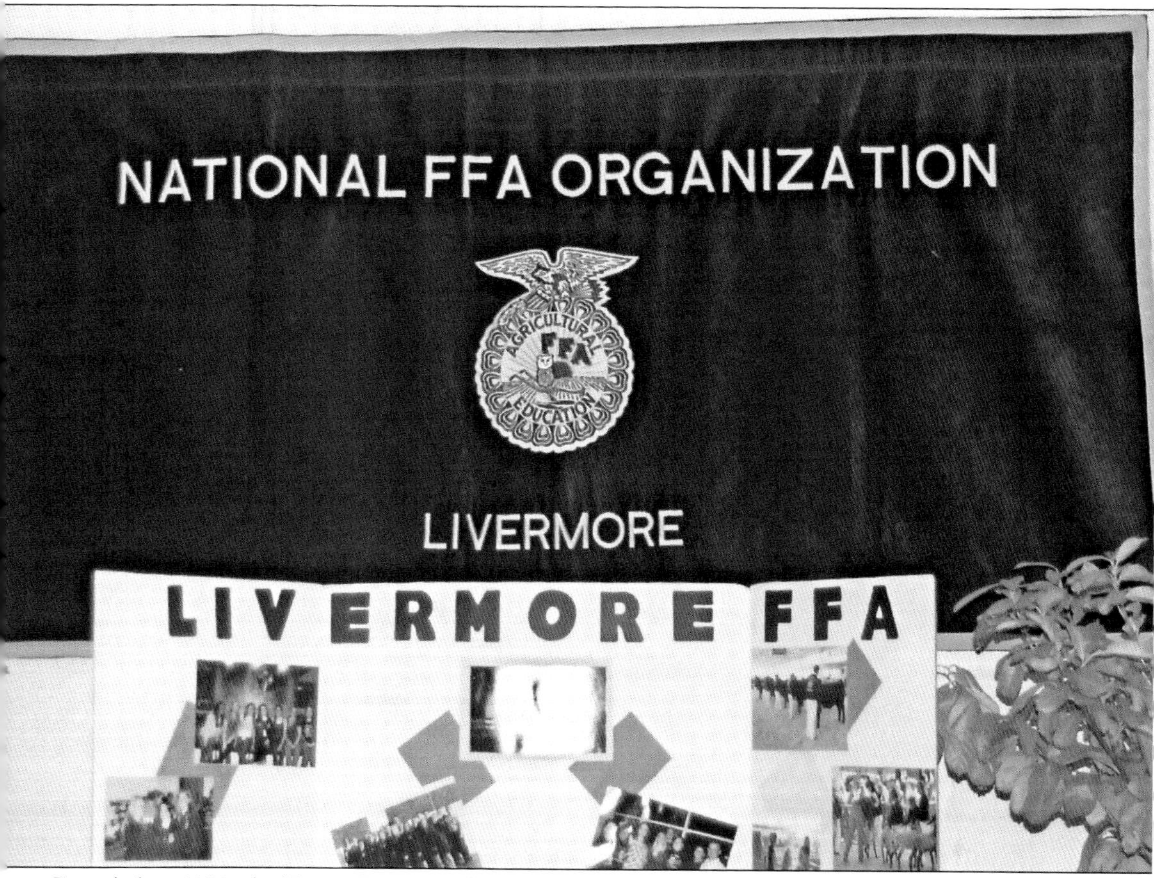

Founded in 1928, the Future Farmers of America's goal is to promote "achievement in premier leadership, personal growth and career success through agricultural education." The FFA emblem consists of five symbols: a cross section of corn, which represents American agriculture; the rising sun, which represents the promise of a new day; the plow, which represents labor and America's strength; an eagle, which represents freedom; and an owl, representing wisdom and success.

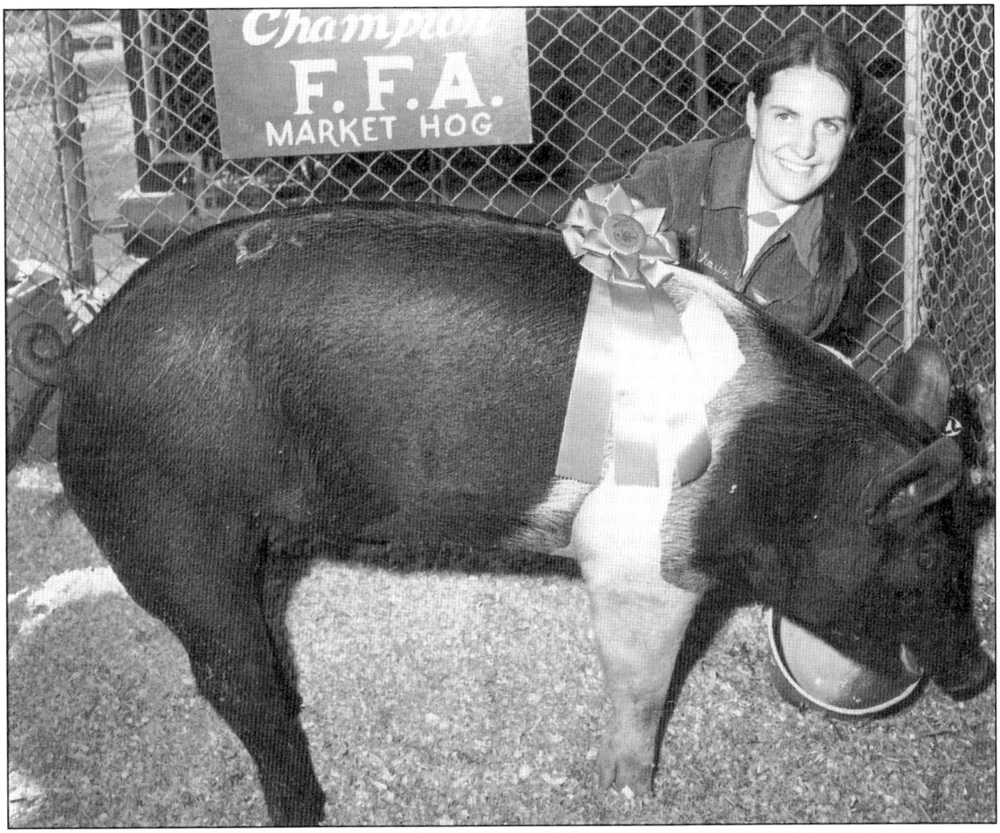

In the 1970s, members from Livermore, Fremont, and Pleasanton represented the FFA at the fair. Ranging in age from 14 to 21 years, members were required to take agricultural classes in high school and plan a project each year. Livestock is not the only option for city kids; the FFA also offered guidance in vegetable gardening and raising rabbits and poultry.

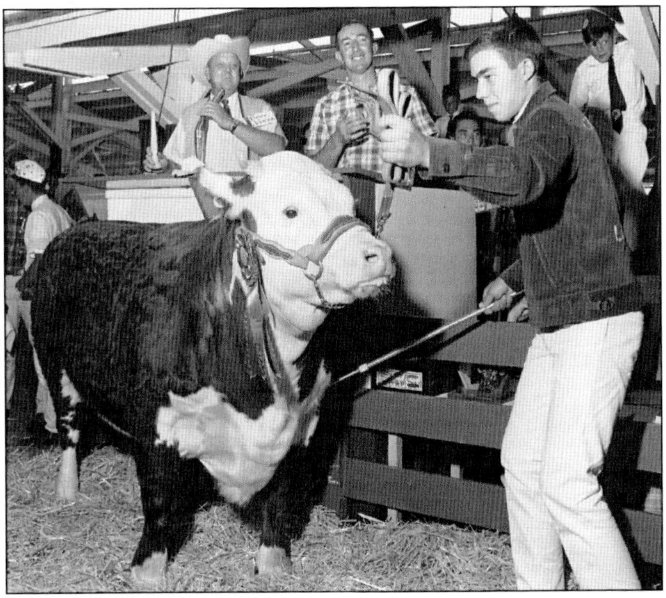

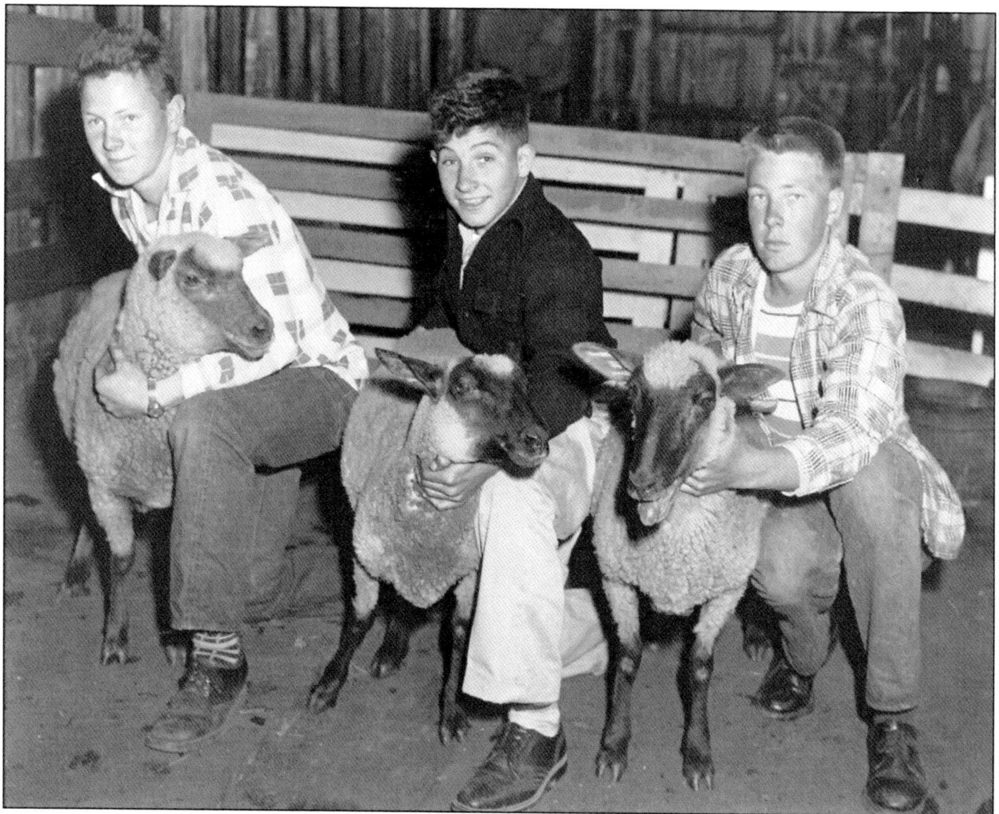

The fair's program from 1945 states, "District and county agricultural fairs in California are made possible largely through money received from the state, directly obtained from pari-mutuel funds derived from horse racing in California. The state's share of the monies is used for the advancement and improvement of agriculture, and is made available for payment of premiums at fairs and for certain construction and maintenance costs at the fairgrounds."

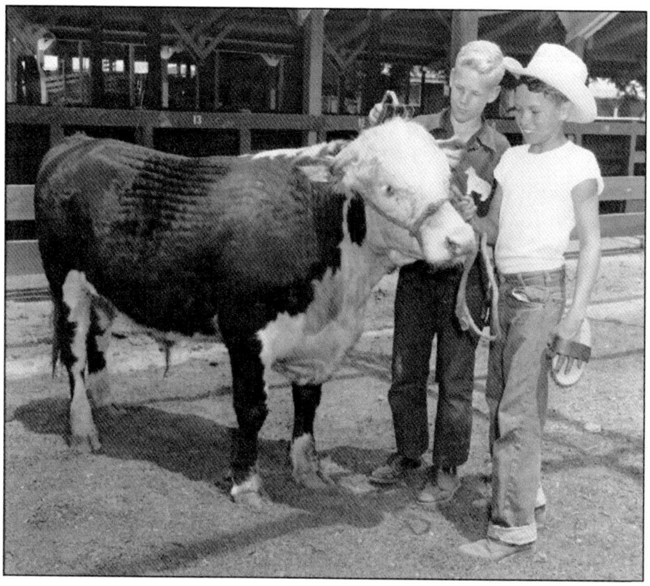

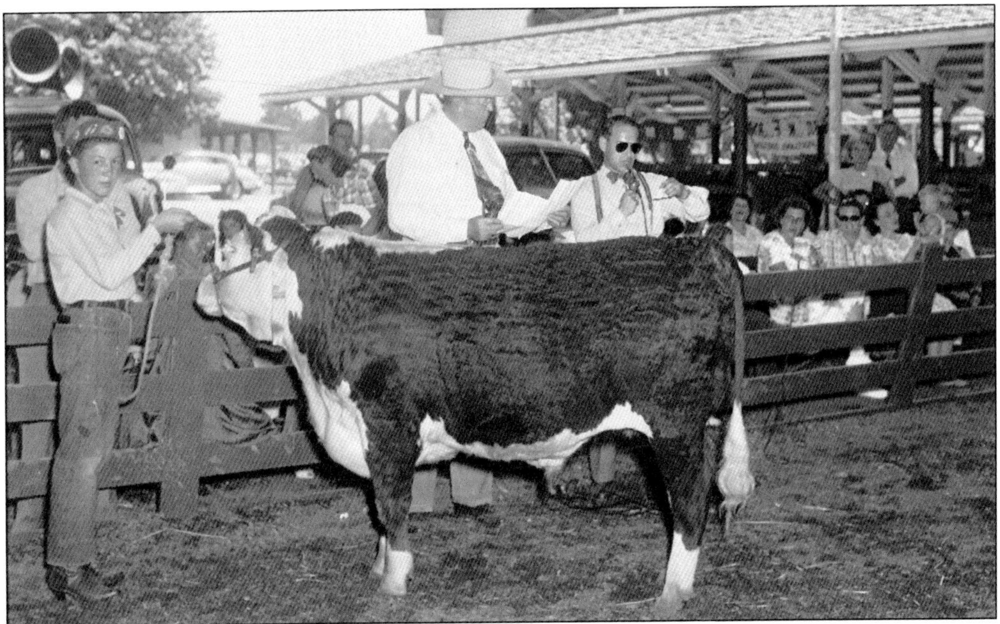

In 1948, there were more than 600 entries in the livestock division, and the first Junior Livestock Auction was held. The prize-winning steer weighed 970 pounds and was sold for $368 by owner Vic Lund of Pleasanton.

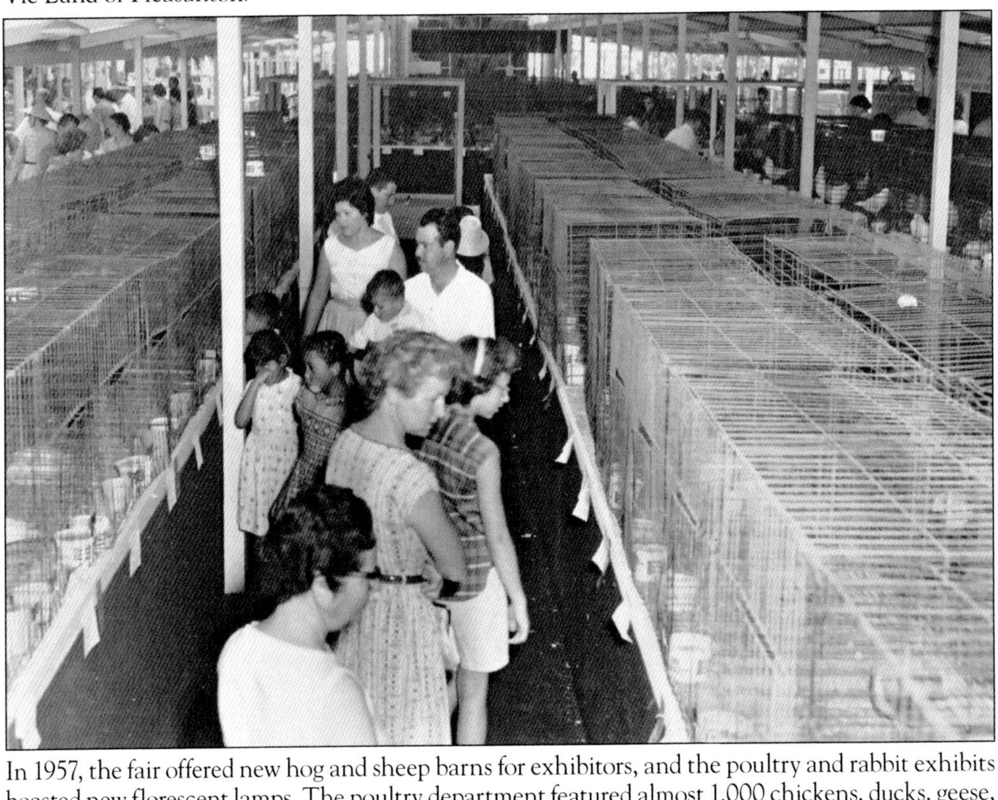

In 1957, the fair offered new hog and sheep barns for exhibitors, and the poultry and rabbit exhibits boasted new florescent lamps. The poultry department featured almost 1,000 chickens, ducks, geese, and turkeys, as well as 700 pigeons and 400 rabbits, all competing for $7,000 in premiums.

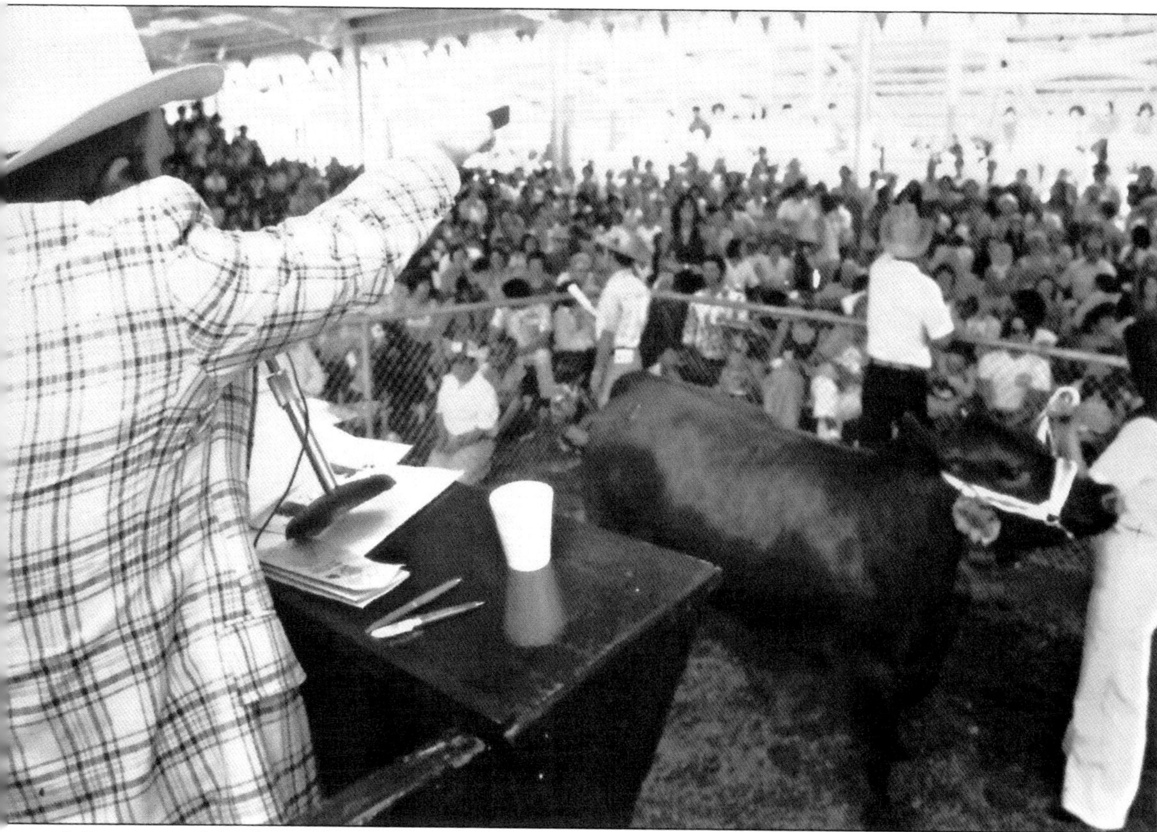

A large part of the fair is the promotion of livestock by youths involved in the FFA and 4-H clubs. The clubs' members participate by first choosing an animal to raise. They purchase and care for their animals for a year prior to competing at the fair, which culminates on the fair's final day at the Junior Livestock Auction, where the animals are sold to the highest bidders. (Courtesy of Peter Bailey.)

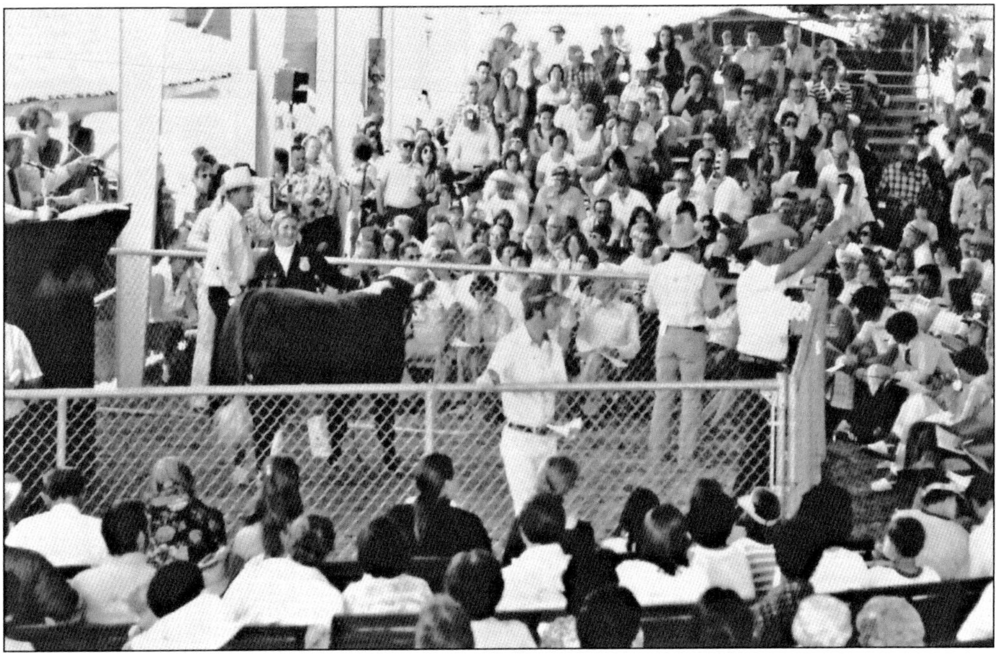

In 1963, more than 1,000 fair patrons attended the Junior Livestock Auction, and the top prize of 72.5¢ per pound went to Susie Silva of Union City for her steer. In 1971, there were 45 4-H clubs represented at the Alameda County Fair. In comparison, there were only 13 4-H clubs present in 2010.

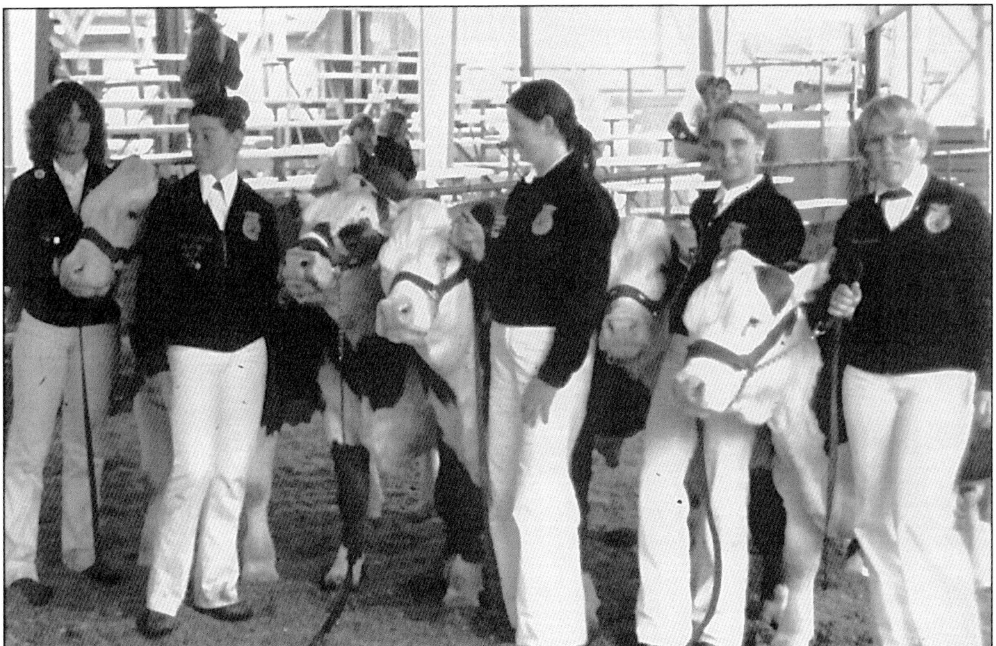

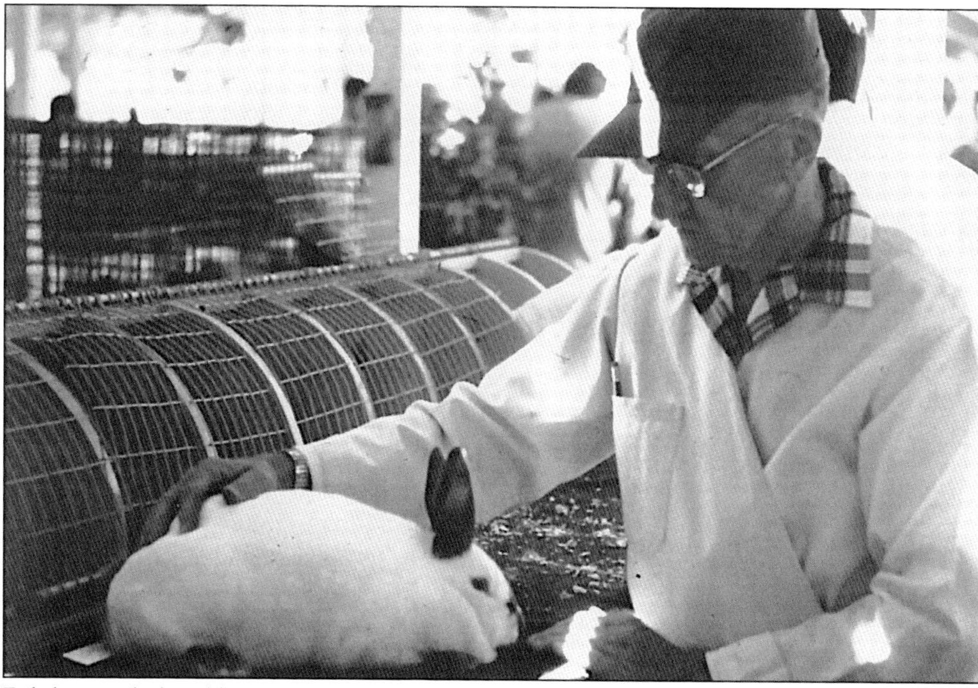

Exhibits include rabbits, poultry, pigeons, swine, sheep, beef, dairy goats, horse, guide dogs, beekeeping, blacksmithing, flower arranging, and sheepshearing demonstrations. The very first rabbit auction was held at the fair in 1964. (Courtesy of Peter Bailey.)

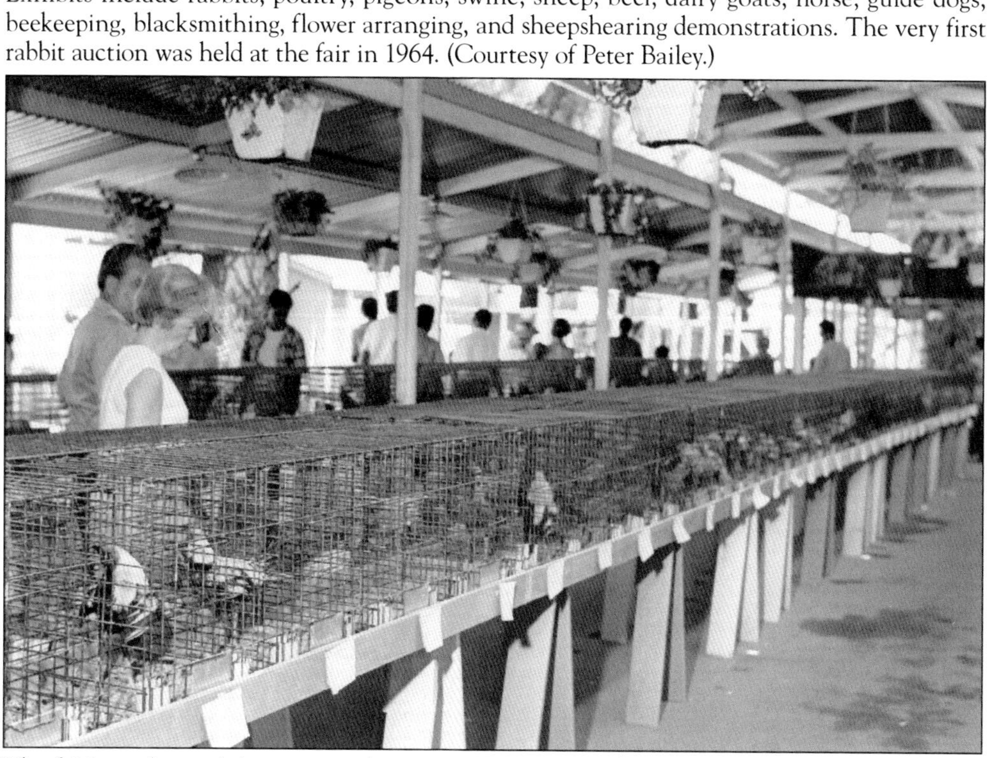

The fair's poultry exhibit was nearly nonexistent in 1962 due to a poultry disease that killed thousands of birds in California. The Pageant of Feathers and Fur was offered again in 1963 and included all breeds of chickens, duck, geese, pigeons, and rabbits. (Courtesy of Peter Bailey.)

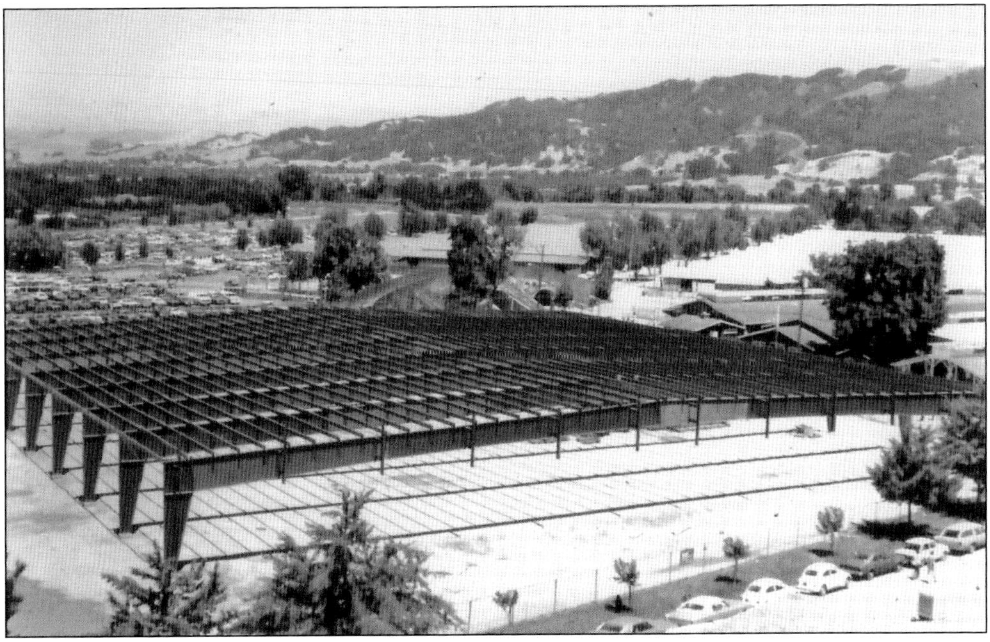

Built in 1980, the Amador Pavilion is a 46,200-square-foot open structure and includes portable stalls, an exhibition ring, and auction area. The pavilion was a wonderful improvement to the old barns and stables previously used to house the fair's annual livestock exhibit. The cost to build the new pavilion was $750,000.

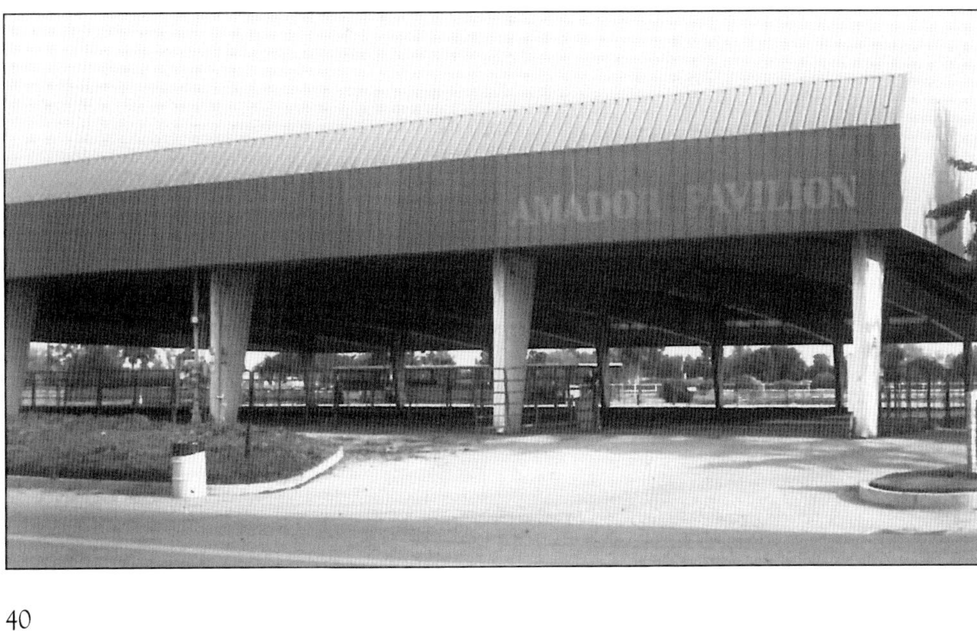

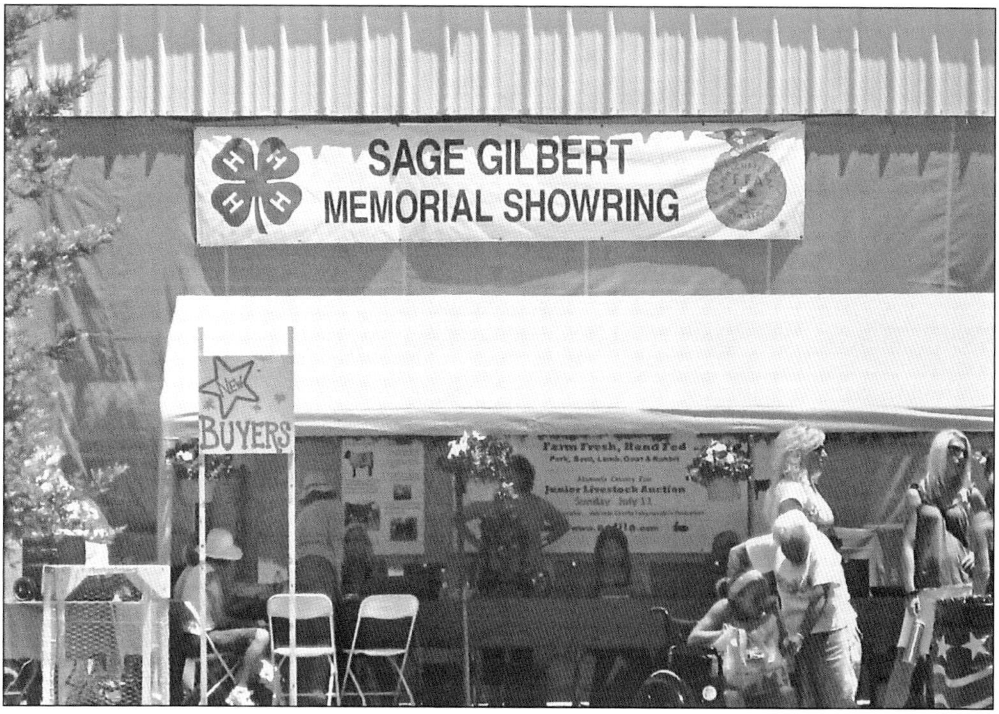

The Amador Pavilion was recently dedicated as the Sage Gilbert Memorial Show Ring. All animals exhibited at the fairgrounds must pass a health inspection by an official fair veterinarian. Competitions include open beef cattle, junior beef cattle, open breeding beef, open dairy goat, junior swine, open swine, junior sheep, open sheep, commercial cattle, open small animals, cats, guide dogs, dog obedience, and showmanship. (Above, courtesy of Ario Ysit.)

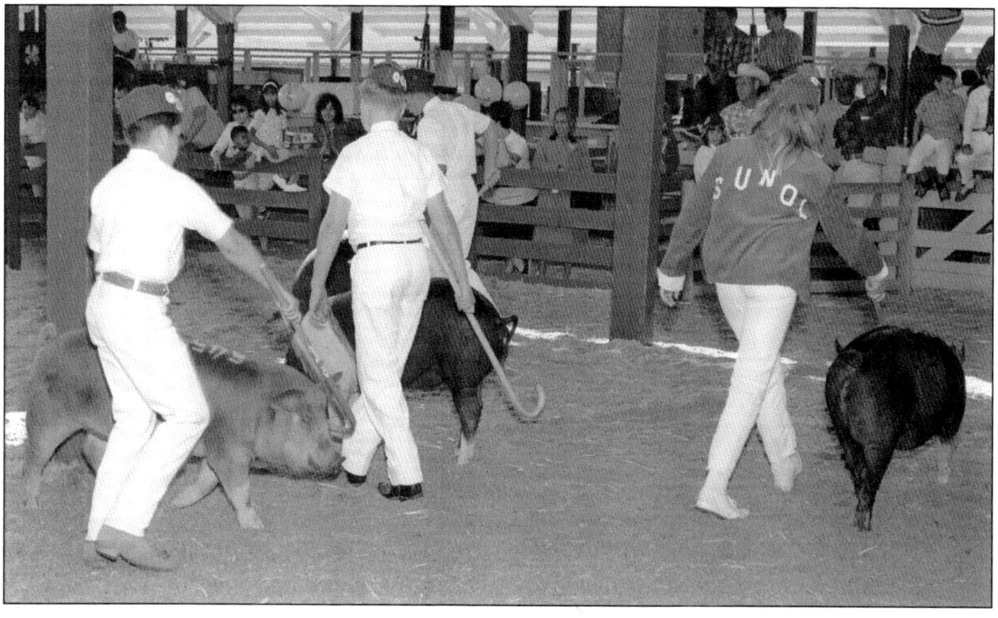

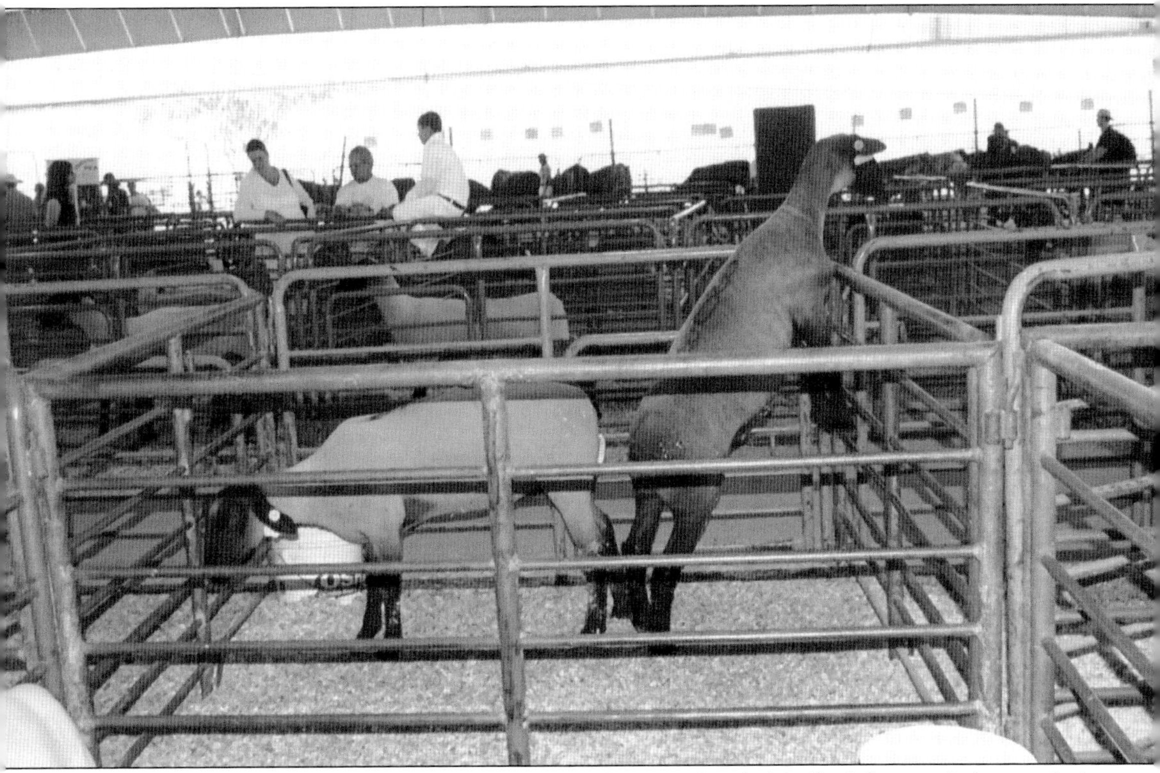

The Amador Pavilion is arranged with movable pens that hold all of the youths' animals for judging competitions. It is also where they care for the animals before and after the contests. In the early years, youths actually slept overnight in the barns with their animals. That's no longer the practice, but the kids and their families spend many hours at the arena during fair time.

Three

Blue Ribbon Exhibits

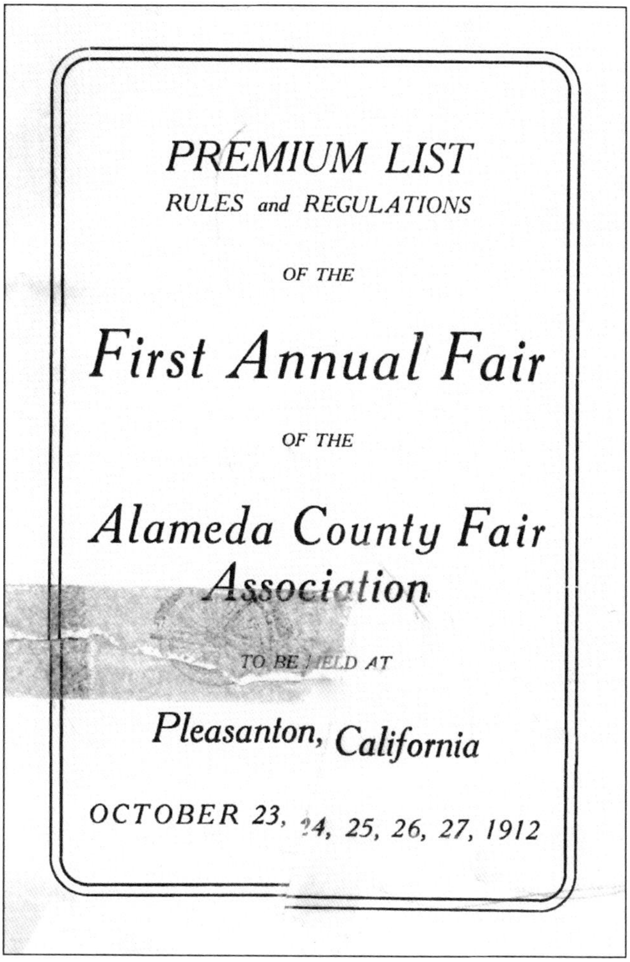
PREMIUM LIST
RULES and REGULATIONS
OF THE
First Annual Fair
OF THE
Alameda County Fair Association
TO BE HELD AT
Pleasanton, California
OCTOBER 23, 24, 25, 26, 27, 1912

In 1912, the fair's exhibits included draft horses, farming equipment, and creamery equipment, as well as butter, cheese, fruit, vegetables, grain, needlework, stenciling, painting, leather, photography, gopher traps, rag carpets, and copper work.

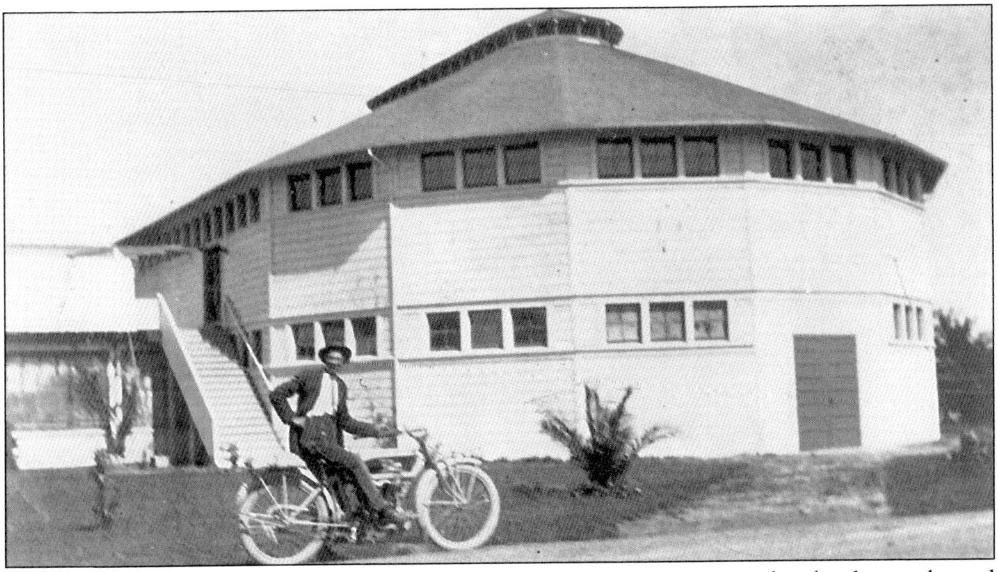

The fair of 1912 featured fine art exhibits such as oil painting, watercolor, leatherwork, and photography. Contests included a spelling bee, relay races, chariot races, bronco busting, donkey riding, and ball games. Pictured above is one of the original exhibit buildings.

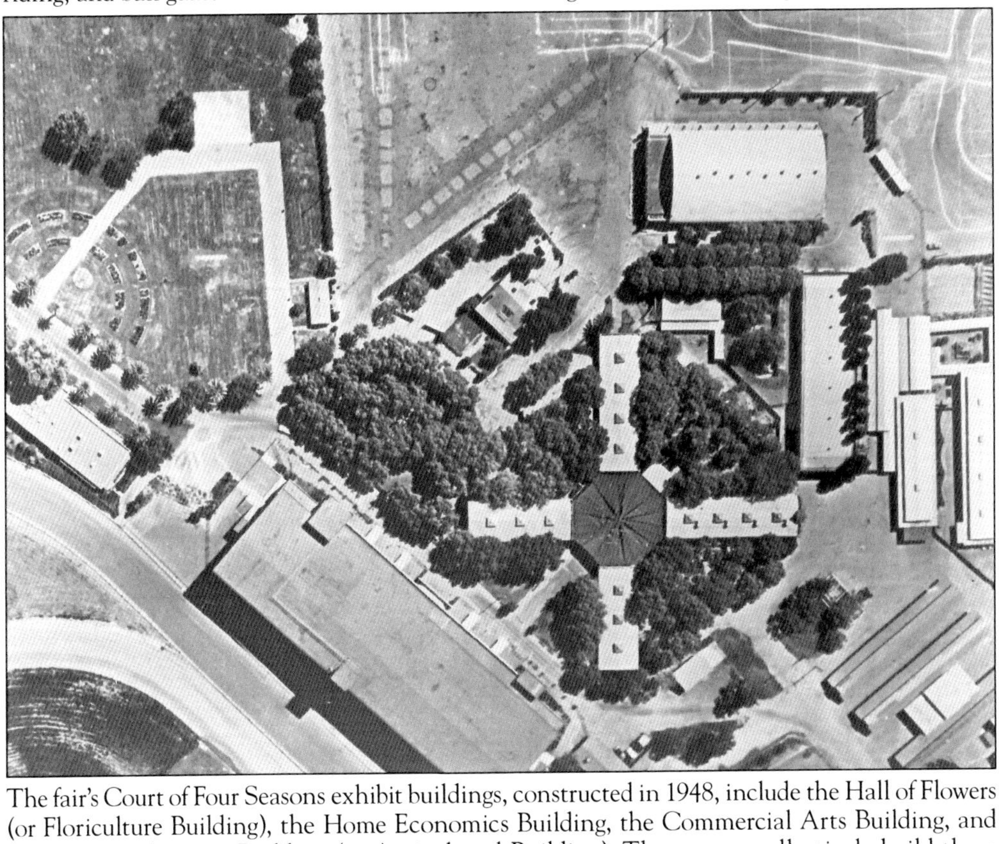

The fair's Court of Four Seasons exhibit buildings, constructed in 1948, include the Hall of Flowers (or Floriculture Building), the Home Economics Building, the Commercial Arts Building, and the Farm Implements Building (or Agricultural Building). The cost to collectively build these structures was approximately $250,000. (Courtesy of Peter Bailey.)

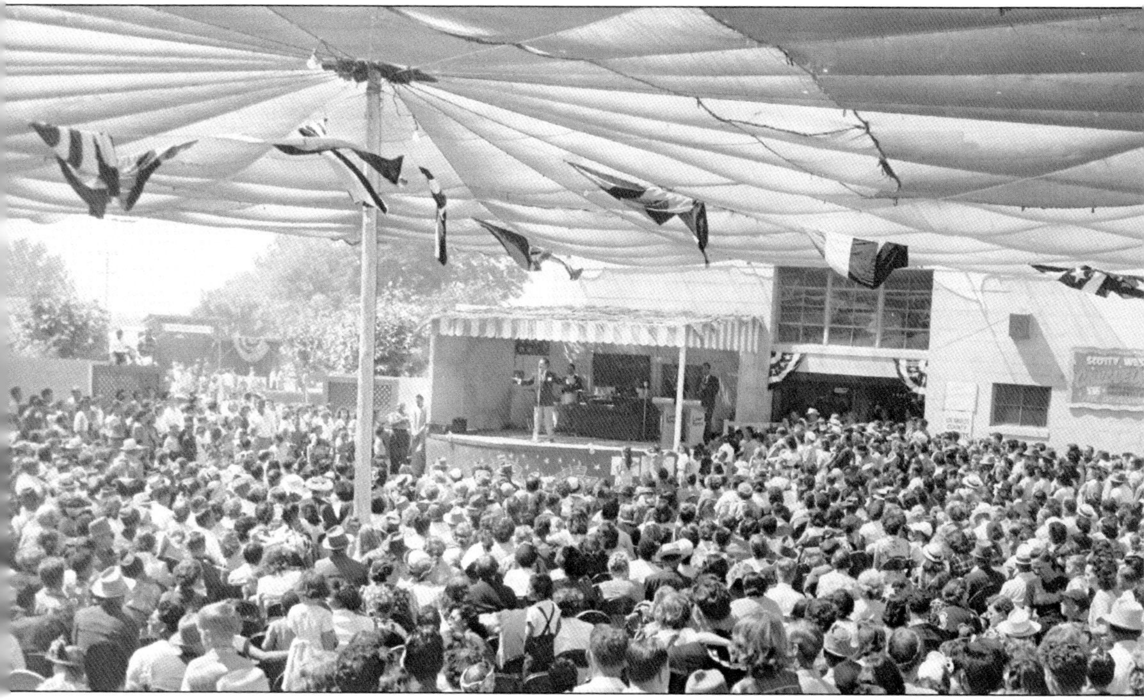

In the center of the four exhibit buildings is the Court of Four Seasons area. A small stage that sits to one side was the central location of all entertainment before the amphitheater was built. The stage is still used for smaller entertainment purposes and has been more recently equipped for cooking demonstrations.

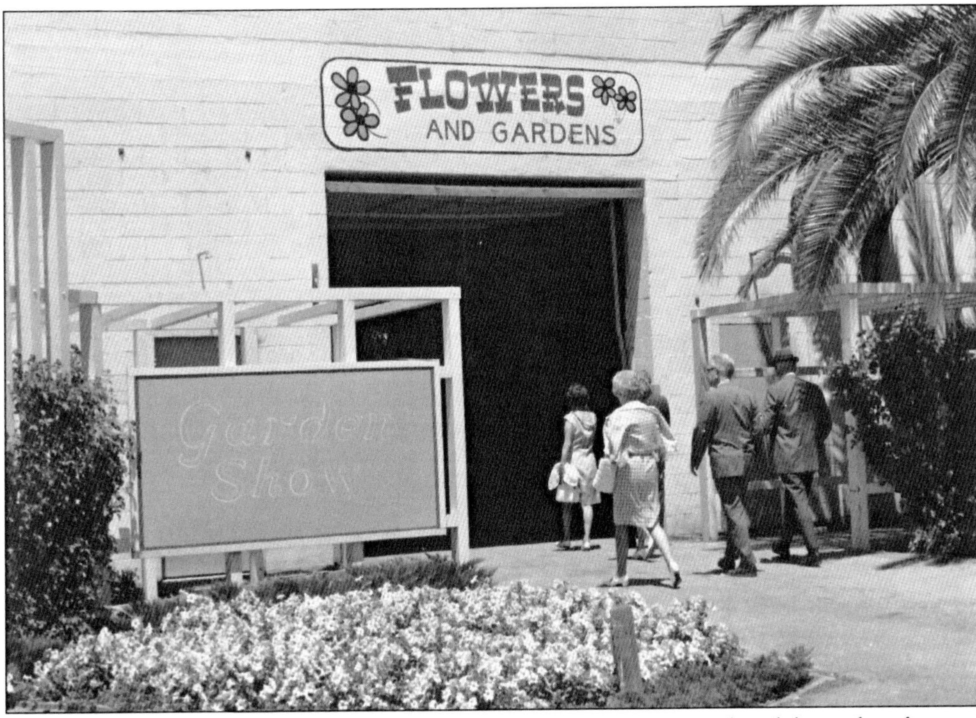

The Floriculture Building features cut flowers, potted plants, amateur garden clubs, and professional nursery exhibits. The indoor waterfall, built in 1960, provides relief to those seeking refuge from the hot summer fair days. The waterfall is the main attraction in the Floriculture Building, but it also houses various other exhibits. A small wooden bridge that leads to the garden displays crosses a portion of the waterfall's pond.

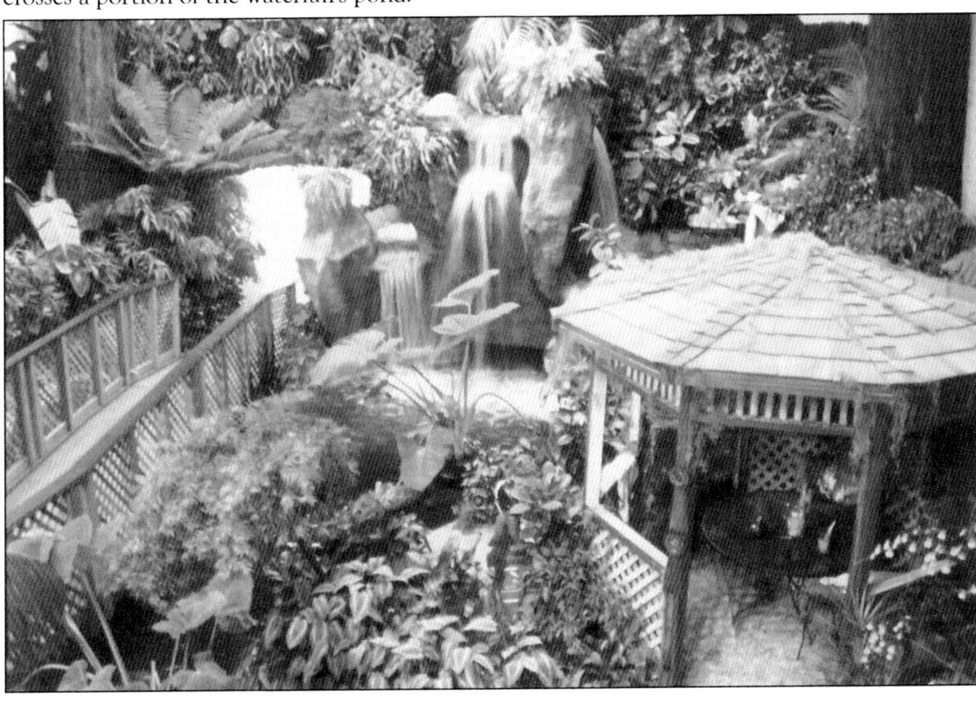

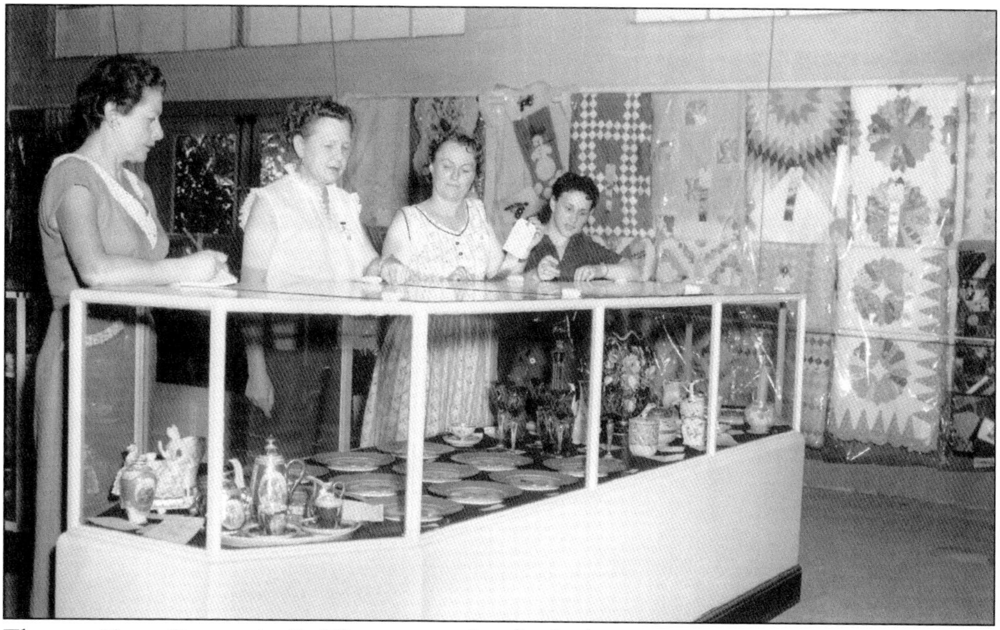

The new Home Economics Building was used to display knitting, sewing, arts and crafts, oil and watercolor paintings, photography, antiques, and baked and canned goods.

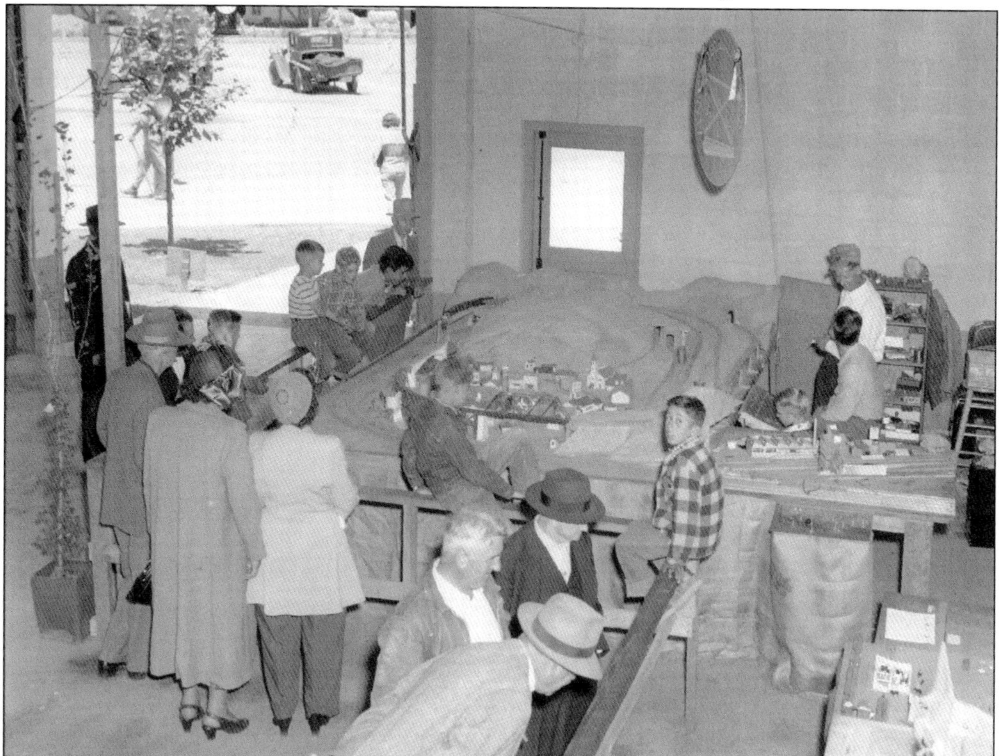

July 11, 1948, was designated as Model Railroaders Day. The event was held in conjunction with a picnic sponsored by the Alameda Model Railroaders club and was open to the public. Seen here is a $3,000 model train as displayed by the Alameda Model Railroaders.

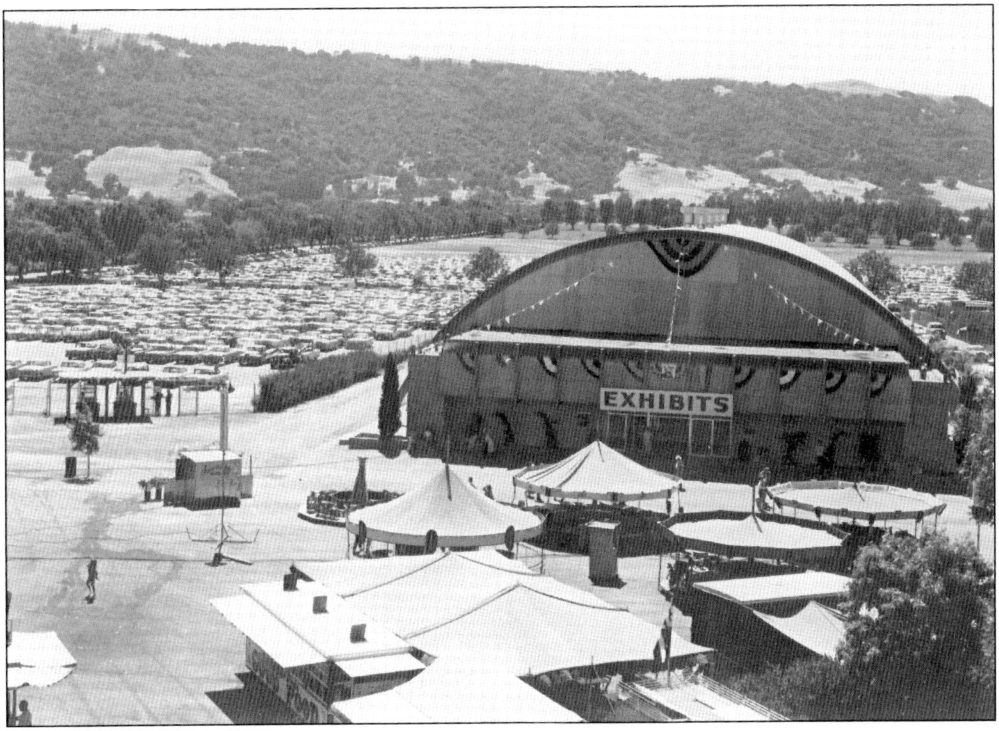

The Main Exhibit building, erected in 1956, measures 220 by 100,feet, has air-conditioning, offices, rest rooms, and seating for 1,800. Once the fair's biggest building, it provides an ample amount of space for off-season events such as arts and crafts festivals, RV shows, and home and garden shows. Below is a newer image of the west side of the Main Exhibit Hall facing the large parking lot. (Both courtesy of Peter Bailey.)

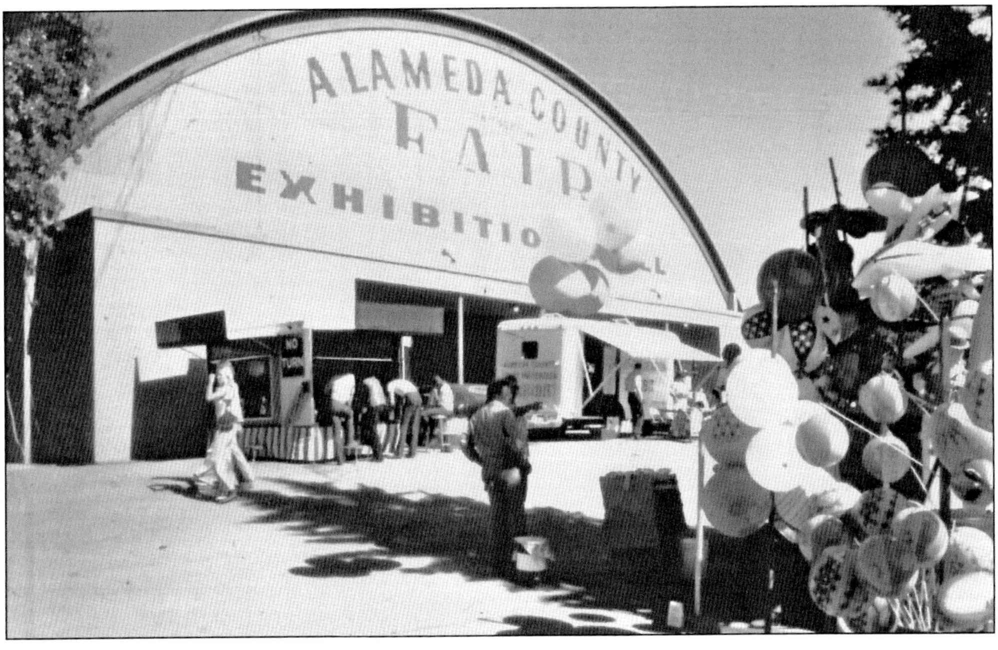

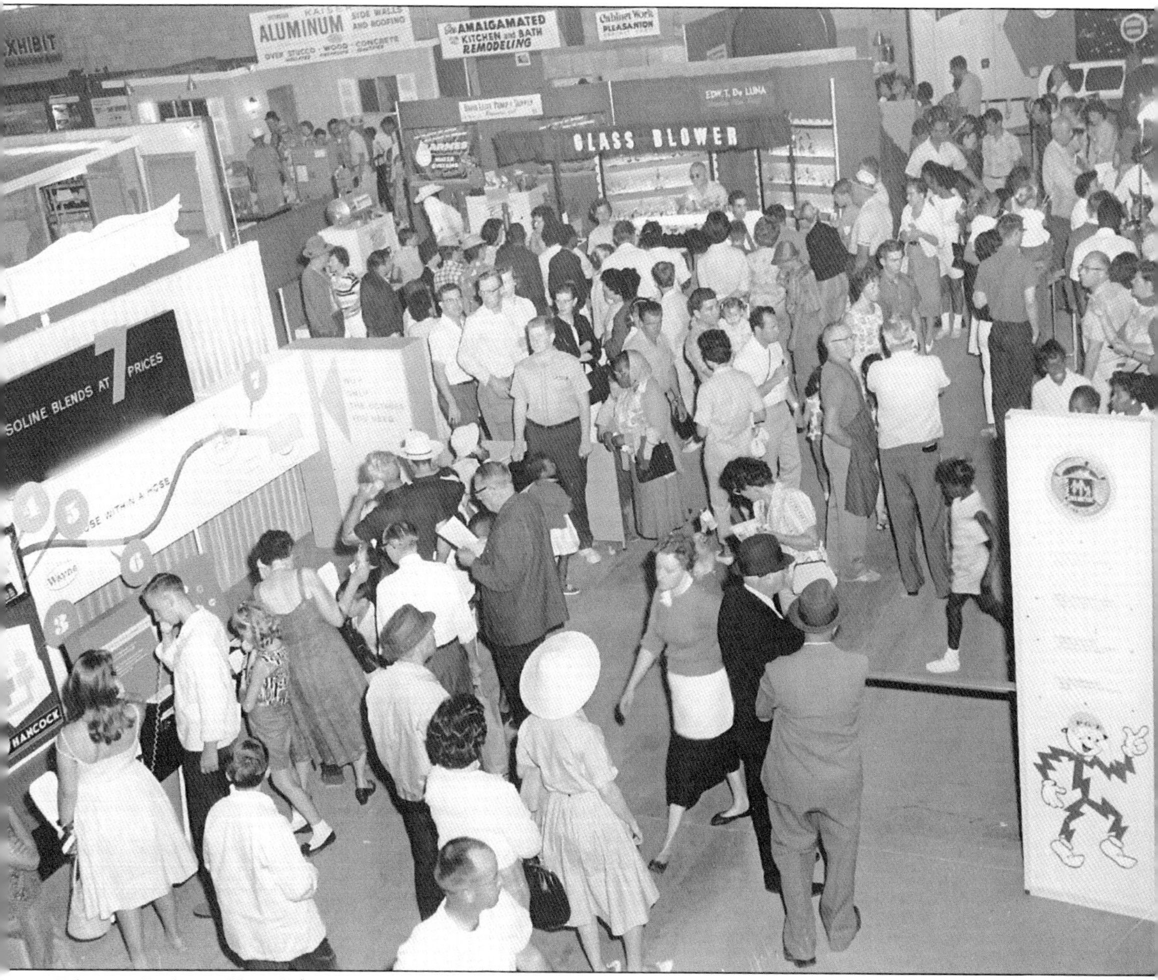

The 1957 fair offered $100,000 in premium money—the all-time highest total awarded for exhibits that included livestock, agriculture, horticulture, floriculture, art, photography, wine, home economics, mining, mineral, poultry, FFA, and 4-H. The commercial building included more than 100 displays of economic and industrial progress in Alameda County. (Courtesy of Peter Bailey.)

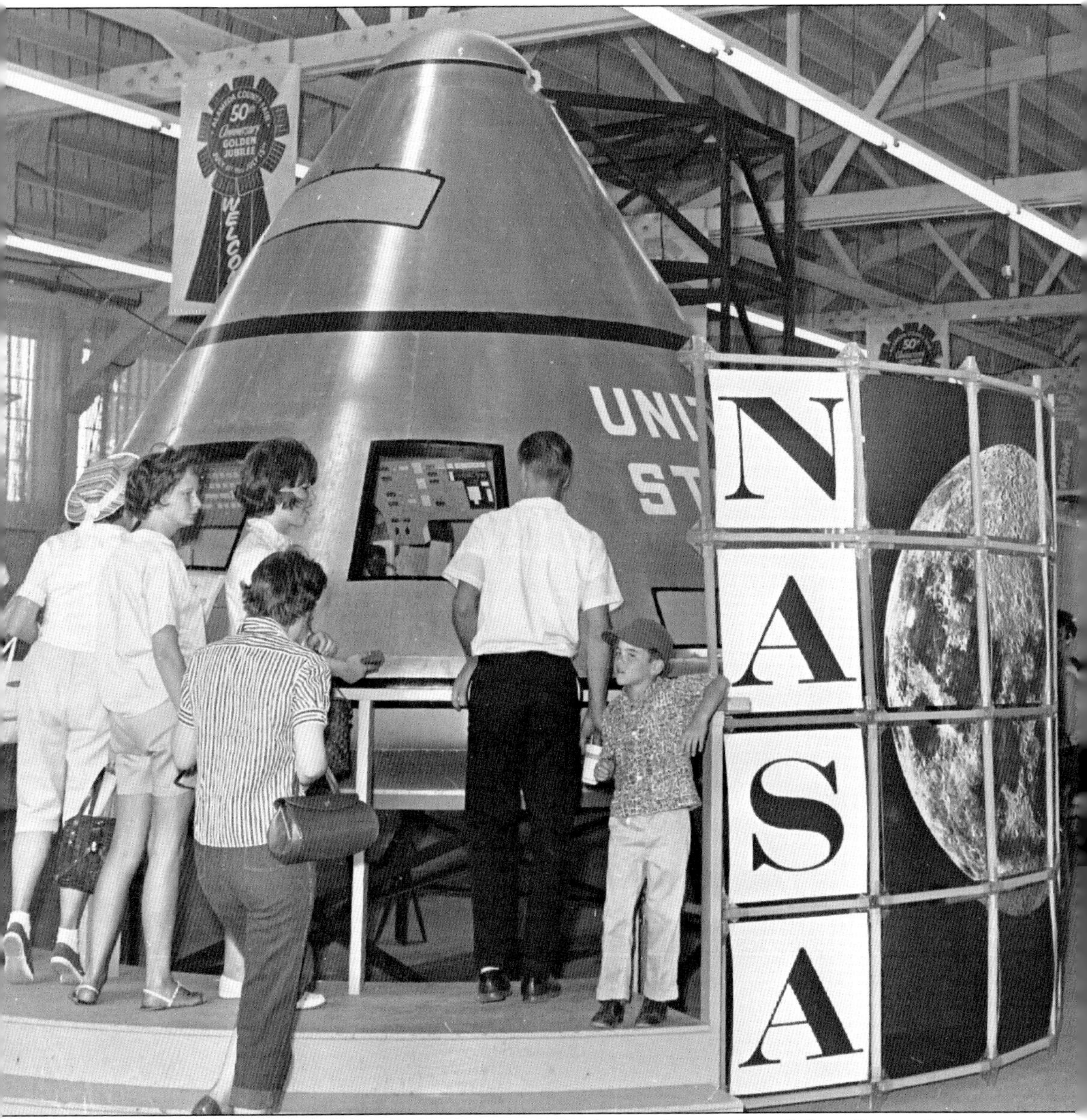

The Technology Building housed interesting and advanced scientific exhibits. Pictured above is a NASA exhibit from 1962. In 1978, the home computer was displayed for the first time. The local newspaper the *Tri-Valley Herald* reported that, "The appearance of the computers may surprise many fairgoers. The central unit resembles the keyboard of an electric typewriter and a video display screen resembling a television set is also needed. The third component, for the simpler model, is a tape recorder."

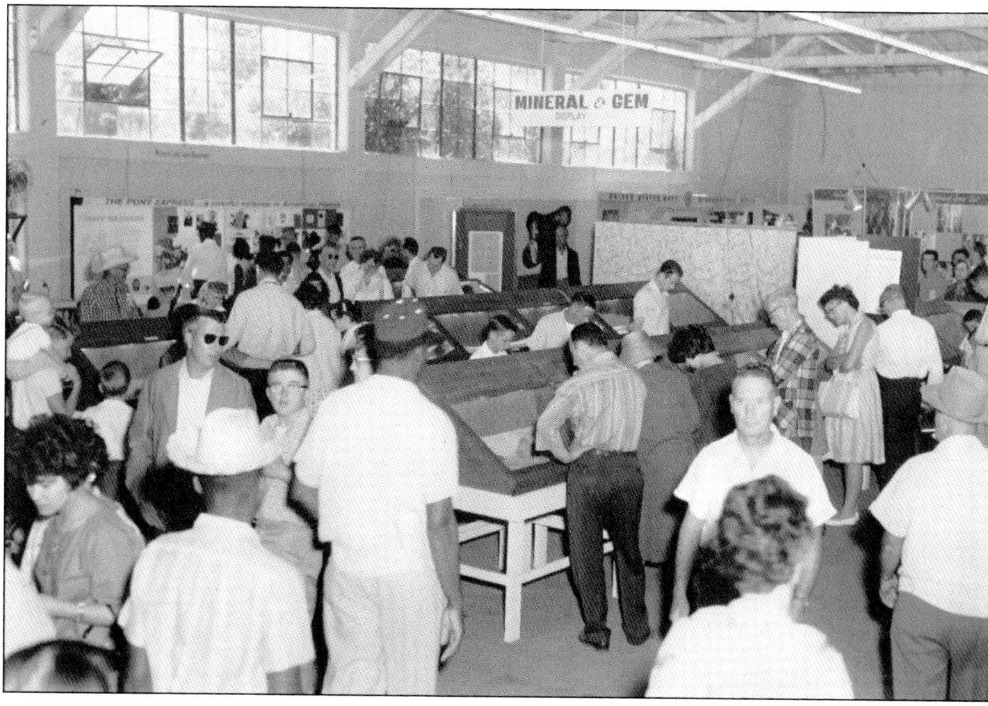

In 1973, the Gem and Mineral Building, also referred to as the mineral and mining department, was considered the largest exhibit of its kind at the fair in more than 25 years. There were 16 exhibit classes that included American Indian artifacts, educational displays, crystals, fossils, petrified wood, antique bottles, gemstones, and jewelry. More than $200 in premiums was offered to competitors.

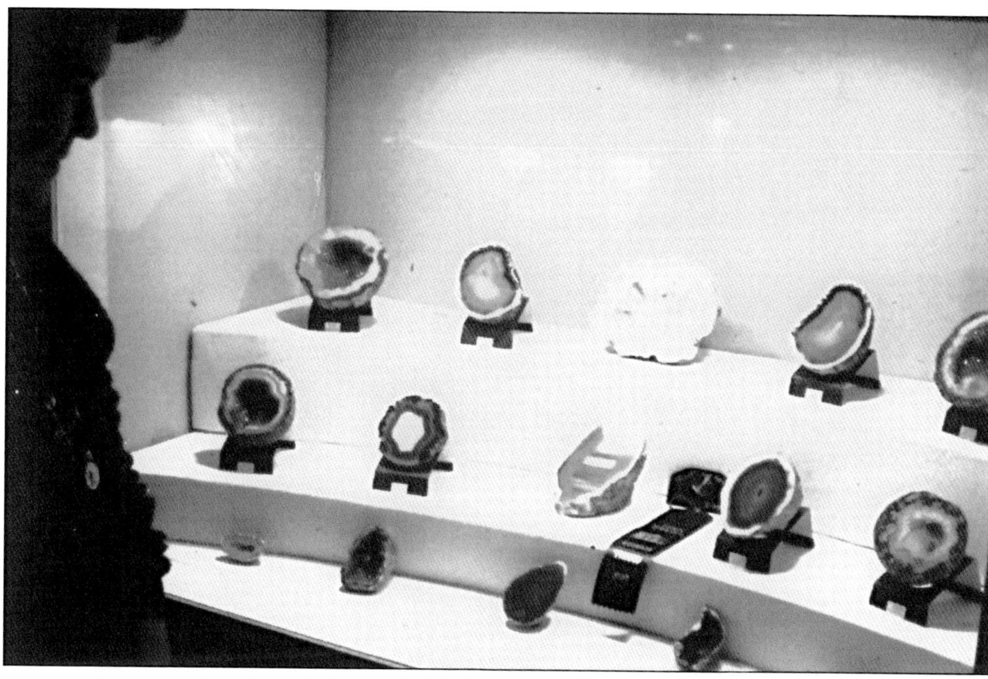

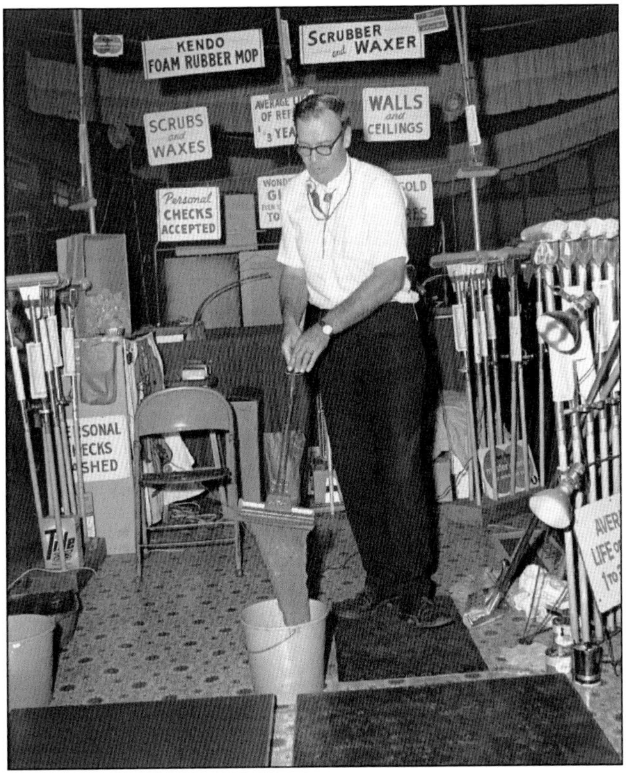

In the fair's early years, there was never enough space to accommodate the growing number of exhibits, but by 1968, there were six designated buildings and areas for exhibits such as industrial, outdoor, lawn, home arts, garden, and commercial. A visit to the fair is especially not complete without perusing commercial vendors.

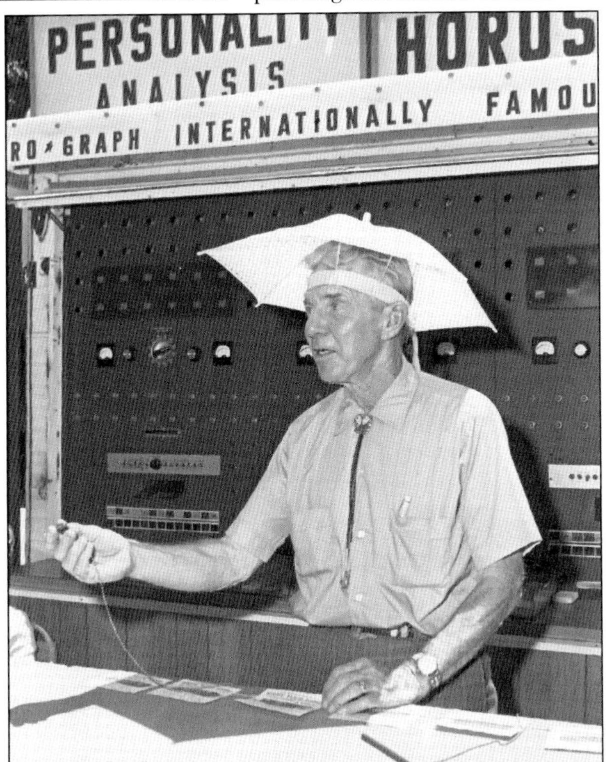

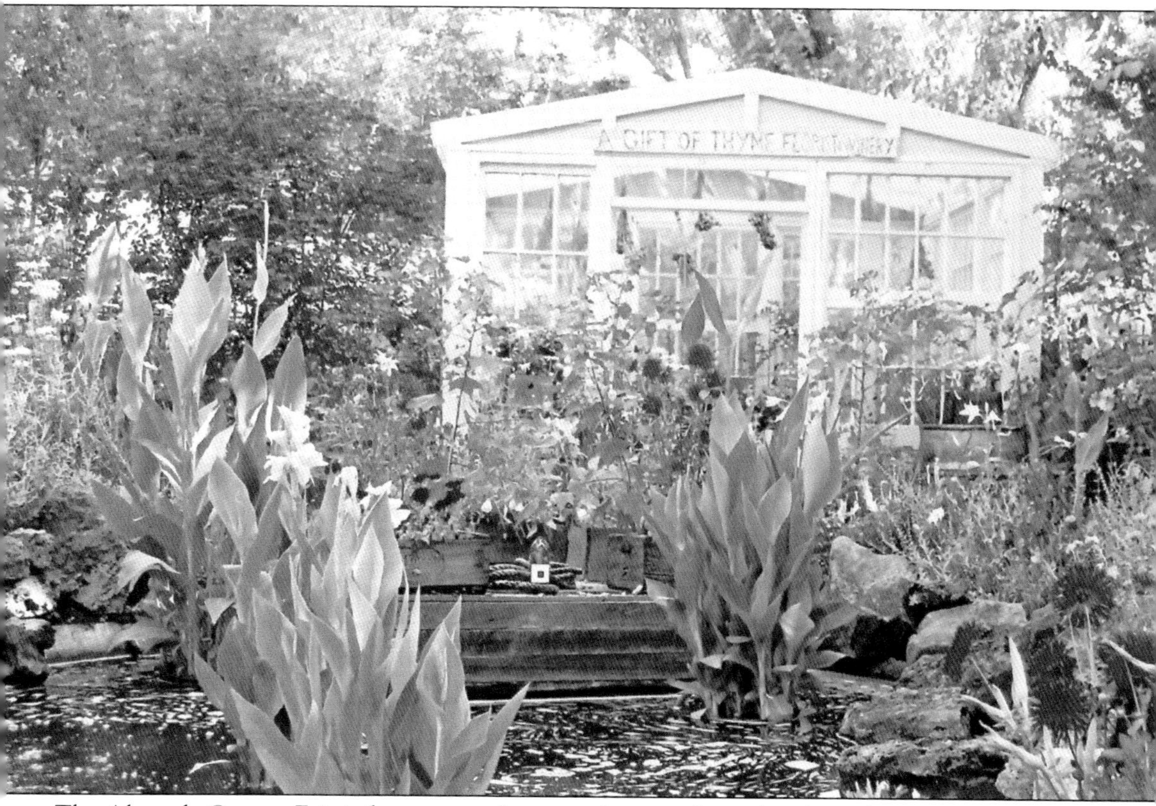

The Alameda County Fair is fortunate to have ample space for its lavish gardens. Community groups, landscape artists, and students compete for awards. Lucky fair guests are allowed to purchase plants from the garden exhibits on the last day of the fair.

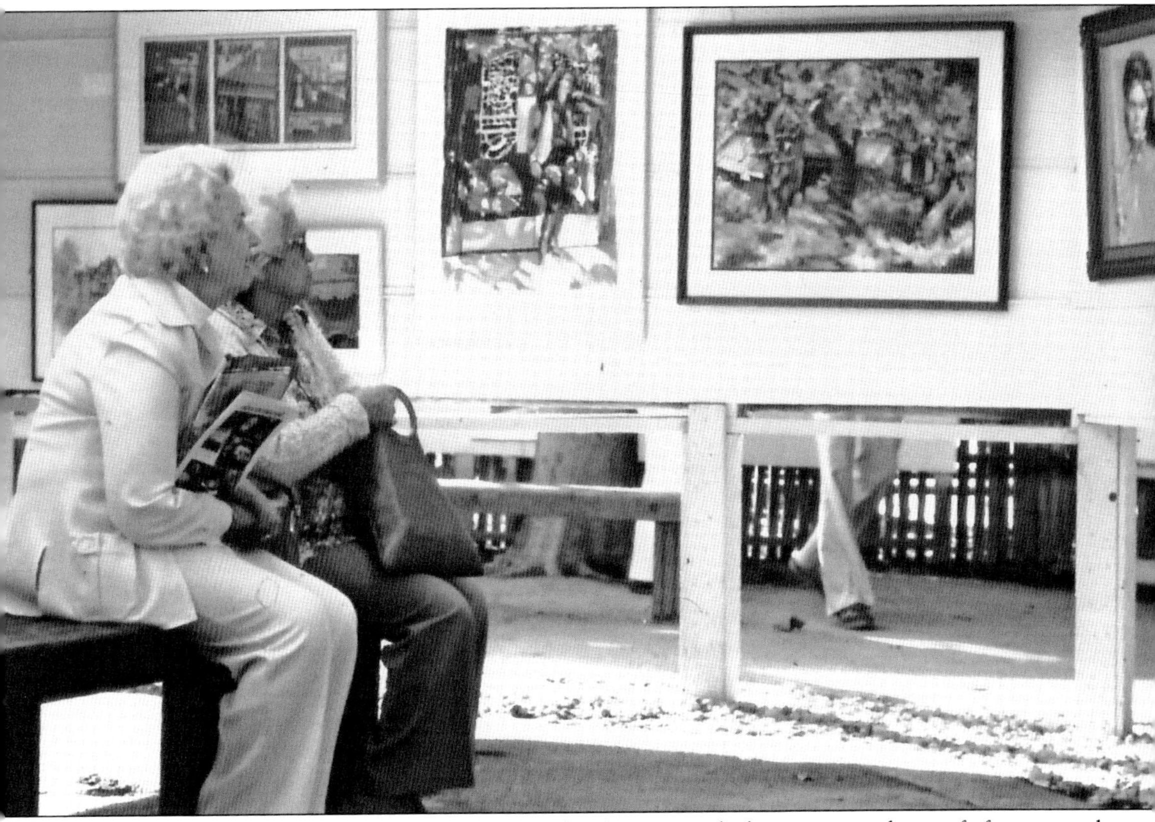

The fine arts exhibit was updated in 1989, and in keeping with the mission style motif of stucco and black wrought iron, it was renamed Plaza Del Arte. Local artists enter their paintings, drawings, and photographs and compete to win the coveted blue ribbon award.

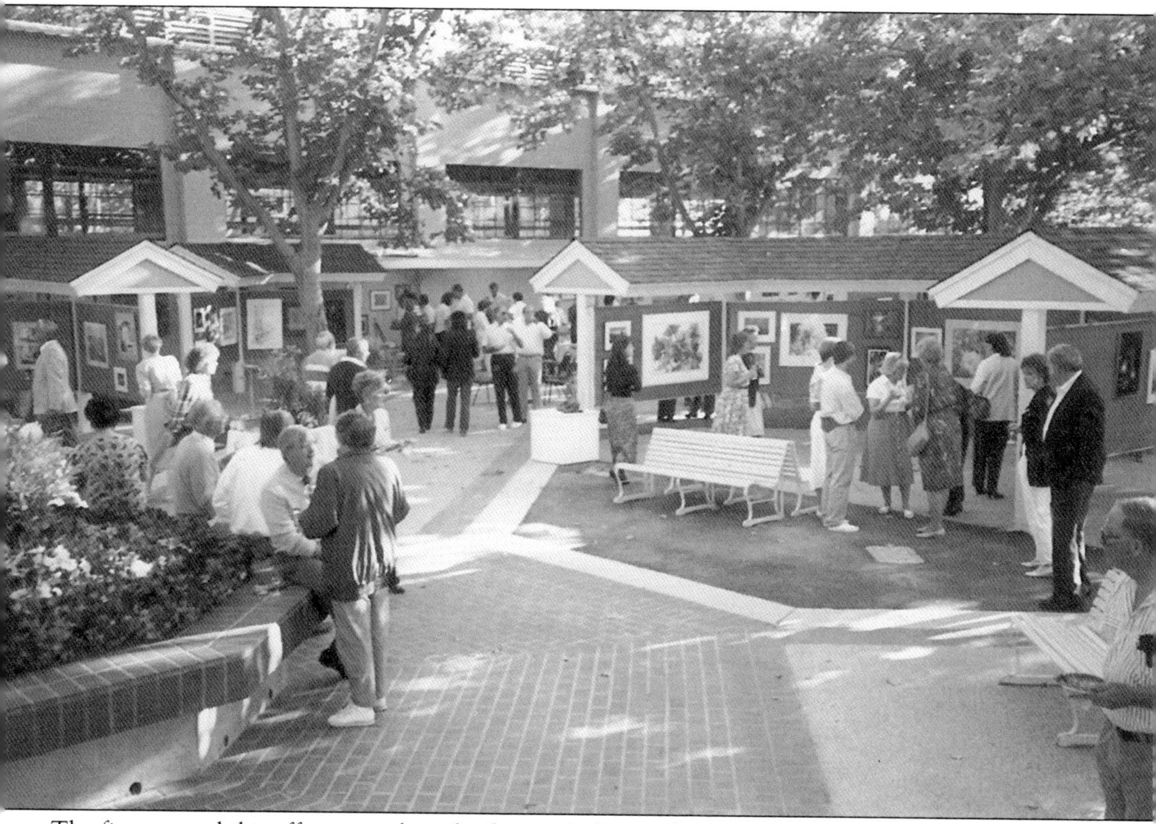

The fine arts exhibit offers a sneak peek of artwork during the annual Fair Preview Gala, which has benefitted the Children's Hospital of Oakland. Guests view artwork while noshing on small plate appetizers, beverages, wine, and champagne.

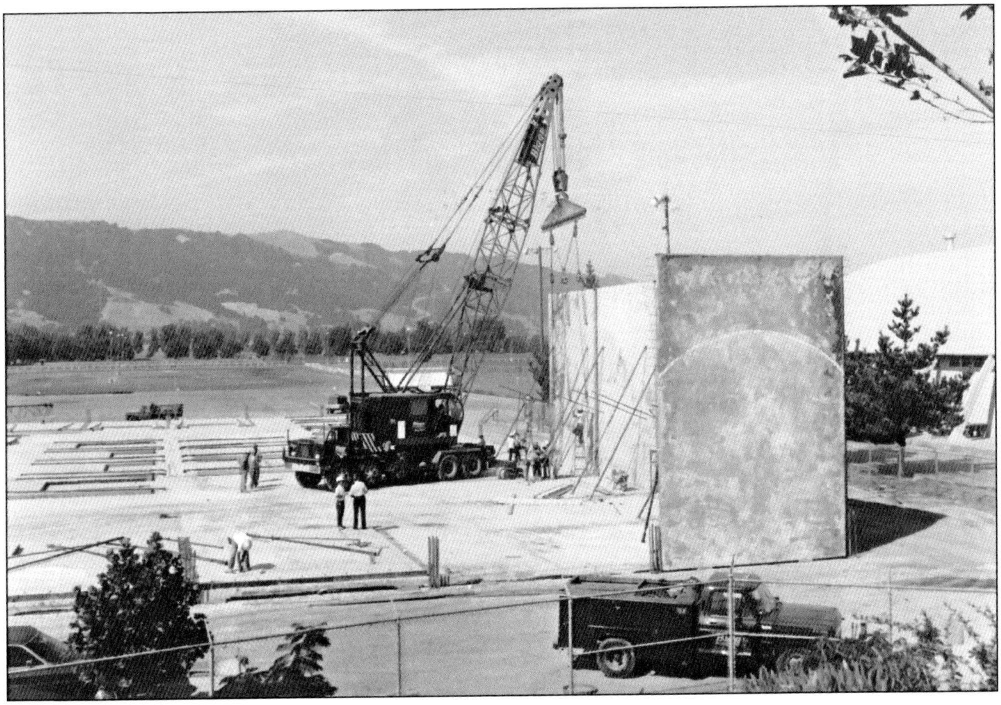

The Young California Building ground-breaking was on August 4, 1974, and the building was completed on June 7, 1975. It hosts exhibits by youths of all ages—including students and 4-H members—ranging from craft, hobbies, and clothing to horticulture and fine arts. At 38,000 square feet, it is the fair's largest exhibit facility. The air-conditioned building also features two separate kitchen facilities and rest rooms. (Above courtesy of Peter Bailey.)

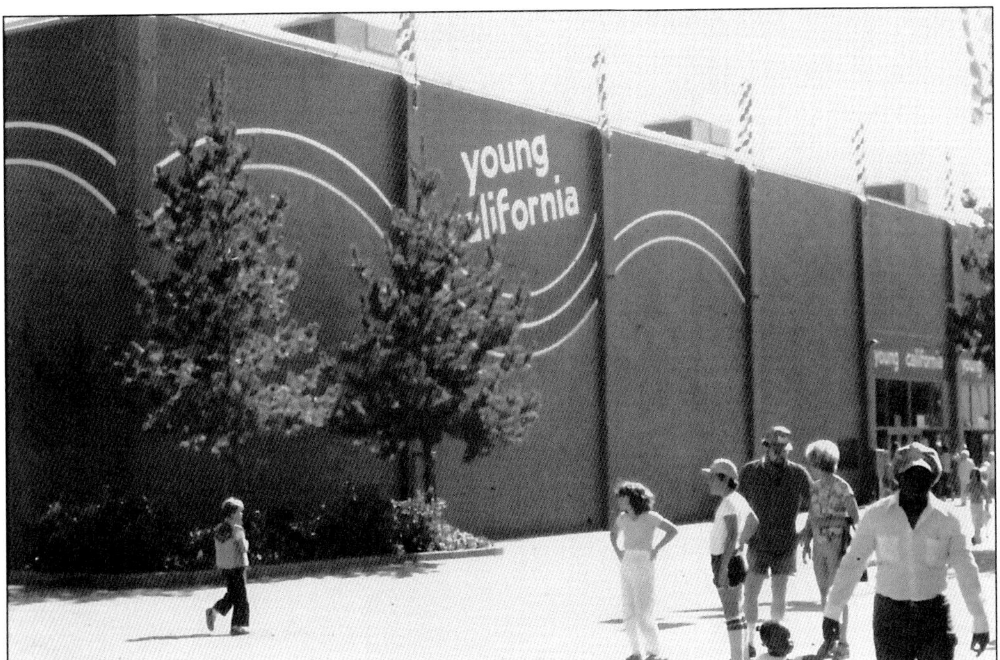

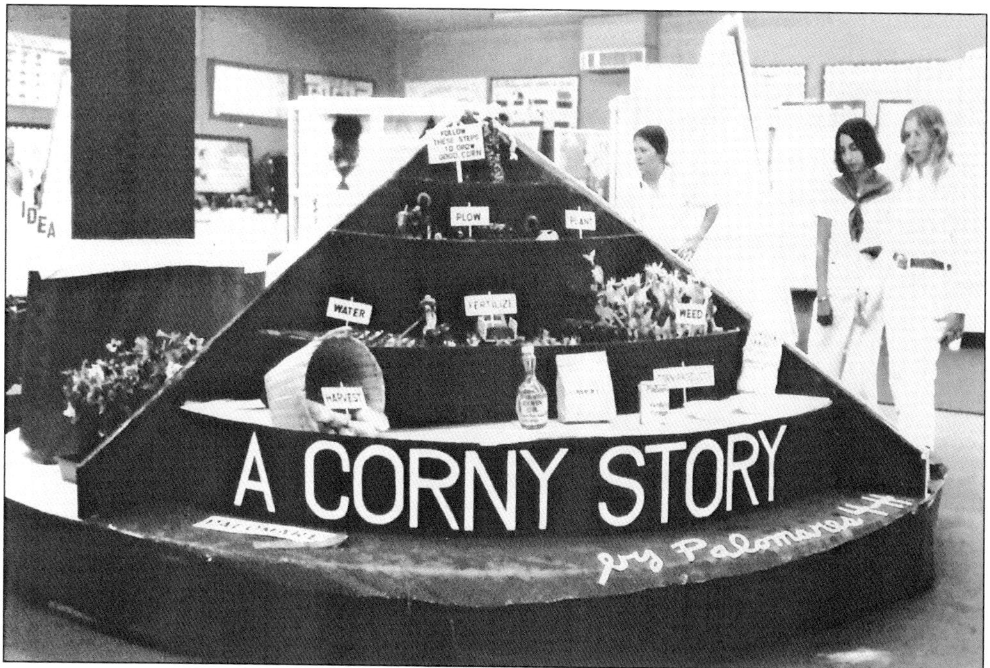

Competitive exhibits in 1975 included hobbies, gems and minerals, collectibles and memorabilia, amateur gardens, a rose show, fine arts, photography, poetry, jewelry, ceramics, winemaking, beer brewing, and creative living for things such as sewing, quilting, baking, jellies, jams, and needlework. The child below gets a demonstration in cow milking.

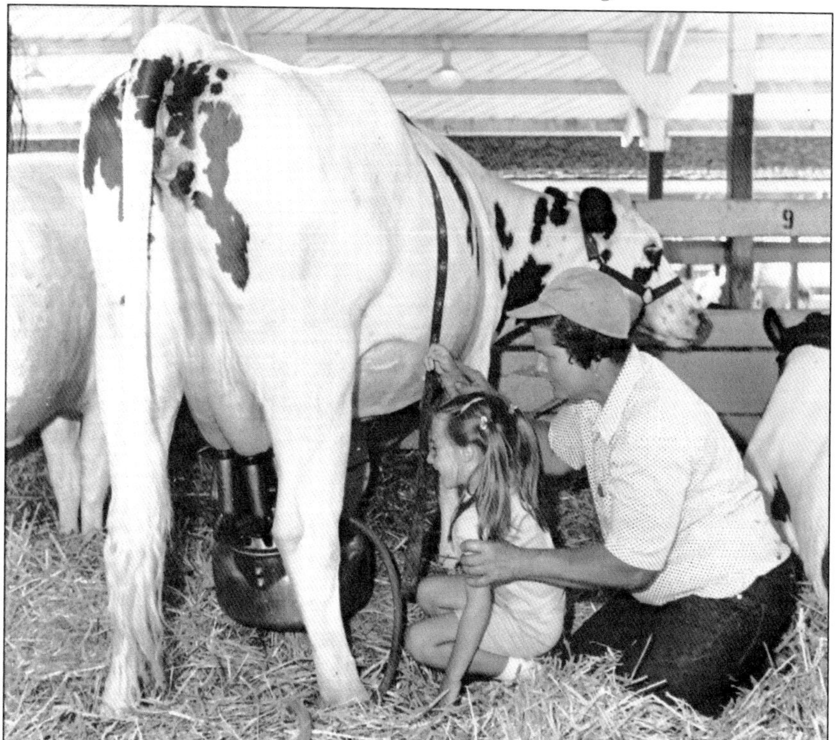

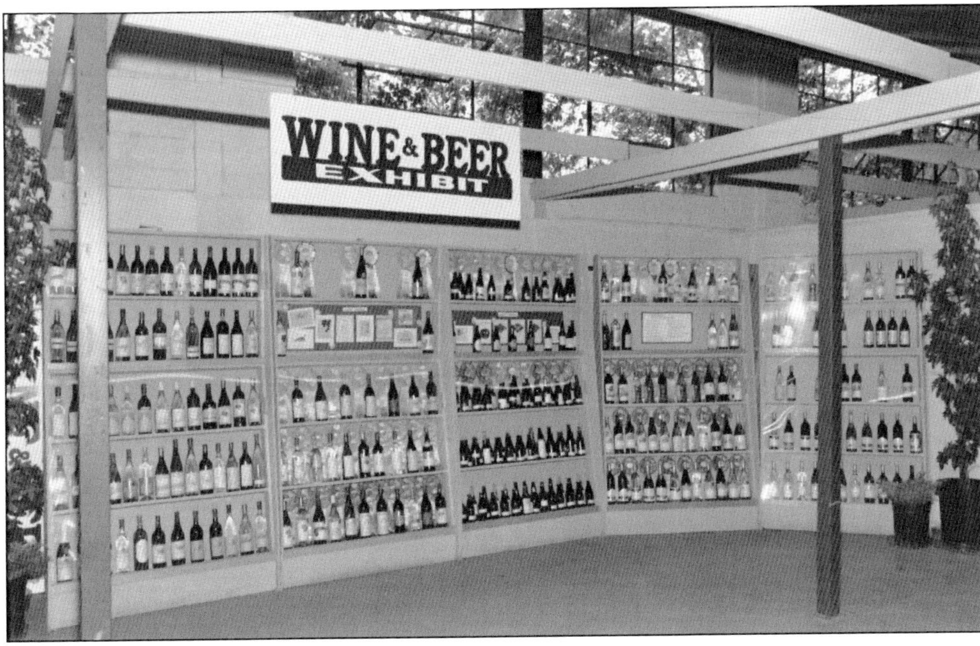

The first amateur winemaking contest was held in 1981. Forty-seven wines were judged, compared to the 2010 Best of the Bay wine competition, in which 274 wines from 64 wineries were judged.

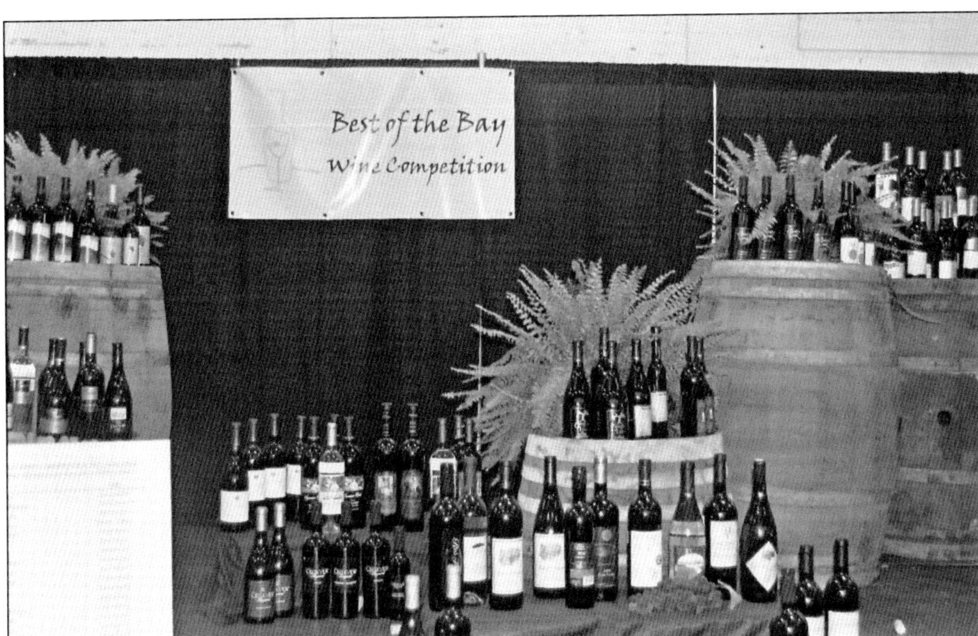

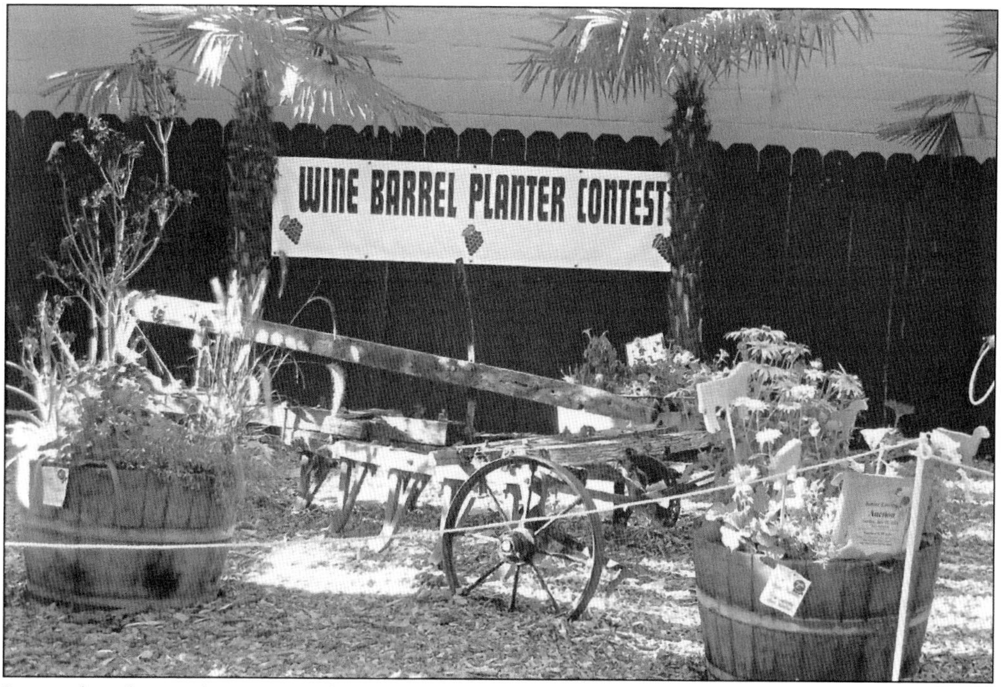

Located in the southeast area of Alameda County, Livermore and Pleasanton are just far enough away from the coast to provide the daytime heat required to allow the area's grape vineyards to thrive, yet they still maintain cool evening breezes. For this reason, the fair's many exhibits include wine, winemaking, and wine-related activities.

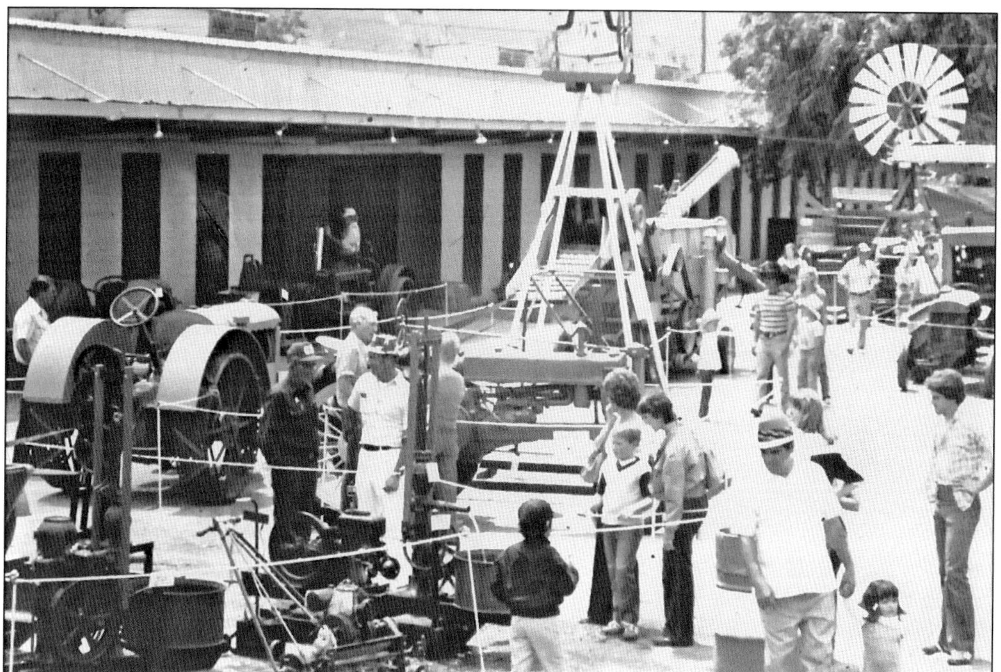

The fair's display of antique farm equipment is located near the small animal pavilion. The display includes a working water pump that allows fairgoers to cool off on hot summer days.

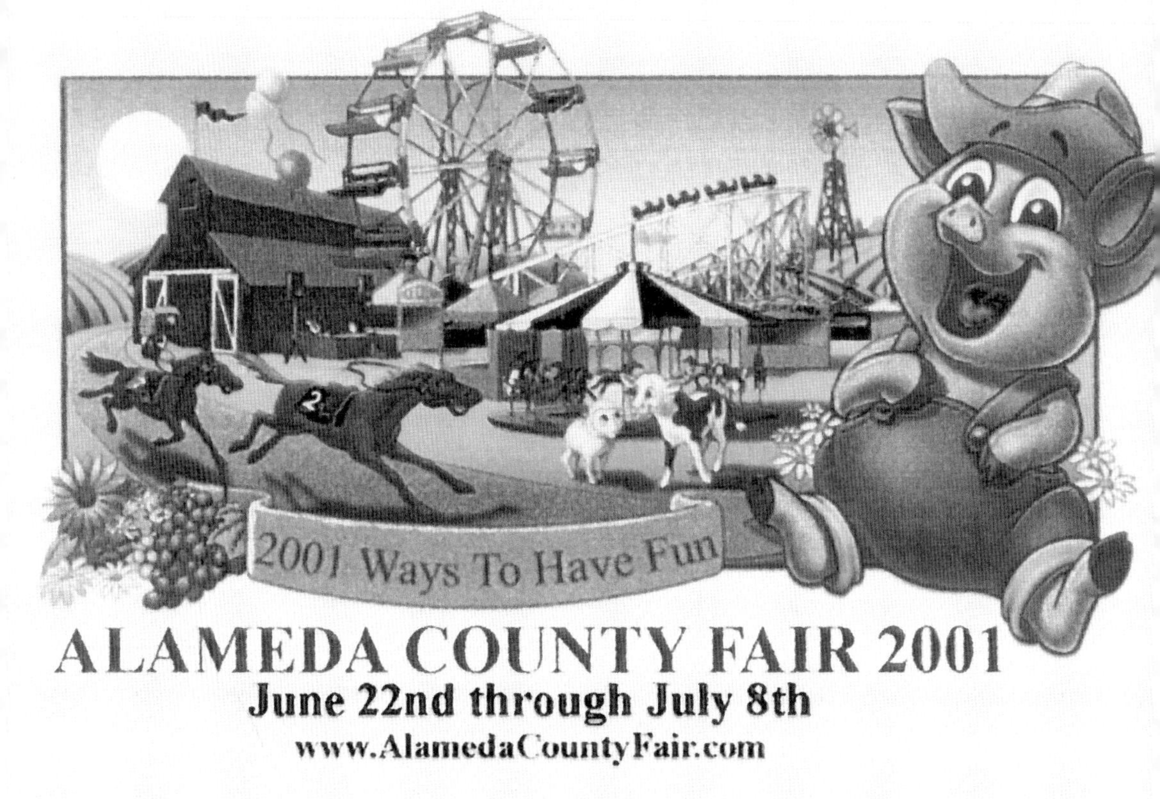

The 2001 fair hosted the usual competitive exhibits, as well as a livestock contest featuring rabbits, poultry, pigeons, swine, sheep, beef, dairy goats, horses, and guide dogs.

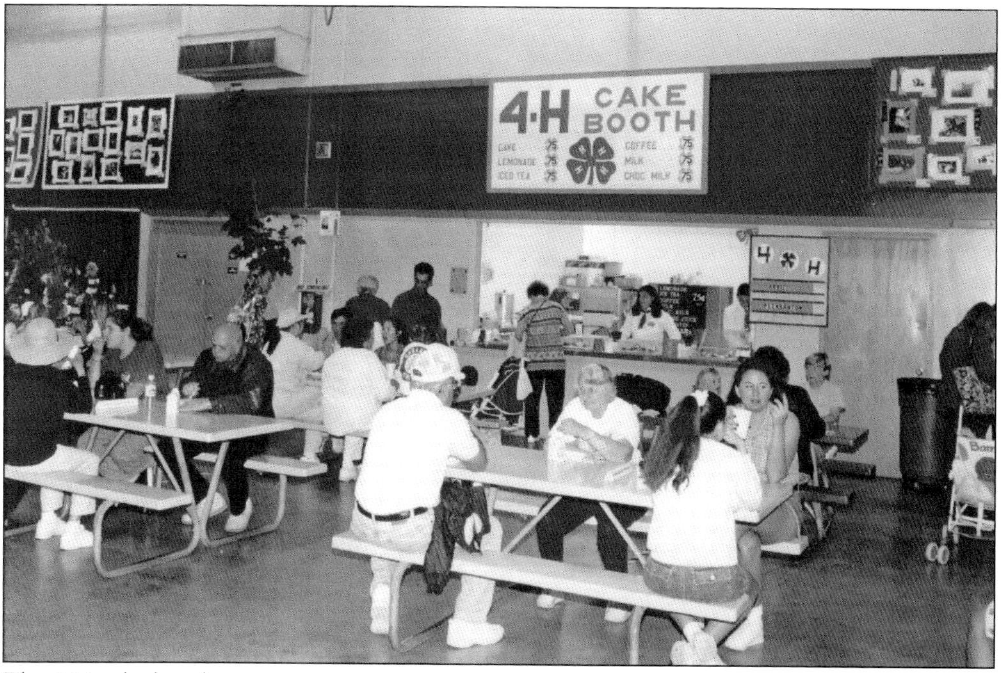

The 4-H cake booth continues to be a favorite fair tradition. The county 4-H community groups take turns manning the popular booth, and fairgoers line up to purchase cake and cookies. The booth is a major fundraiser for the youth groups.

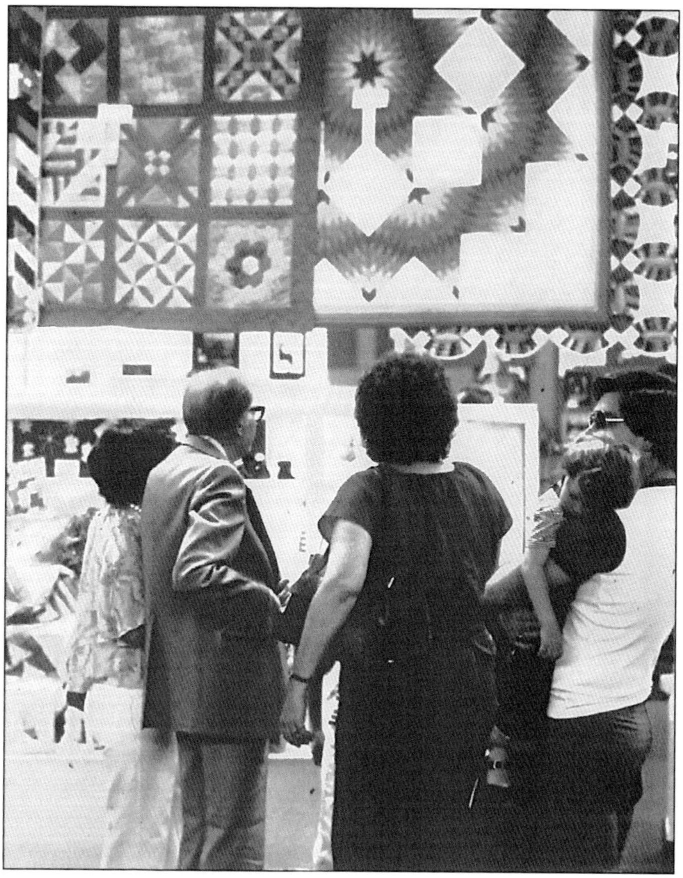

Beautiful quilts, such as those seen at right, as well as other needlework and sewing projects, are located in the Young California Building.

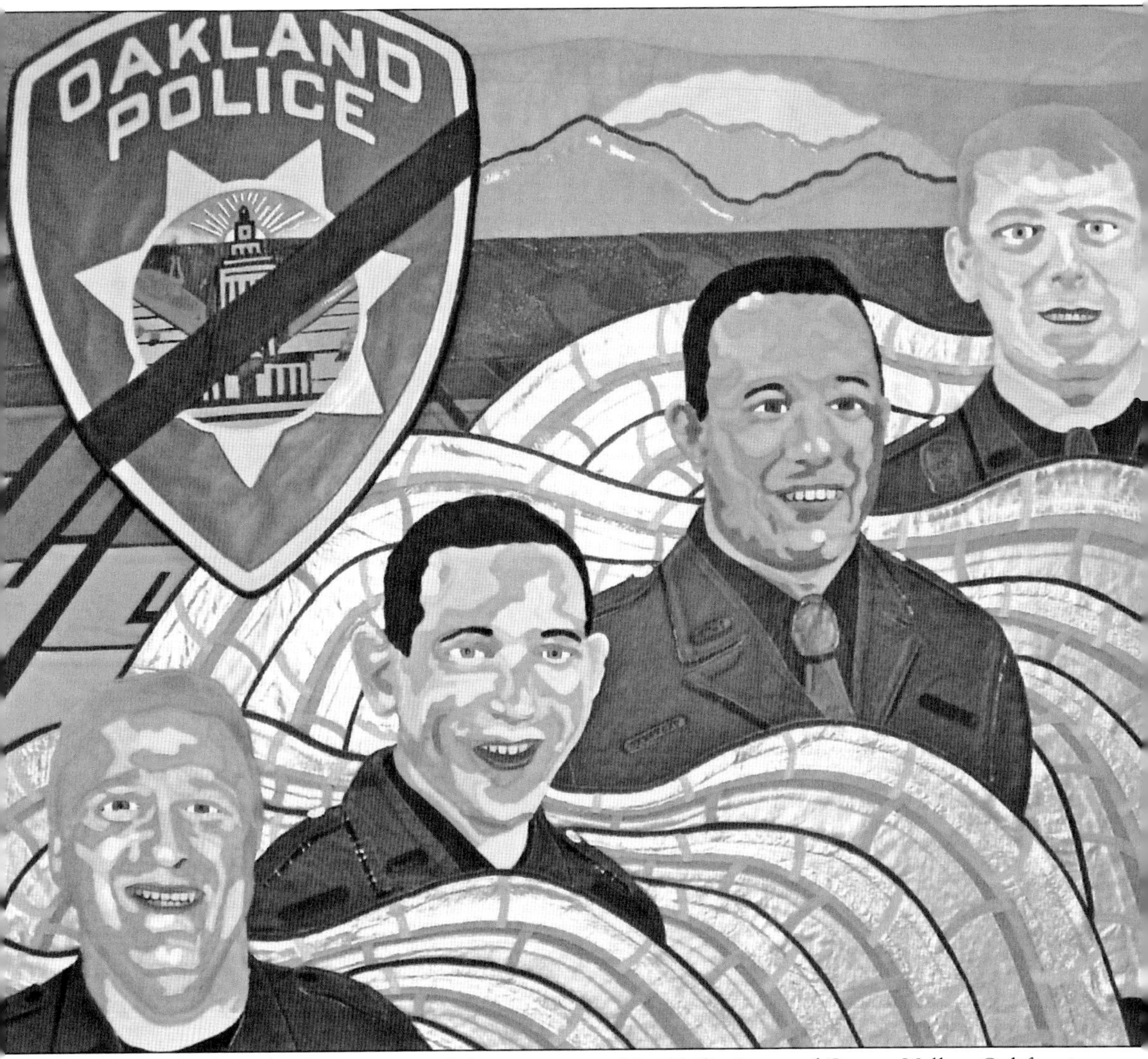

This touching leather mosaic exhibit was created by Philip Long of Castro Valley, California, in memory of four Oakland police officers who lost their lives in the line of duty on March 21, 2009. From left to right are officer John Hege and sergeants Daniel Sakai, Ervin Romans, and Mark Dunakin. (Courtesy of Ario Ysit.)

Four

Horse Heaven

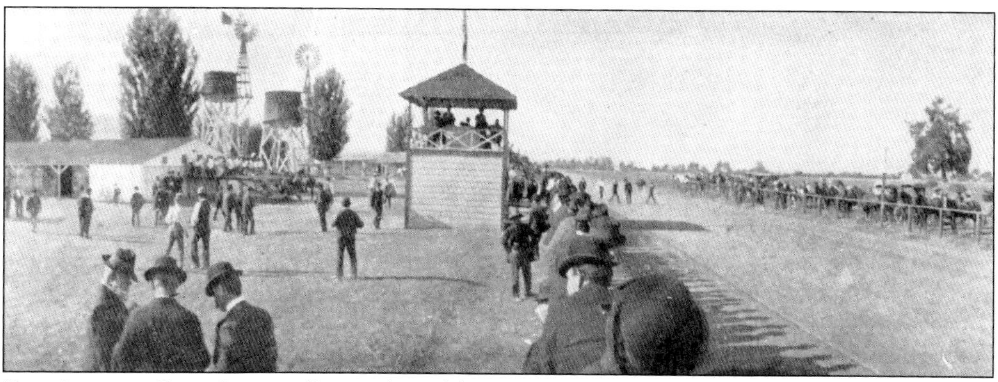

Don Augustin Bernal originally raced neighbors, including Robert Livermore, Jose Amador, and Jose Higuera. Following their father's death in 1872, sons Frederick and Antonio Bernal built a one-mile-long oval track behind the family's ranch in 1874. (Courtesy of Amador Livermore Valley Historical Society.)

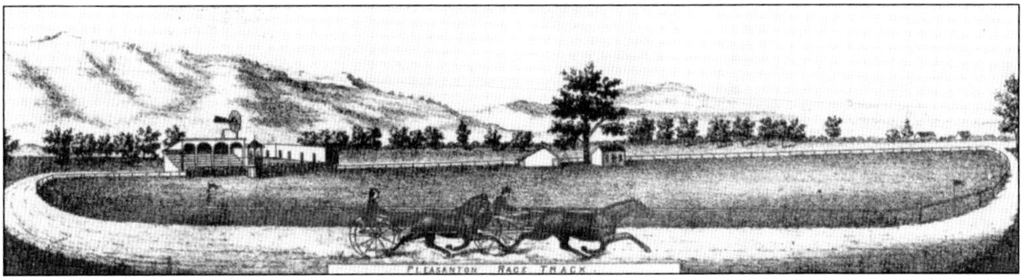

In 1876, the track was sold to Joseph F. Nevis, who formed a jockey club that included members of local ranches. Nevis also built barns, stables, and a small grandstand and renamed the facility Nevis Race Track. (Courtesy of Thompson and West Atlas.)

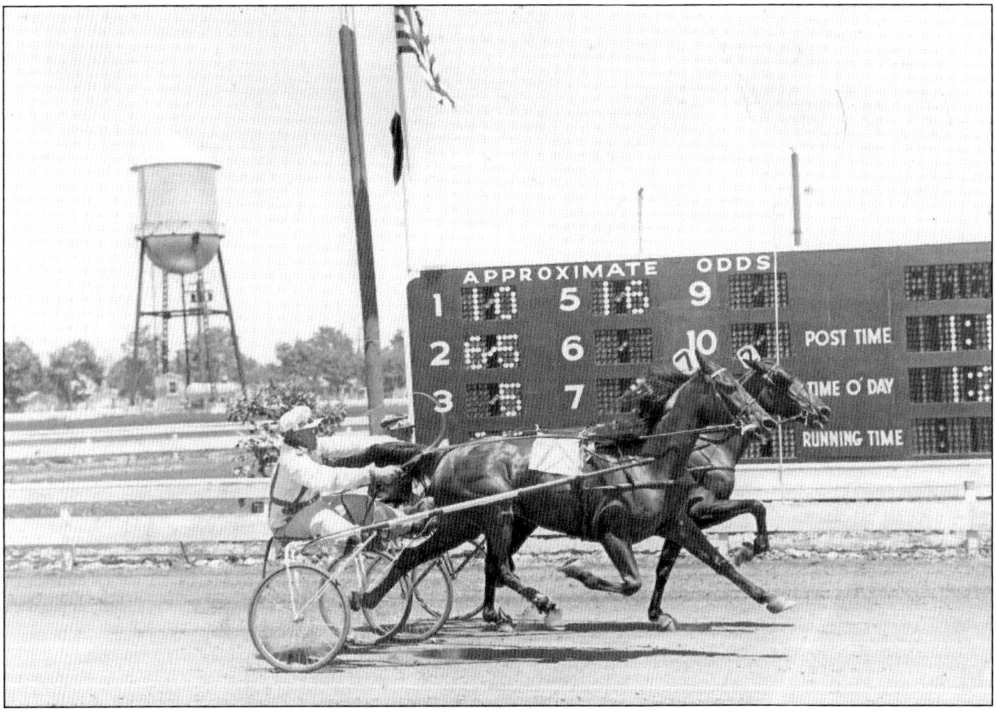

In 1883, the track was purchased by Australian businessman Monroe Salisbury for $25,000 and renamed Pleasanton Stock Farm. The track became popular for spring training facilities for horses from cooler parts of the country. Salisbury specialized in harness racing, and by 1898, the track in Pleasanton was considered a major sporting event arena.

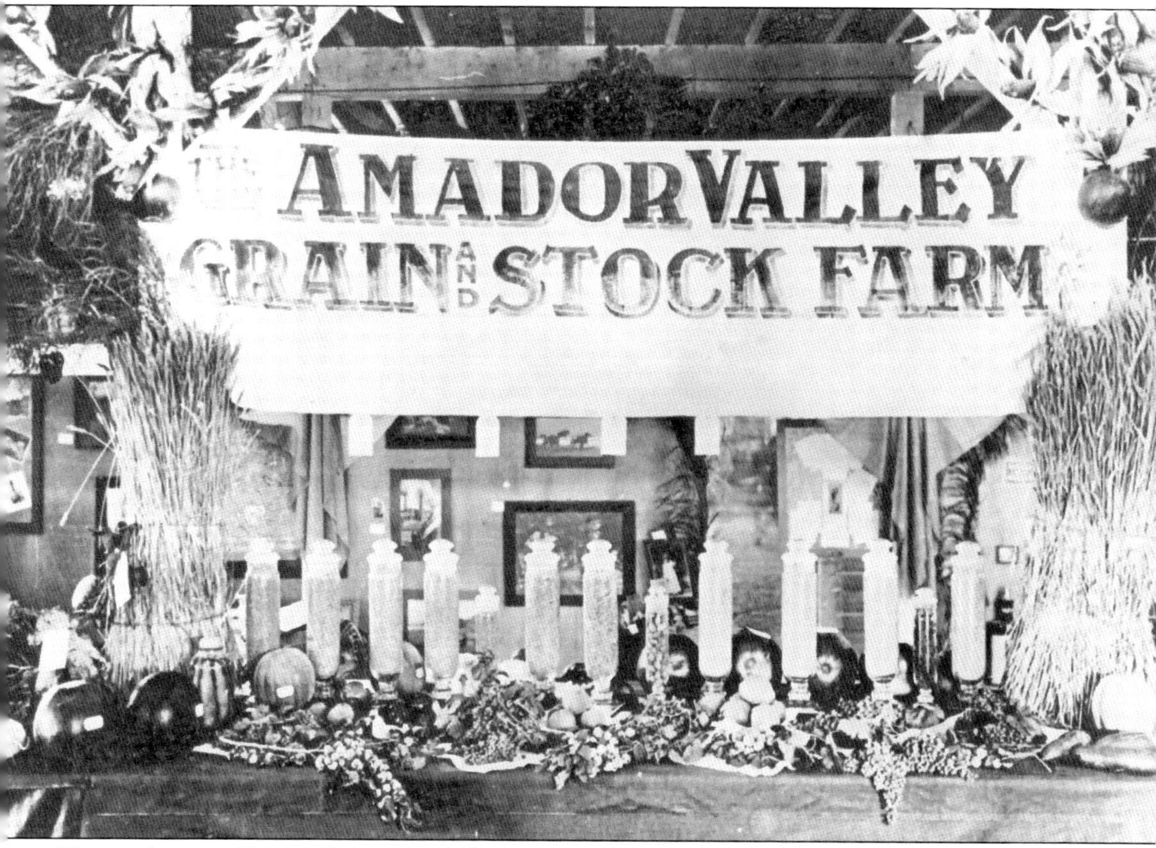

The track was sold several times to different owners over the years. More improvements were made, stables and barns were added, and the track was brought up to state regulations. By 1900, the track, then known as the best winter horse training facility in America, included more than 200 horse stalls. (Courtesy of Amador Livermore Valley Historical Society.)

FIRST ANNUAL ALAMEDA COUNTY FAIR 81

RACING

Wednesday, October 23, 1912

Best two in three. Free for all trot. Prize $100 Cup.

Thursday, October 24, 1912

Best two in three. Free for all pace. Prize $100 Cup.

Running Race

Friday, October 25, 1912

2:20 Pace

Best two in three Prize $100 Cup

Running Race

Saturday, October 26, 1912

Base Ball Game

Sunday, October 27, 1912

Motor Cycle Races

Amateur Races

First 5 miles - - - - - Prize Cup
Second 10 miles - - - - Prize Cup
Third 15 miles - - - - Prize Cup

Professional Race

25 miles - - - - - Cash Prize $150.00

In 1911, the track was sold to Rodney G. Mackenzie, the son of a Canadian railroad tycoon, who spent approximately $250,000 to build the first grandstand, which, underneath, housed elaborate living quarters. He also built stables that held 300 horses. Mackenzie was instrumental in bringing running horses to the track, rather than trotters or pacing horses. But one of Mackenzie's most historical achievements was when he helped host the first Alameda County Fair, which opened adjacent to the racetrack in 1912. An antigambling law prevented folks from betting on horse races, but trotting races were held and $500 purses were awarded. After Mackenzie's death in 1927, the racetrack and surrounding property were held by a trust company until the land was sold to Alameda County for $50,000 in 1941.

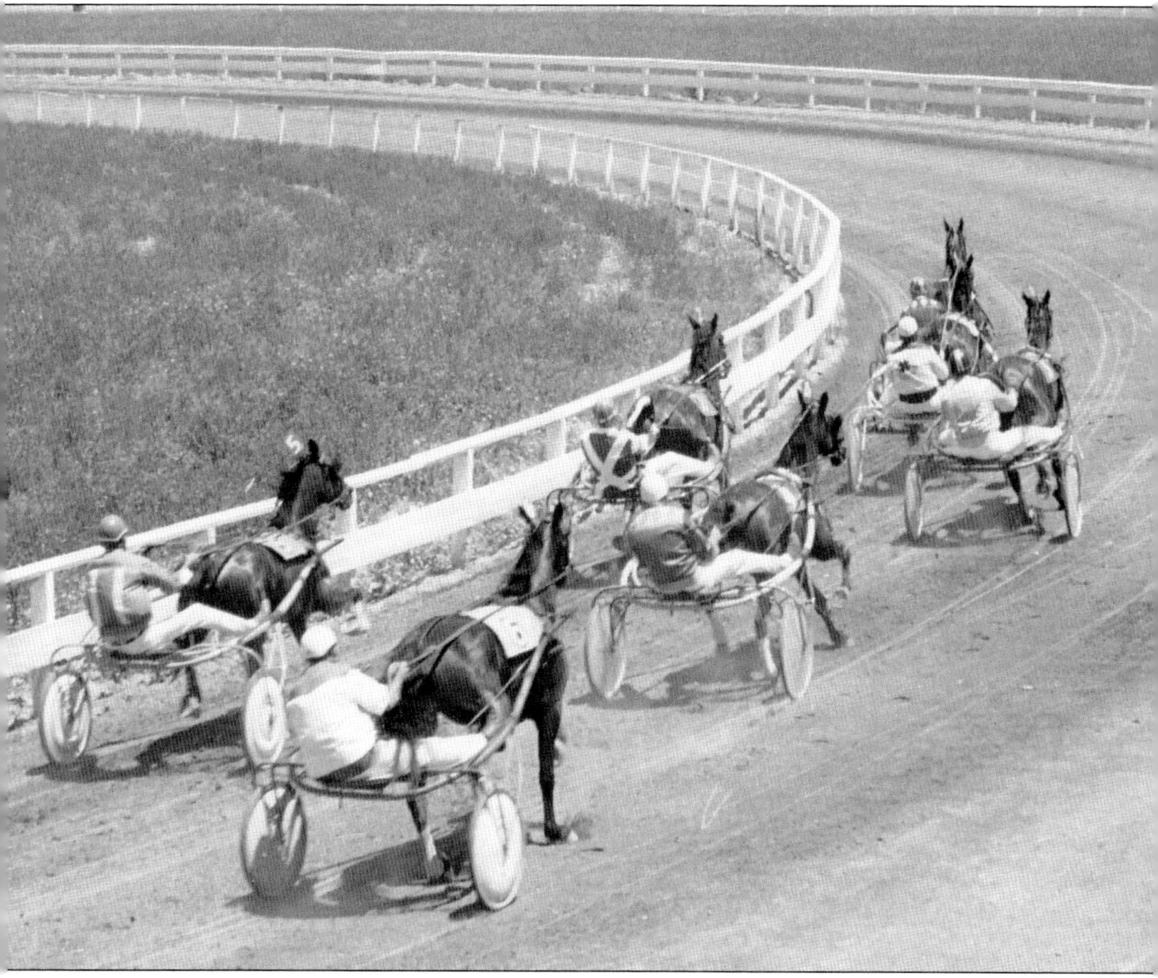

Due to the mild climate, fresh water, alluvial soil, and excellent feed, the racetrack also became a popular spring training facility for horses from cooler parts of the country and was referred to as "Horse Heaven." Nearby creek-bottom sediment and sandy clay soil provided near-perfect track conditions. The natural underground gravel filter beds provided the fresh water, and the foothills supplied the best conditions for growing the area's finest red oat hay. It is rumored that America's champion racehorse Seabiscuit trained in Pleasanton for 10 days during the winter of 1936.

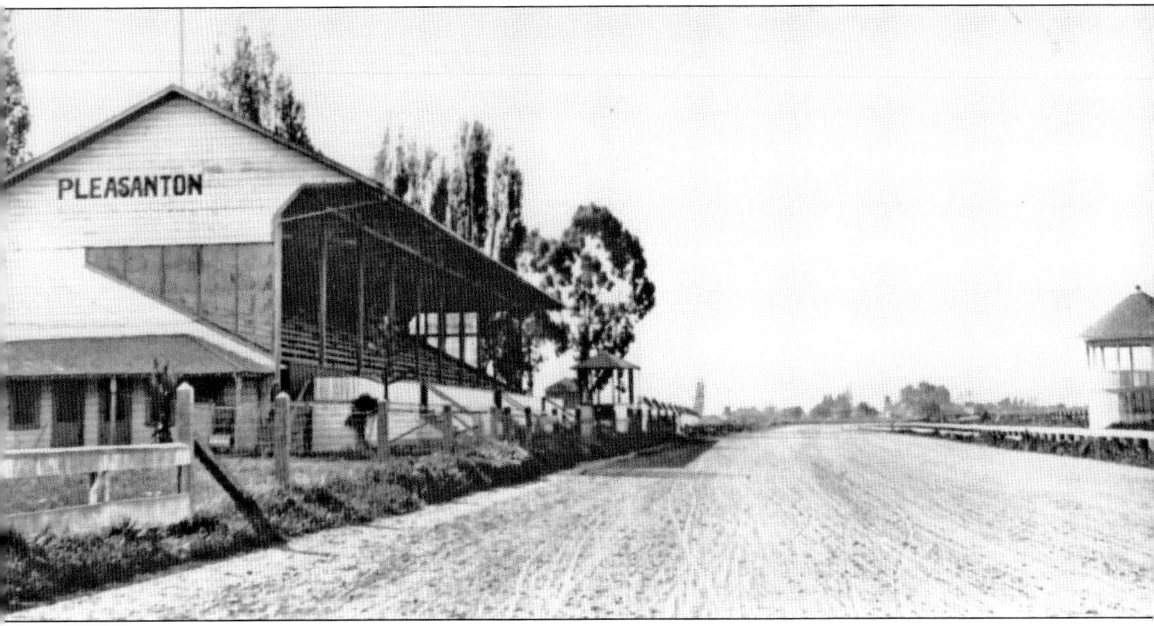

In 1933, California legalized pari-mutuel betting with the intent that taxes would fund the development of agriculture and livestock at the county fairs and promote Thoroughbred racing in the state. Developed in France, pari-mutuel betting is a system of betting in which wagers are pooled together before a race and then distributed based on the outcome. In 1939, a modern fair was established and the first pari-mutuel handle was recorded at $19,800 over a four-day period.

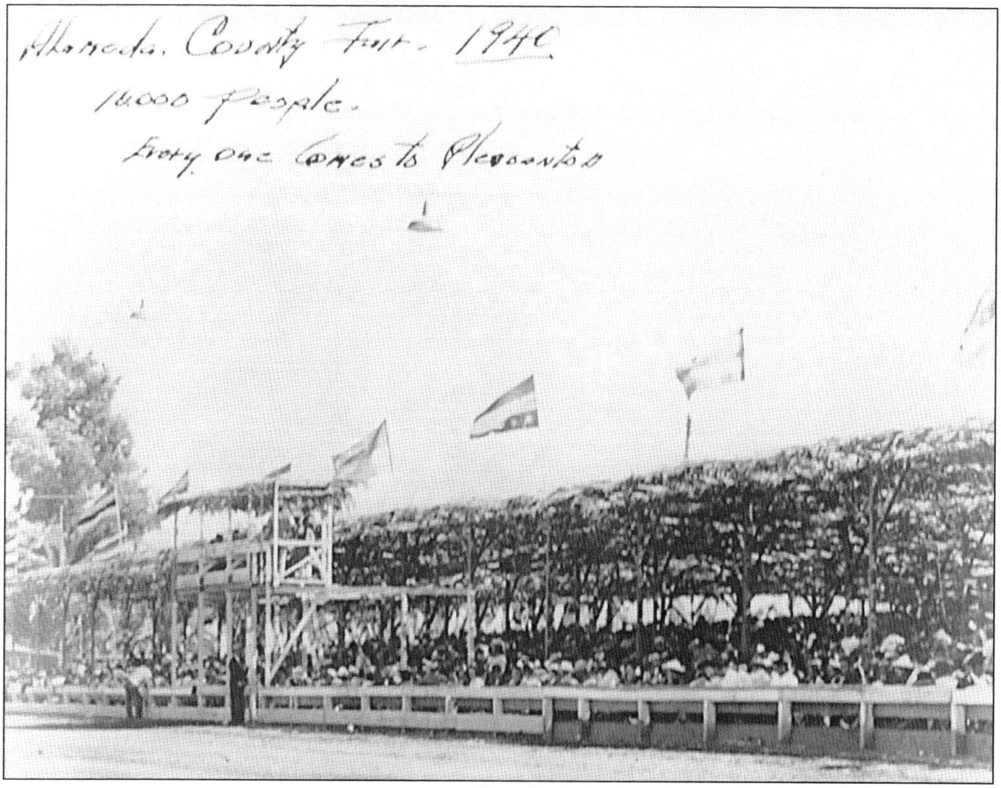

The previous grandstand had burned down, so racing fans used temporary bleachers, as seen above, prior to the new 5,000-seat grandstand (below), which was built for a cost of $69,000 in 1941.

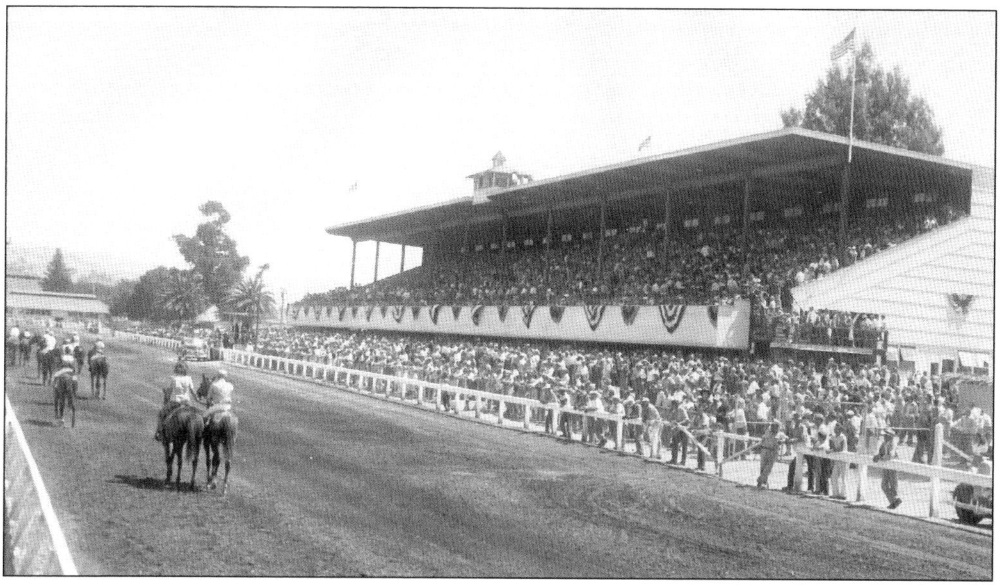

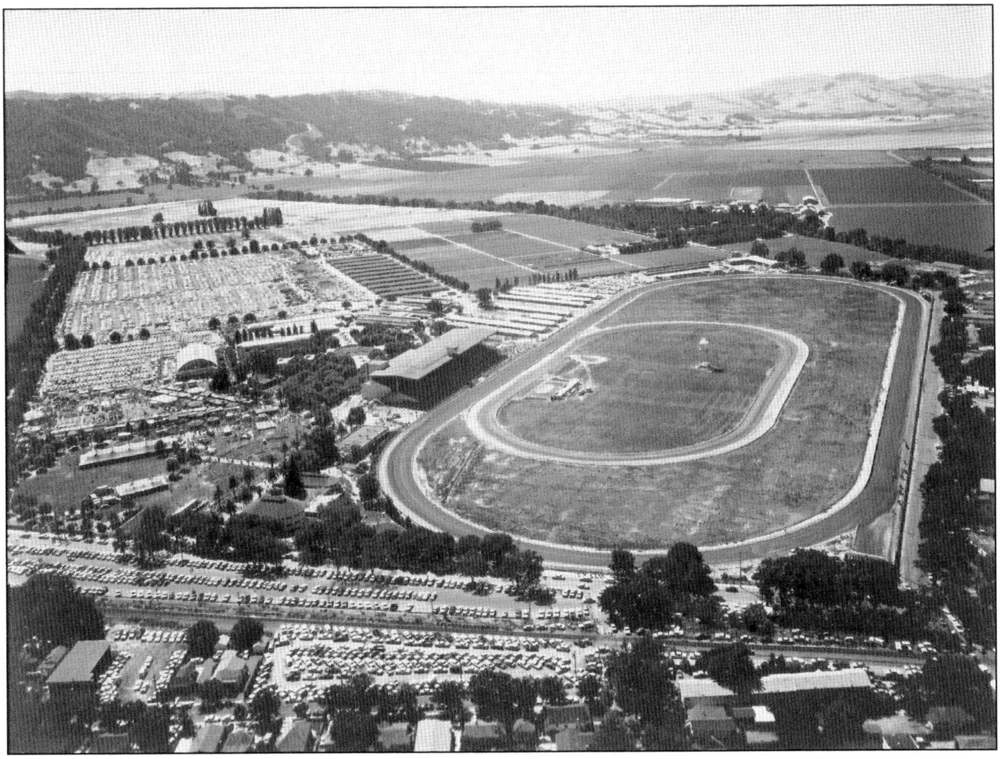

Also new to the 1941 fair was the addition of a half-mile inner track to be used for harness racing. Over the track's nine days of racing, a record $432,000 was wagered.

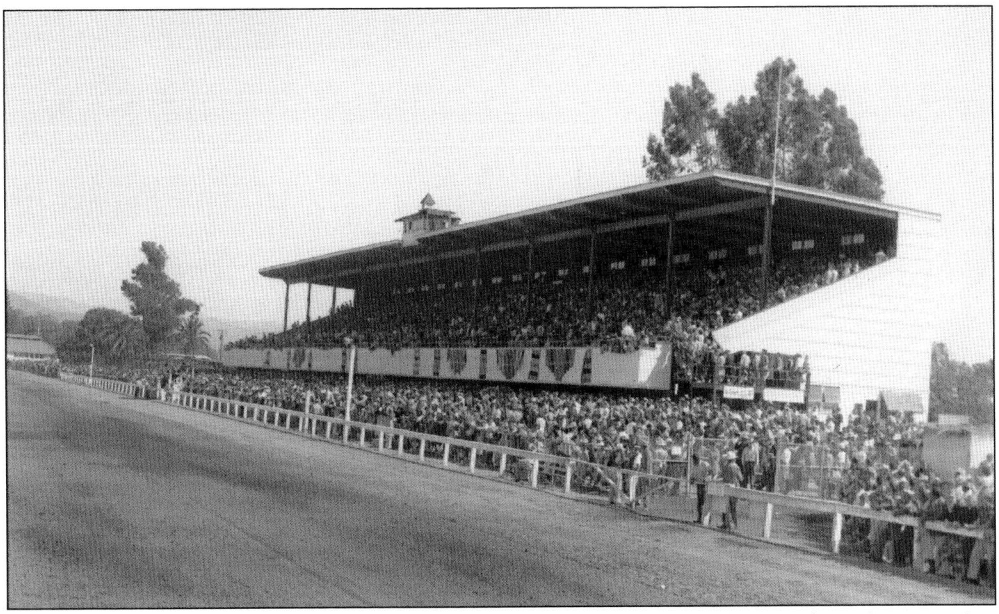

There were no fairs held from 1942 to 1944 due to World War II, but the grandstand was used as a lookout. Local residents took nightly shifts scanning the sky for enemy aircraft.

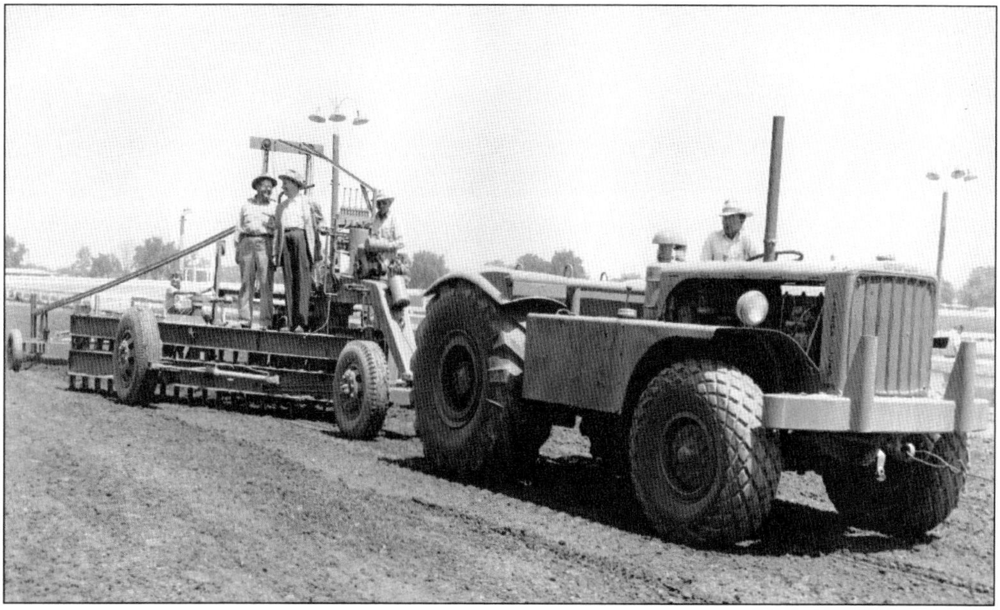

The 1948 fair marked the first time 10 Hawaiian Thoroughbreds were featured during the fair's horse races. Besides the eight Thoroughbred horse races, the track also held four Standardbred races and four harness races daily.

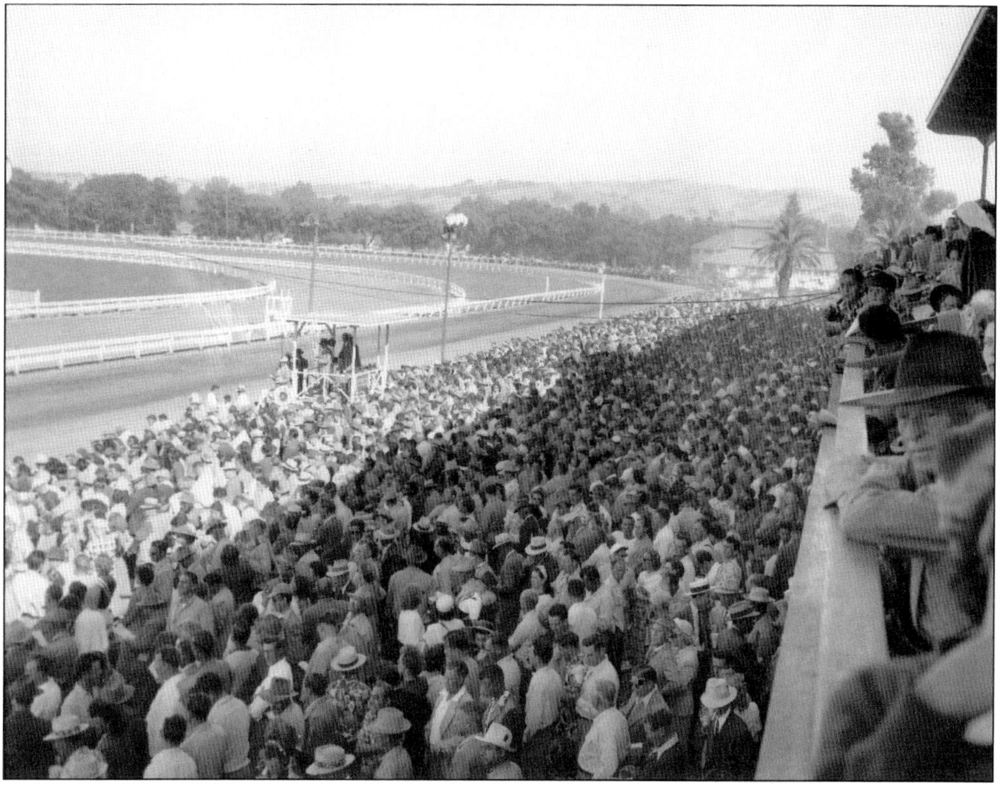

On opening day in 1948, several hundred horses were stabled and ready to race, and more than 3,800 patrons were ready to place their wagers. The last year of harness racing was in 1972.

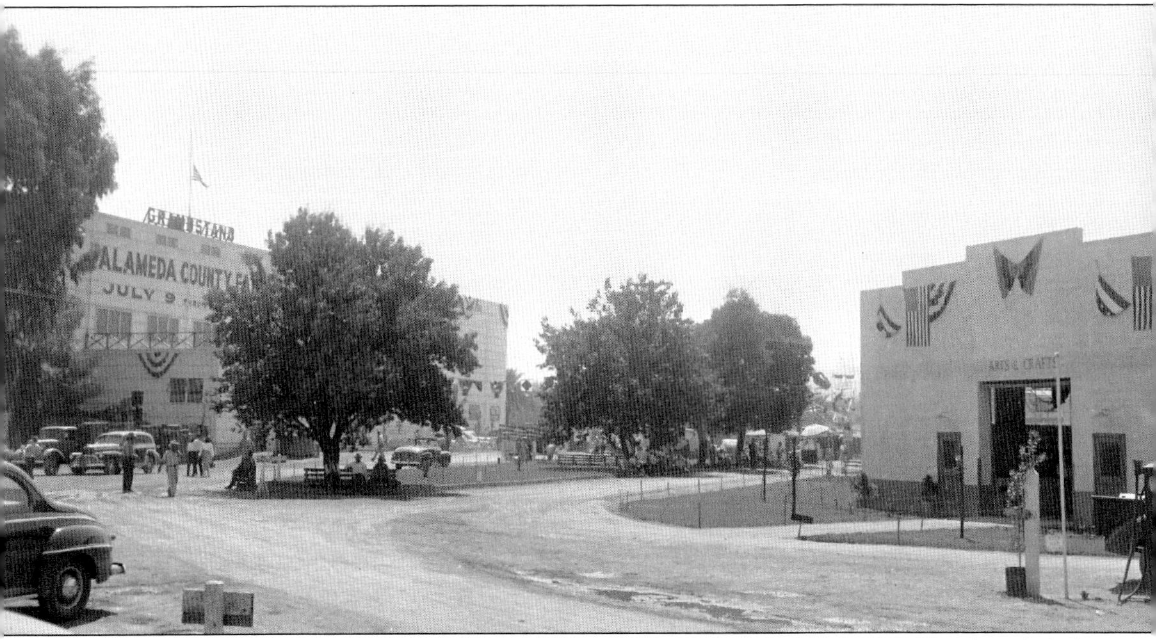

The Alameda County Fair Horse Show was held on Sunday, July 11, 1948, and included a children's class, a hunting class, a parade horse class, a trail horse class, a stock horse class, a harness pony class, and several others. Prizes ranged from $5 for fifth-place contestants to $175 for first-place winners.

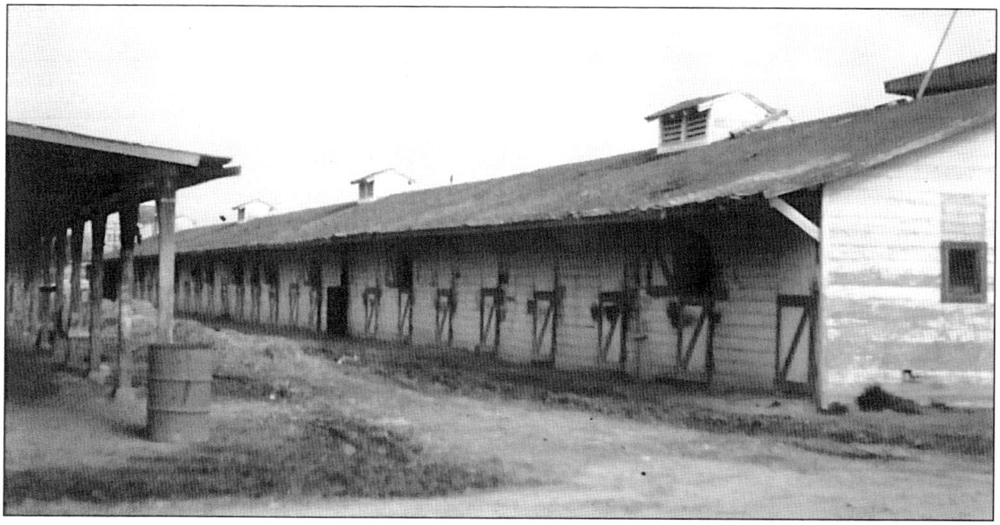

With all of the wooden structures on the property, fire was quite common. Tragedy struck in 1952, when 10 horses were killed and several barns were destroyed by fire. Another major fire on February 10, 1965, burned only one horse barn, but plans were immediately drawn to build new barns by 1970. (Below courtesy of Peter Bailey.)

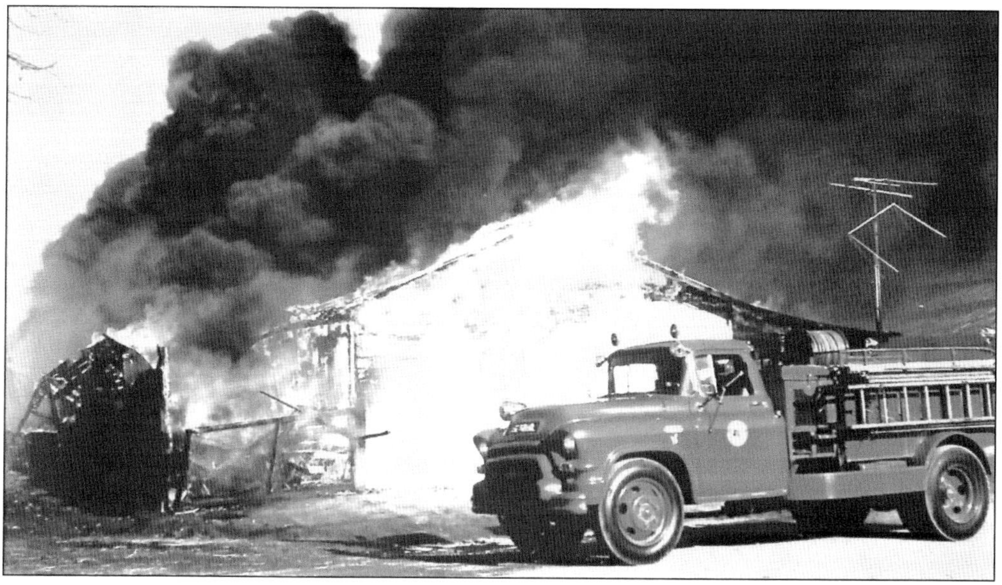

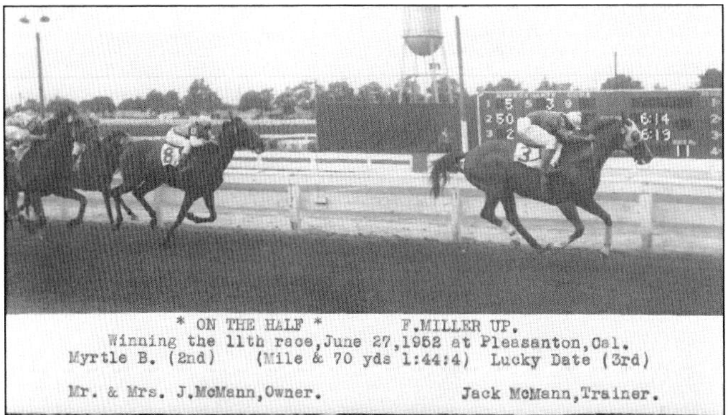

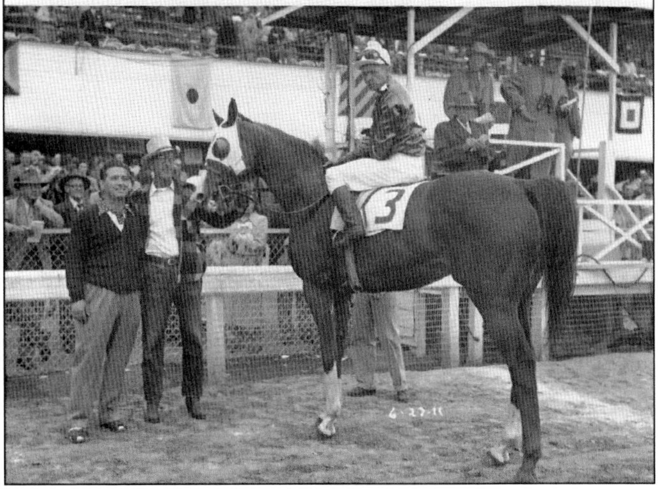

A horse named On The Half was in the winner's circle on June 27, 1952. Owned by Mr. and Mrs. J. McMann, the horse won the 11th race. (Courtesy of Sammy DiLaura.)

Pictured below is the former grandstand that was demolished and replaced with the current grandstand in 1964. In 1963, horse racing attracted 82,000 fans who wagered $5.5 million.

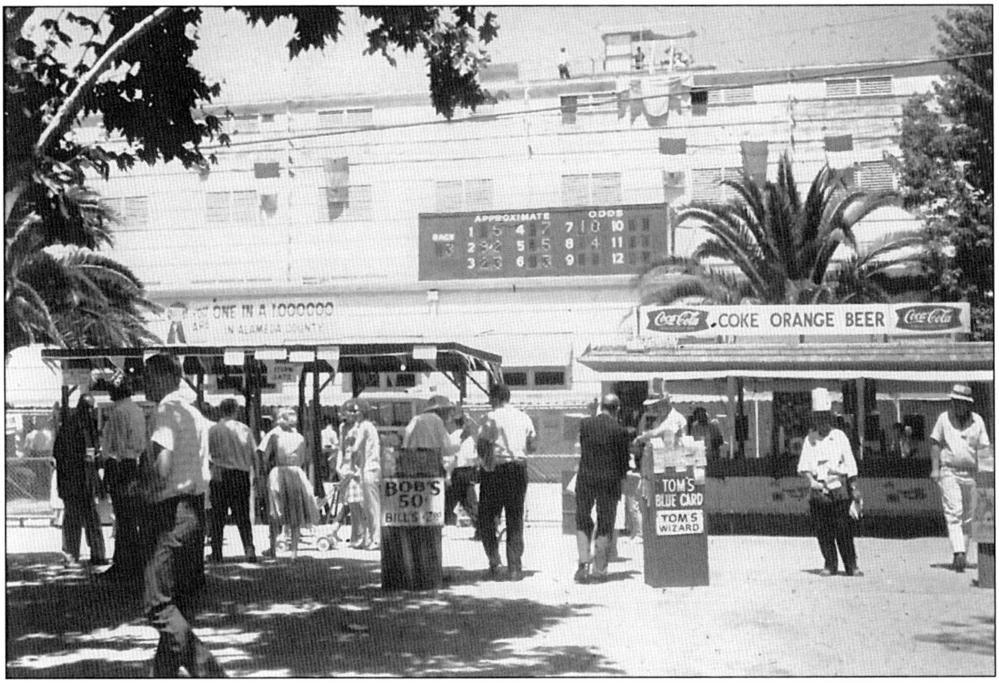

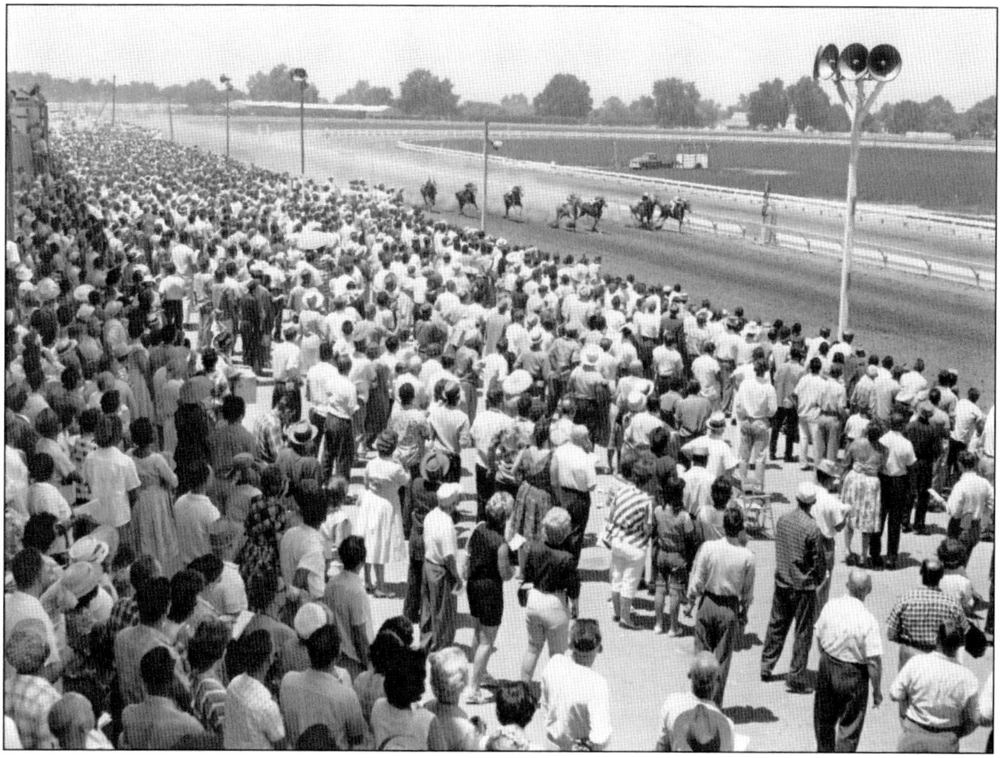

On August 14, 1963, the *Daily Review* reported an increased budget estimate from $1.3 million to $1.6 million for the new steel and concrete grandstand that would seat 6,608 racing fans, with additional standing room for a total capacity of 25,000. Immediately following the 1964 fair, construction began to ensure completion by the 1965 fair.

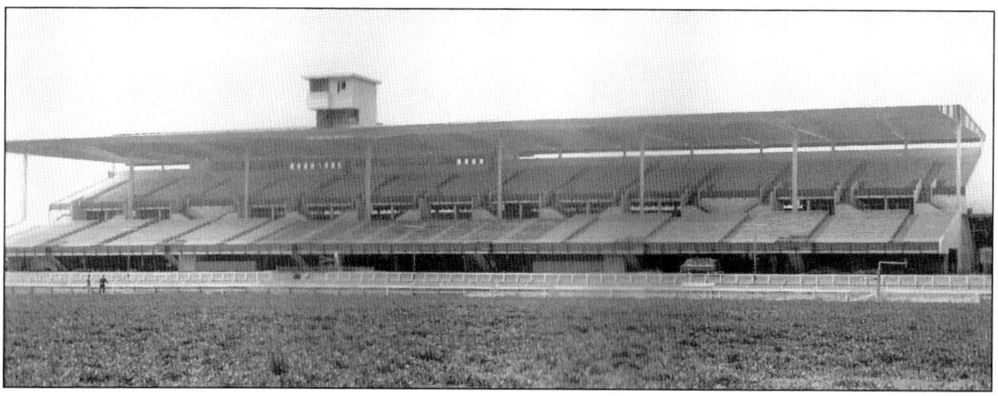

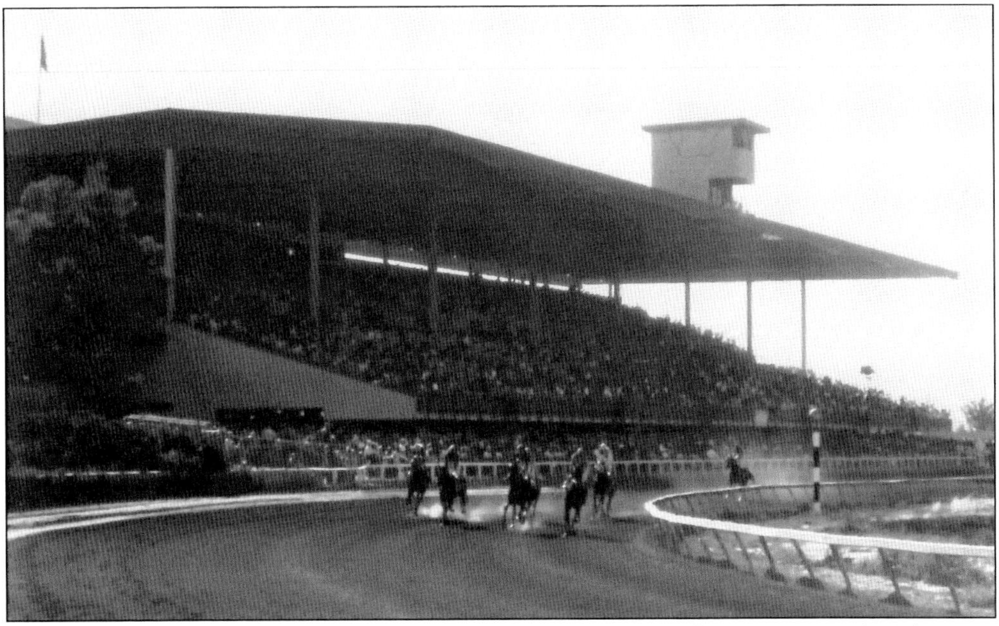

The fair's 15-day run in 1975 proved a smashing success, surpassing all previous records. Admission was up 11 percent, the racetrack's pari-mutuel handle was $11,828.50, and grandstand admission was a record 122,688.

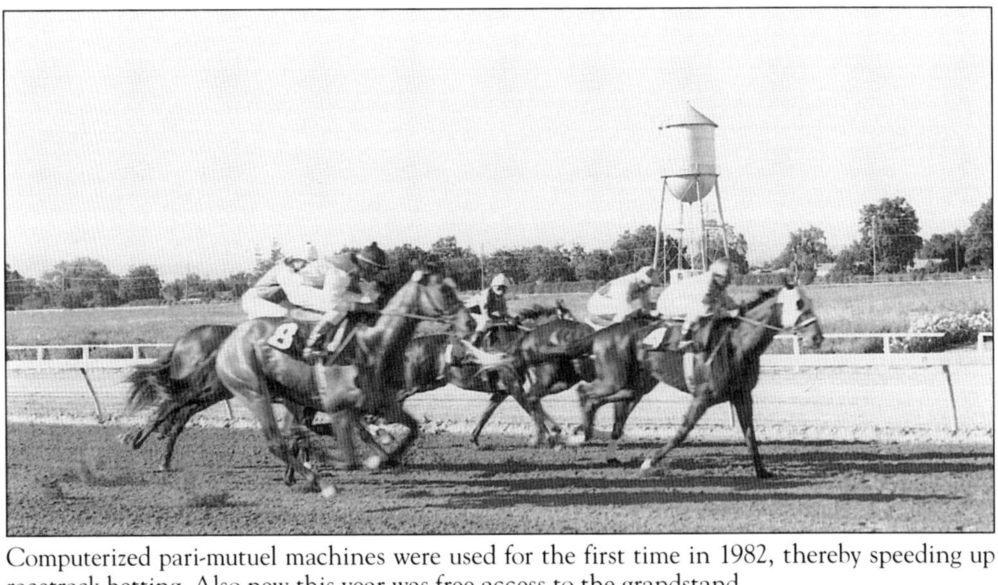

Computerized pari-mutuel machines were used for the first time in 1982, thereby speeding up racetrack betting. Also new this year was free access to the grandstand.

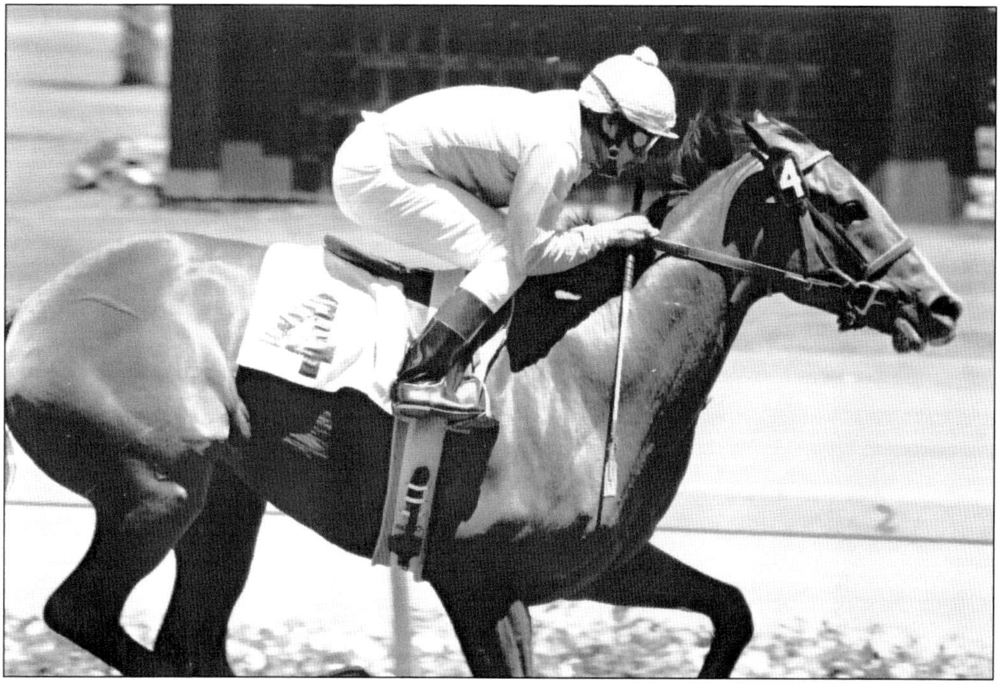

The fair offered a first-time-ever $1-million sweepstakes on July 1, 1985. All guests received an entry form to pick the winners of each of the 13 horse races being held that day. The person who correctly picked the winning horses won the sweepstakes or split the winnings amongst their fellow winners.

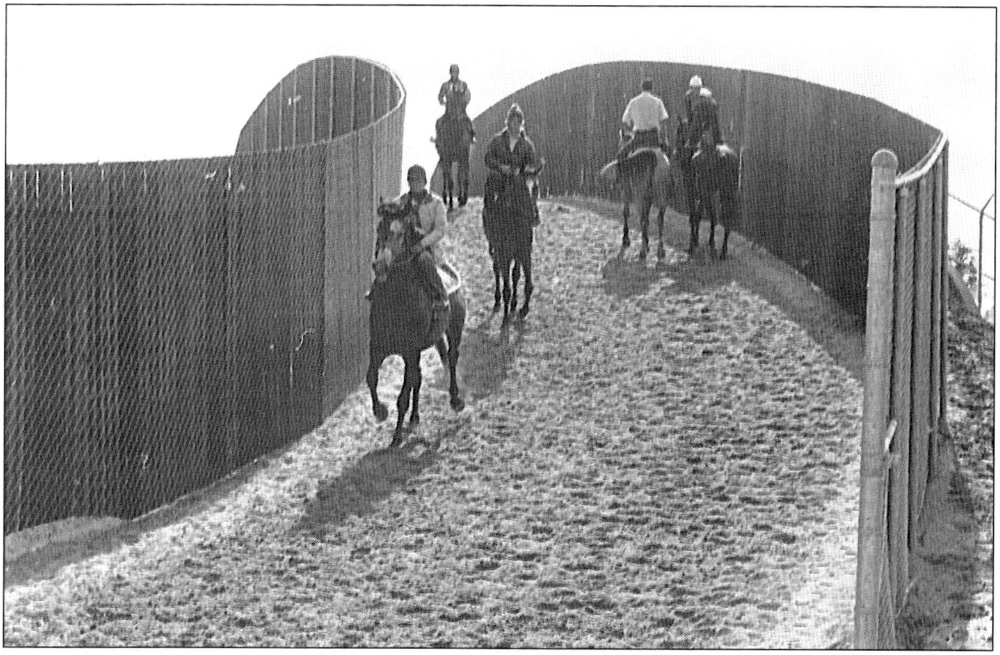

In 1996, the California Horse Racing Board formally reduced the number of racing days at all racetracks in the state from 13 to 11 days. It believed this would allow more horses to be offered for each race held. In comparison, the fair's racetrack hosted 16 days of racing in 2010.

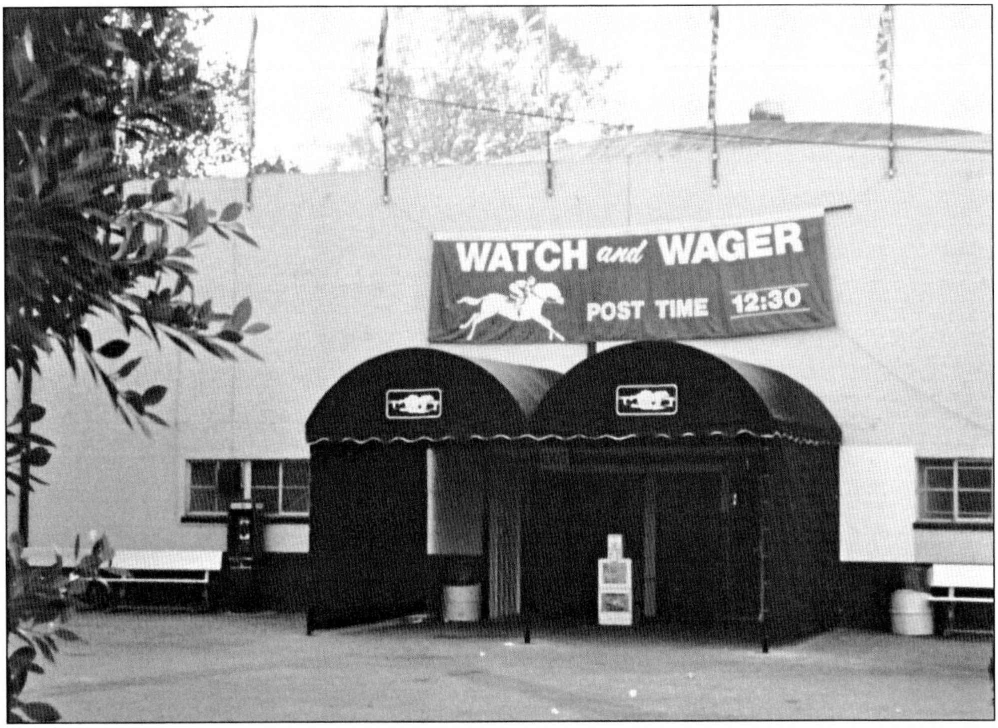

Several other fairs had been very successful in offering offtrack betting, therefore, after a considerable amount of effort by the fair's board of directors, the Alameda County Fair opened the Watch and Wager offtrack betting facility on March 1, 1987.

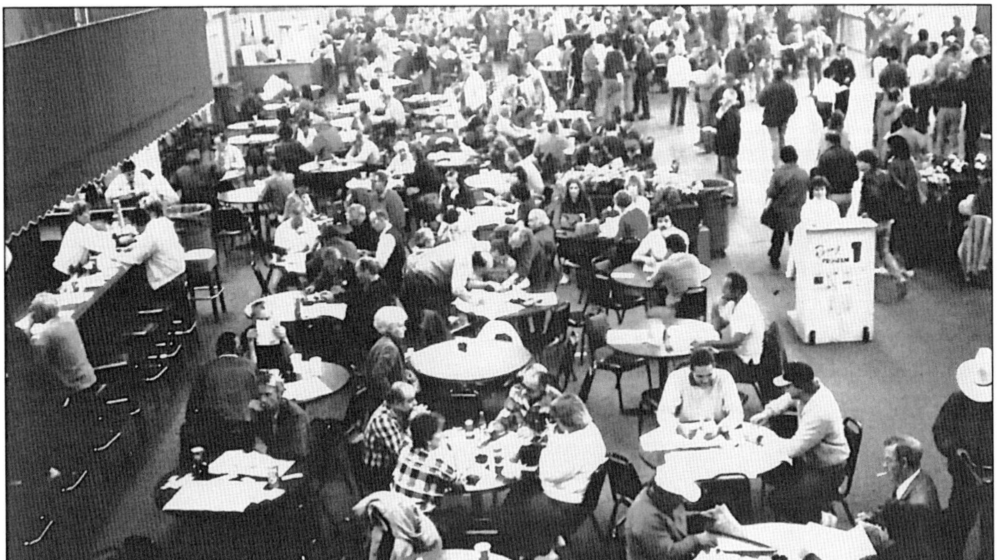

Housed in the Hall of Commerce Building, the facility included tables and chairs, a café, 35 television monitors, 12 betting machines, 32 pari-mutuel betting windows, and two cocktail lounges. Hundreds of race fans flocked to the facility, and by 1990, it was apparent that a more permanent structure should be sought. (Courtesy of Peter Bailey.)

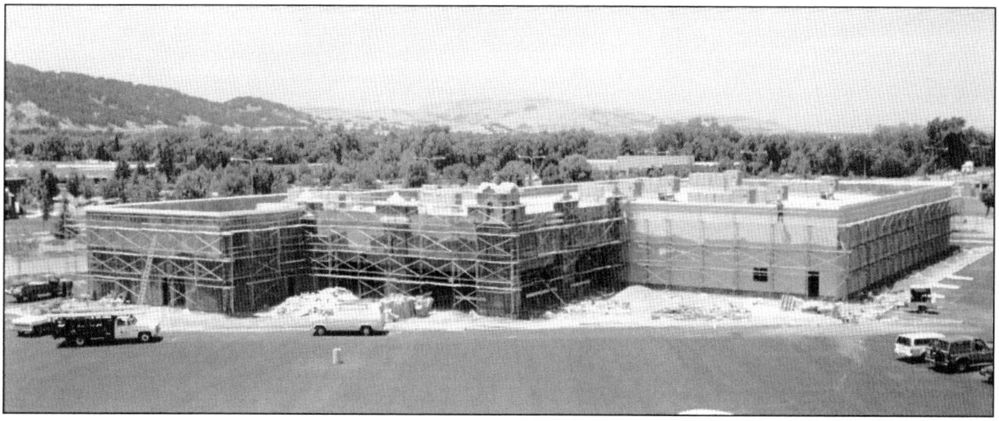

Located on the farthest west side of the fair property is the Satellite Wagering Facility. The facility's grand opening was on October 6, 1992. It includes wagering windows and computerized betting, 114 television sets, a snack bar, a turf club, and an outdoor patio. At 30,000 square feet, the facility can easily hold more than 800 persons. The facility cost approximately $3 million, none of which came from local or state tax dollars.

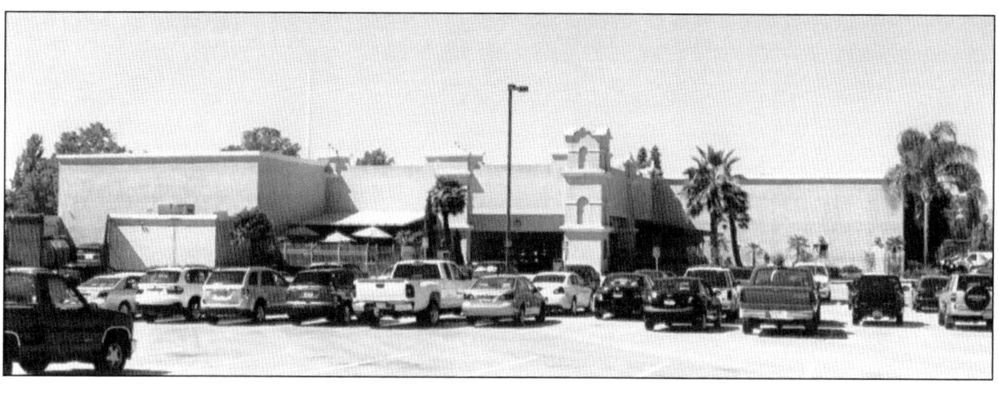

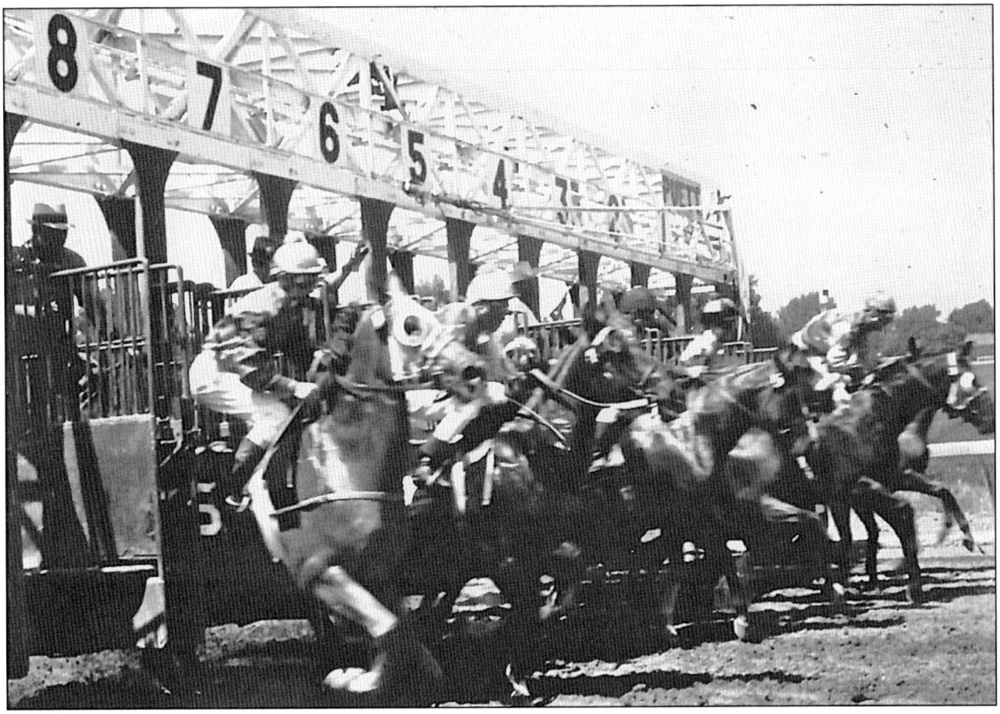

Celebrating its 150th anniversary in 2008, the racetrack at the Alameda County Fair is the oldest continually running track in California and the oldest one-mile track in America.

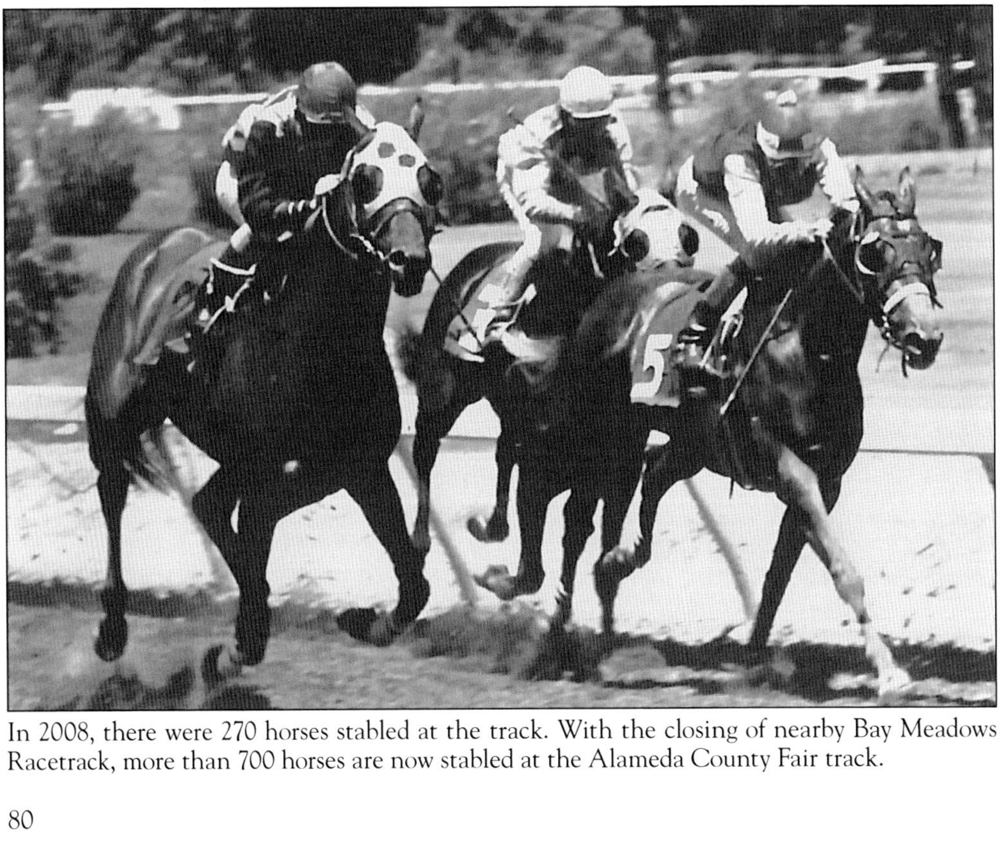

In 2008, there were 270 horses stabled at the track. With the closing of nearby Bay Meadows Racetrack, more than 700 horses are now stabled at the Alameda County Fair track.

Five

THRILLING RIDES

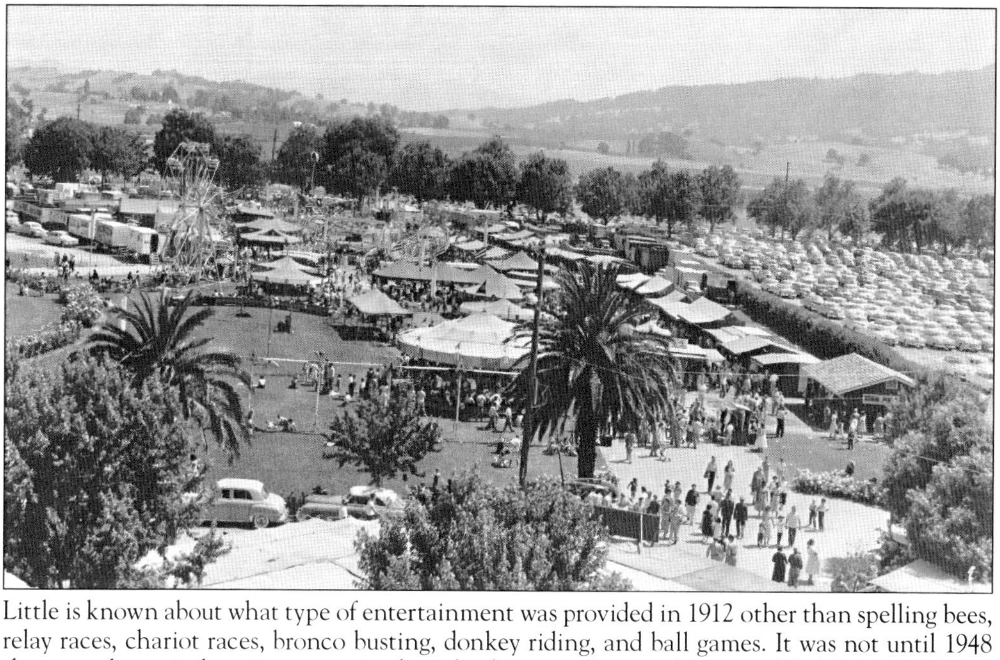

Little is known about what type of entertainment was provided in 1912 other than spelling bees, relay races, chariot races, bronco busting, donkey riding, and ball games. It was not until 1948 that actual carnival equipment arrived on the fairgrounds, compliments of Golden West Shows of San Francisco. At that time, there was also no admission fee to the fair except for entering the grandstands for horse races. The view above of the carnival area was taken in 1948.

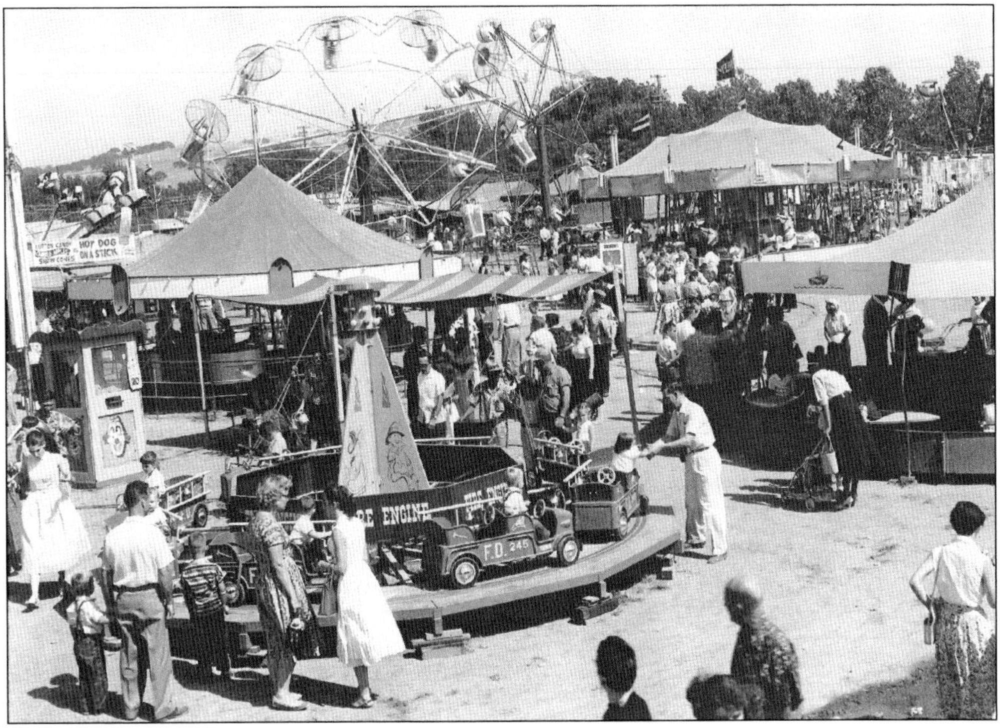

The carnival may have started out with only four rides, but by the late 1950s, there were dozens. Most of the mild rides, such as the carousel and Ferris wheel, were replaced by larger, faster, more thrilling rides.

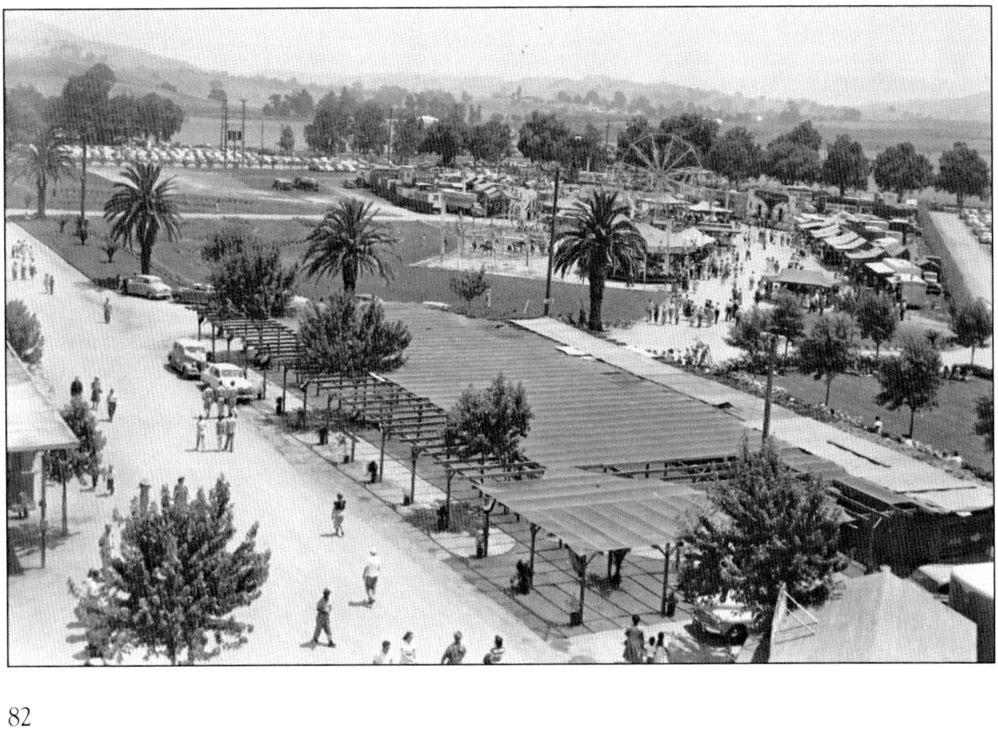

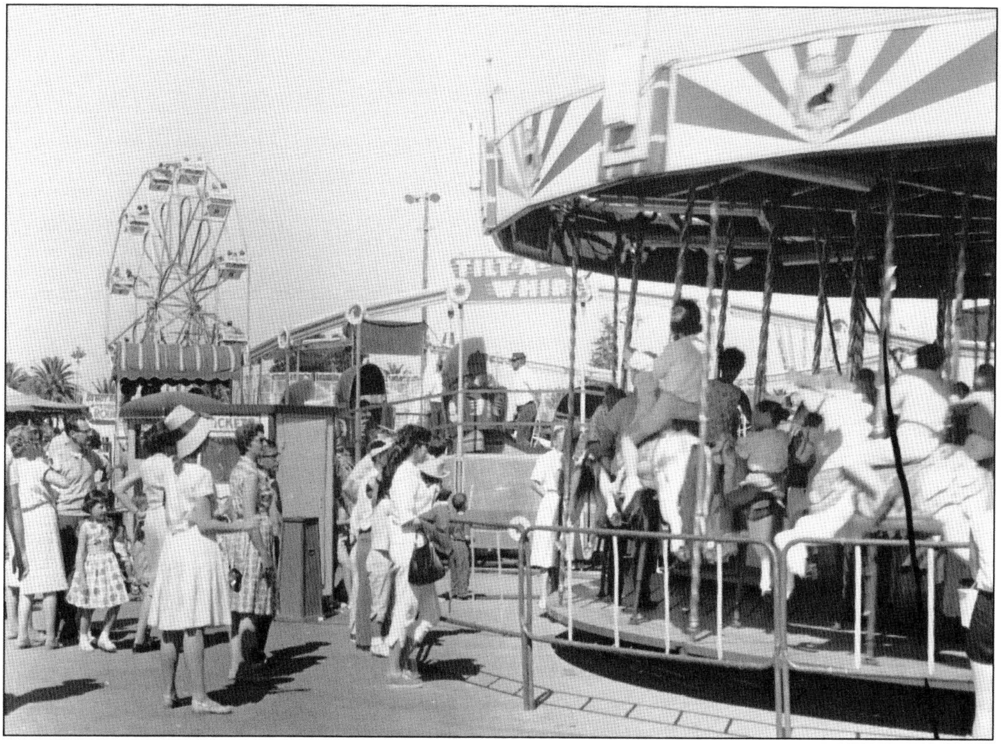

For several years, the Foley and Burke Carnival Company arrived by train on a track located adjacent to the fair's main entrance. In 1973, the Blash & Hilligoss carnival provided $2 million worth of rides and games for the fair such as the Tilt-A-Whirl, bumper cars, and a fun house.

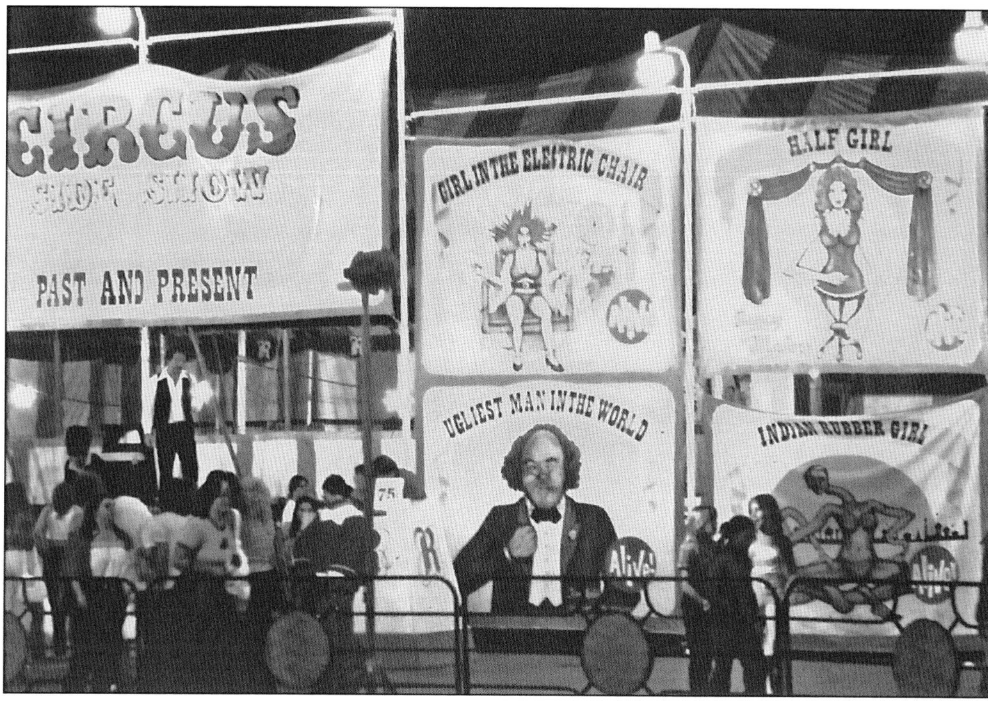

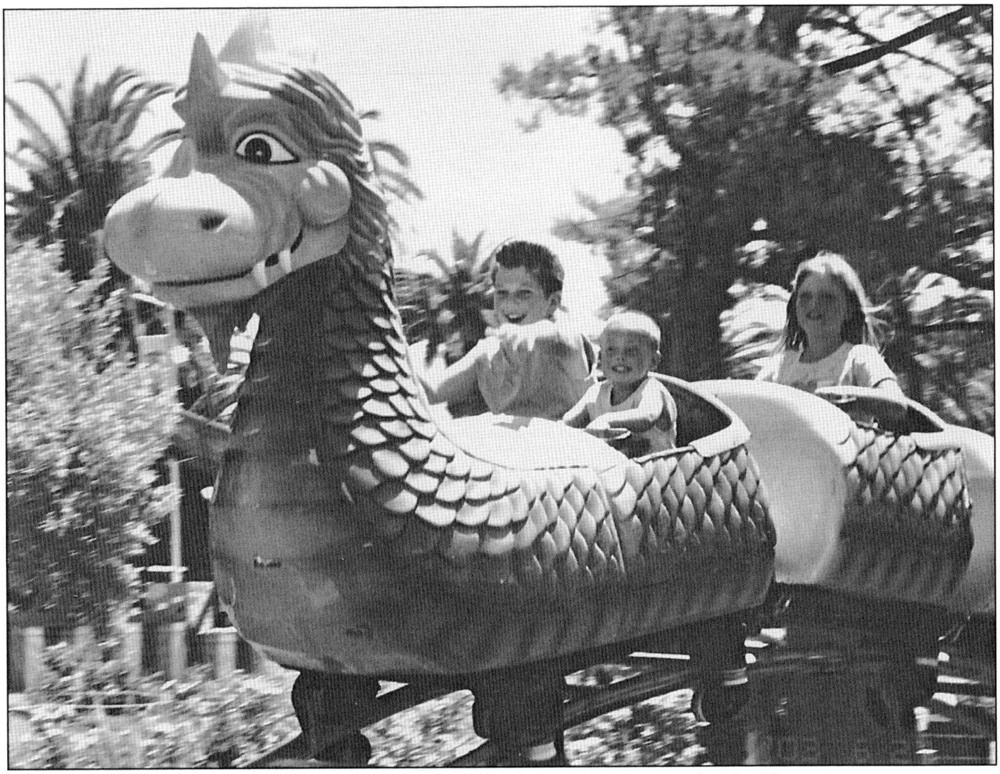

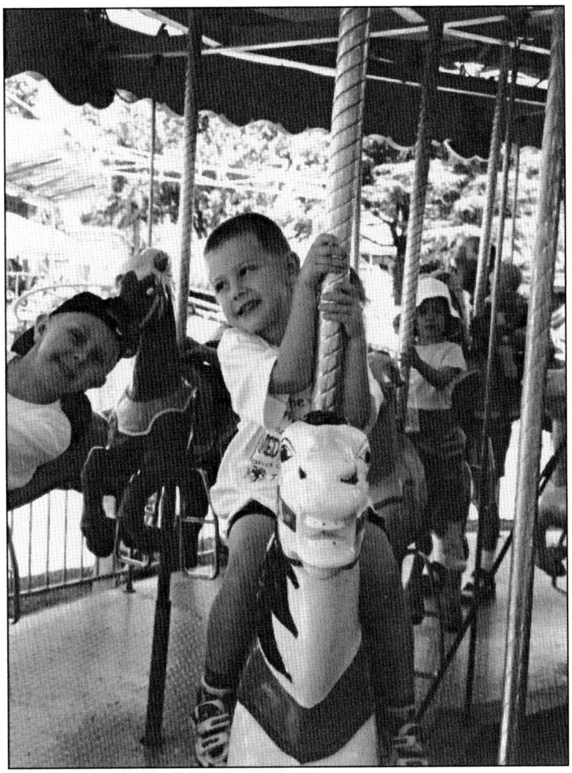

In 1999, the kiddie rides were moved away from the large carnival area to the lawn area near the main gate. This provided a unique environment just for children.

Eventually, a kiddie park was established, offering games, science projects, animal acts, themed entertainment stages, arts and crafts, pony rides, and a petting zoo. Pictured in the 2001 photograph at left are Brandon (left) and Colton McCullough. (Courtesy of Bonnie Bruton.)

Butler Amusements, Inc., has had a profound relationship with the fair since 1999. George "Bud" Butler and his son Earl "Butch" Butler founded the carnival in 1970, but Bud had already begun acquiring games and rides since 1960. By 1972, the duo owned eight rides. Only a year later, in 1973, the Butlers had 13 rides, though the number of rides continued to increase. By 1996, they had amassed 130 rides.

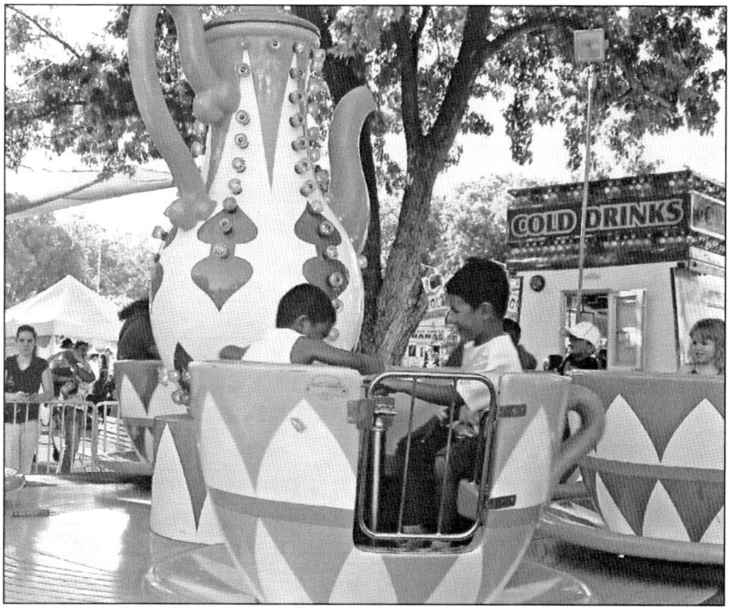

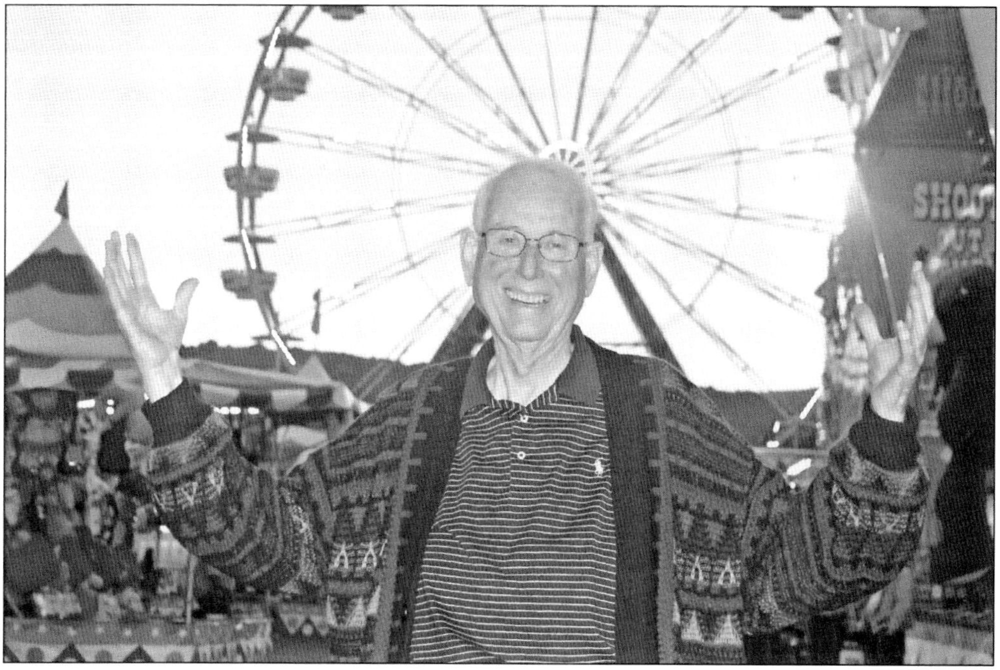

Butch Butler continues to manage the carnival with the help of his five adult children and their families. The family-owned and family-operated Butler Amusements' motto is "The Cleanest Show in the West." In 2008, a milestone of serving 1,000 fairs in 40 states was reached—three times more than any other amusement company on record. (Courtesy of Victoria Christian.)

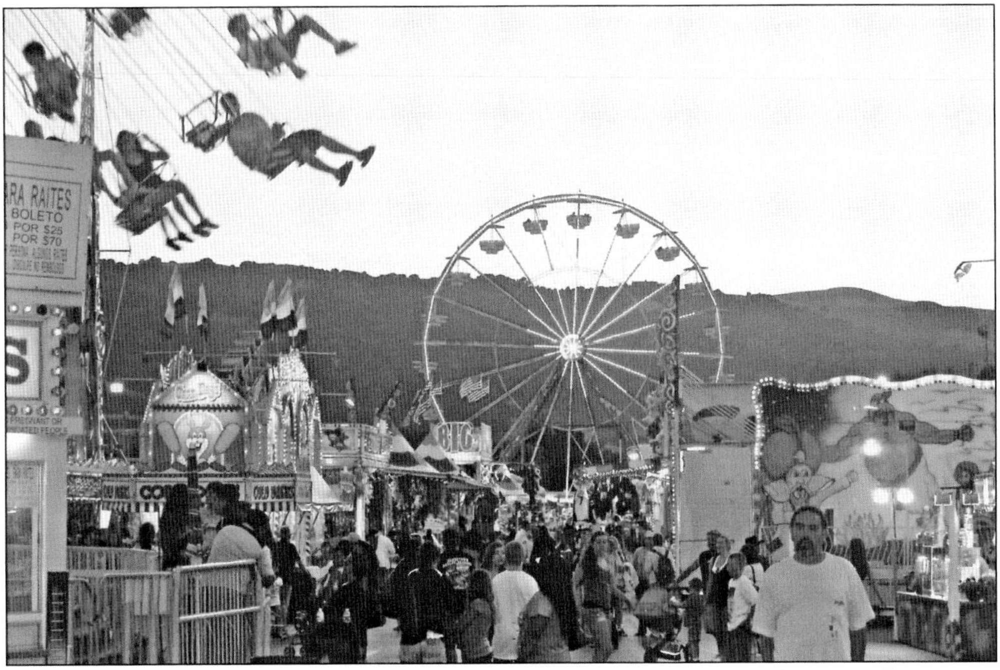

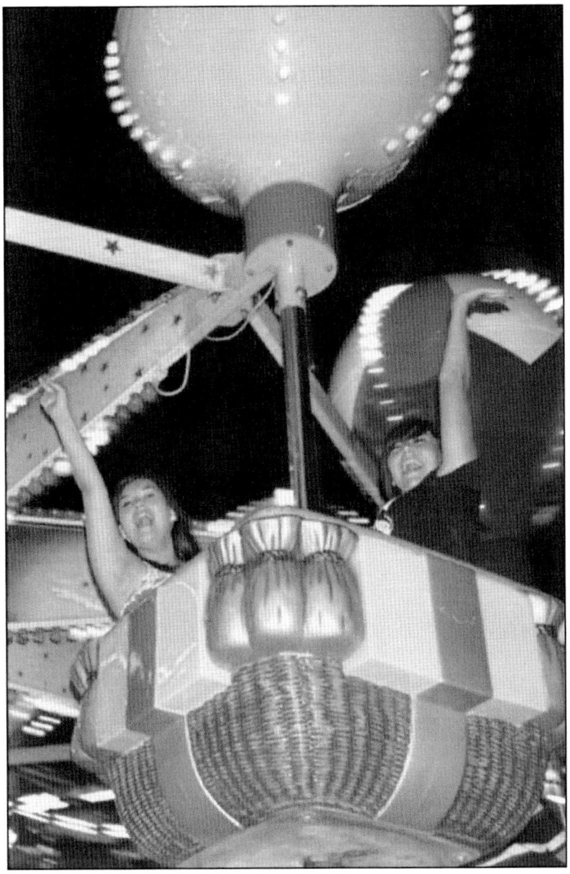

In serving more than 12 million people in six western states, safety is the number one priority with Butler Amusements. The company's highly experienced and trained maintenance staff regularly inspects and maintains all rides. (Courtesy of Victoria Christian.)

Made in Italy, the Balloon Samba ride made its first appearance at the fair in 2009. Butler Amusements purchased the ride, along with several others, during an auction at the late entertainer Michael Jackson's acclaimed Neverland Ranch near Santa Ynez, California. (Courtesy of Ario Ysit.)

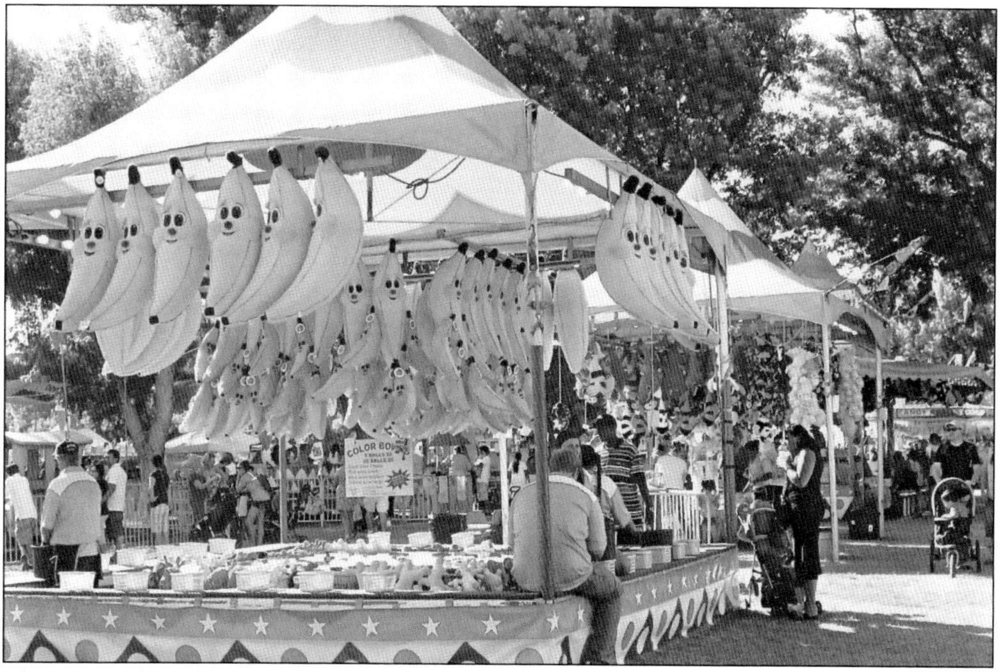

The carnival's games are a large part of the amusement park theme, and Butler Amusement faithfully maintains its wholesome appearance.

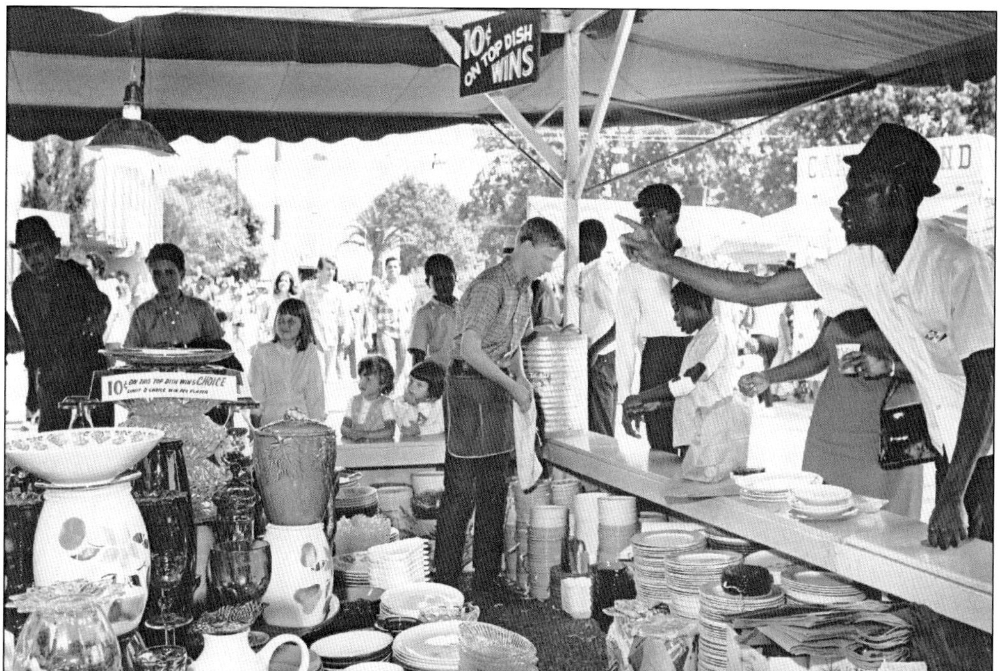

Many can't resist the call of the carnival worker as they pass by. Exciting and challenging, everyone wants to snag that giant stuffed animal to proudly carry around the fair.

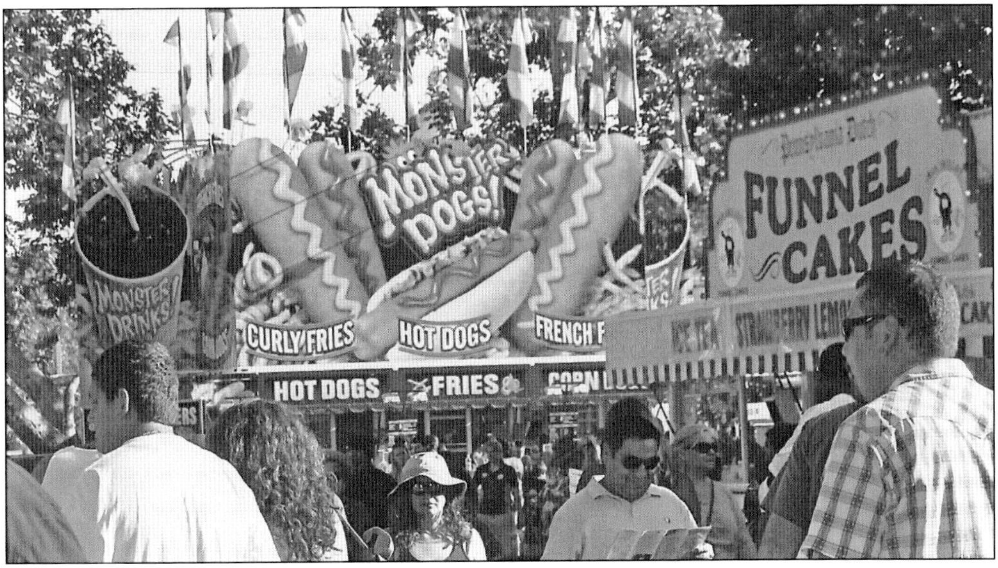

Fair food! In an era when most unique fair food is either deep-fried or covered in chocolate, the 2010 fair introduced something new—chocolate covered bacon. Some liked it but most found it unappetizing. In 2010 alone, fairgoers consumed an astonishing 79,882 corn dogs, 21,437 funnel cakes, 10,312 shaved ices, 5,026 turkey legs, and 5,113 cinnamon rolls.

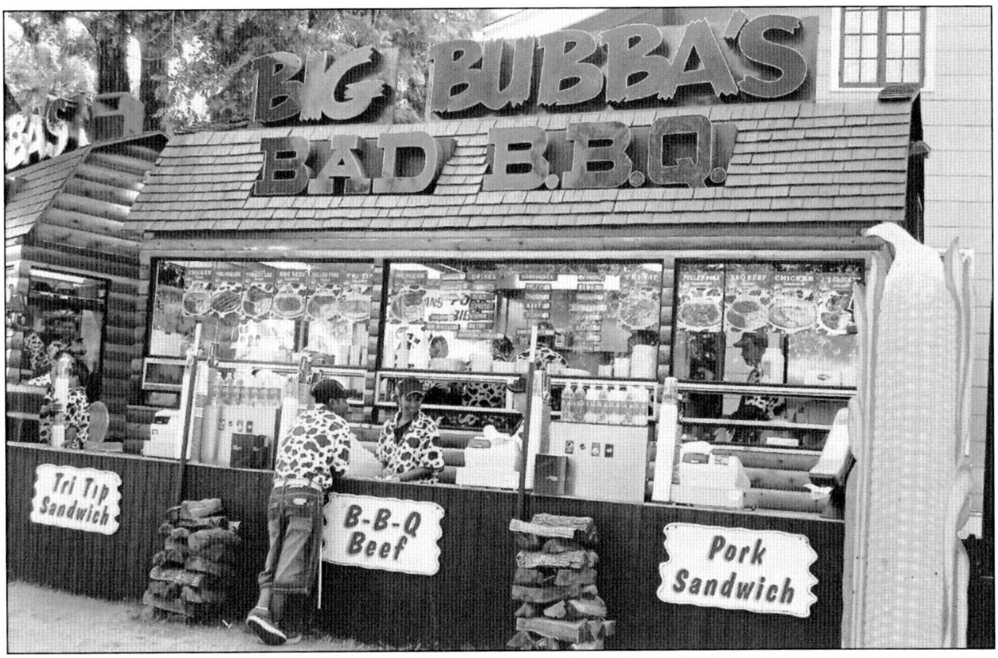

Still hungry? More fair food includes barbecue beef, chicken, funnel cakes, roasted corn, ice cream, cinnamon rolls, cotton candy, shaved ice, turkey legs, churros, dill pickles, sno-cones, frozen yogurt, pie, baked potatoes, chili-cheese fries, lemonade, fish and chips, doughnuts, smoothies, sandwiches, french fries, deep-fried Twinkies and Oreos, fried artichokes, caramel apples, candy apples, pizza, beer, margaritas, falafel, chocolate-covered strawberries, bananas, apples, marshmallows and cheesecake, popcorn, caramel corn, kettle corn, pink popcorn, corn dogs, hot dogs, nachos, and burgers. The fair also offered Italian, Mexican, Greek, Chinese, and Thai meals.

Six

Entertainment for All

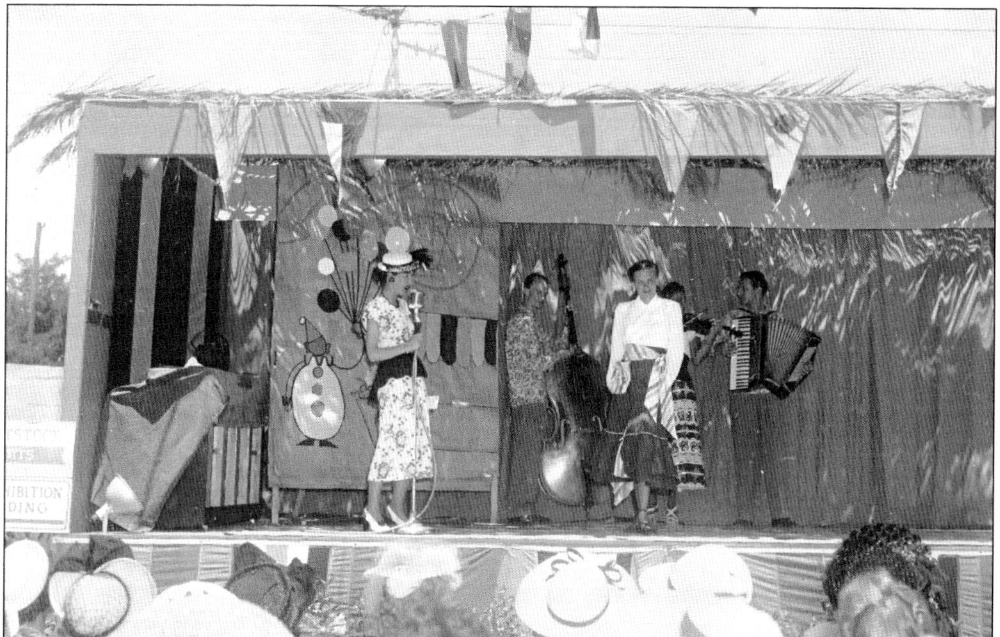

The only entertainment provided in 1912 were a few kids' games and contests. In 1939, vaudeville acts took to the stage to entertain racetrack patrons between races.

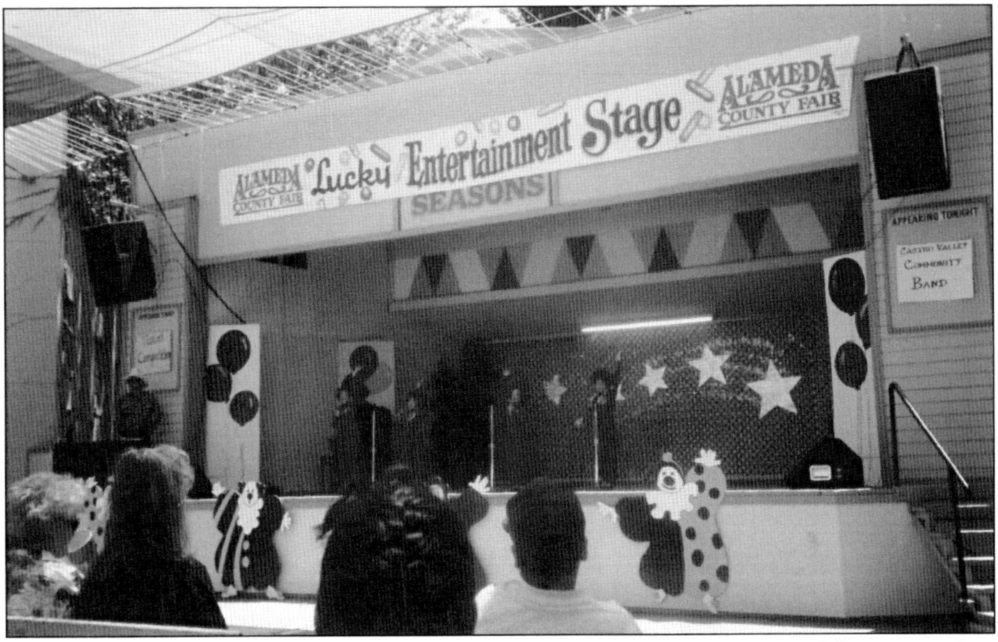

Built in 1948, the Court of Four Seasons stage was to be placed in the center of the surrounding exhibit halls, but a temporary stage was built on one side and eventually became permanent.

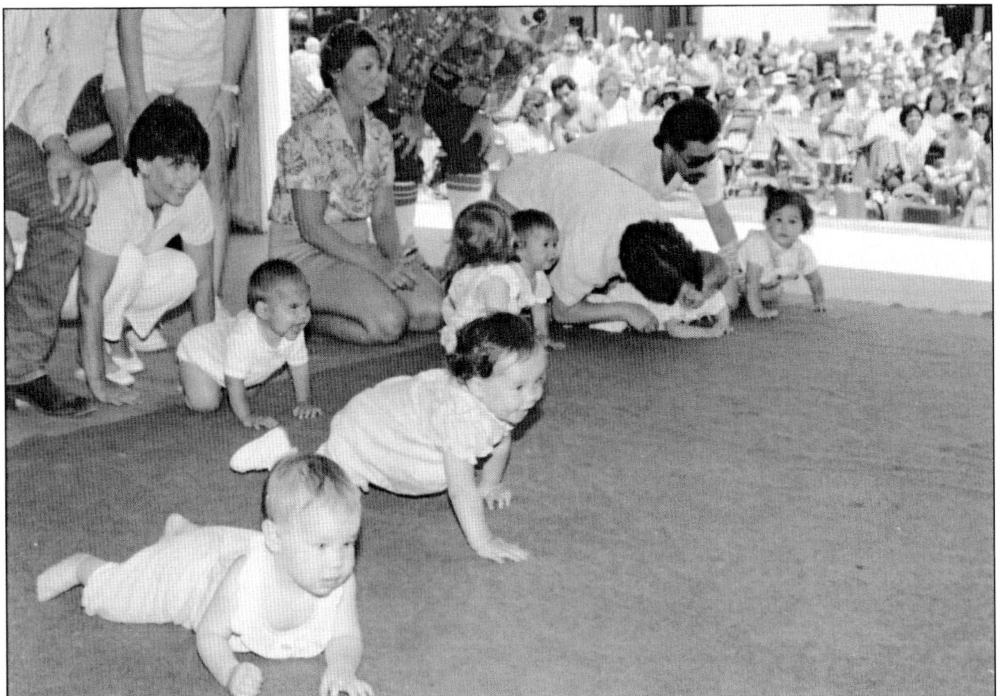

Held at the Court of Four Seasons stage, the Diaper Derby began in 1962 with participants aged one year old or younger crawling a distance of 12 feet across the stage. The tot was disqualified if he or she stood up or walked. The fastest crawler ever recorded was the 1981 winner, nine-month-old Rusty Smith, who crossed the finish line in a record six seconds.

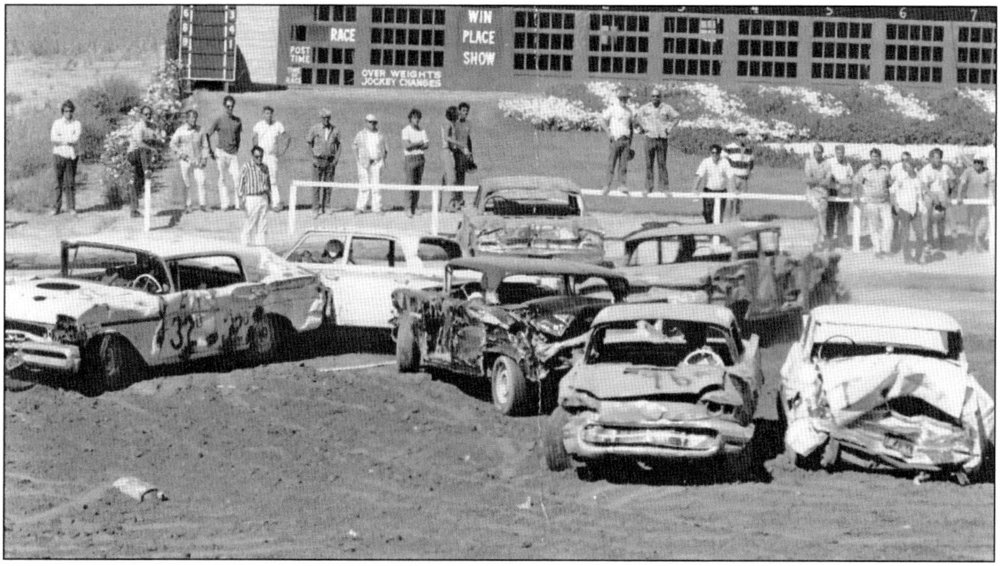

Always a crowd favorite, the Destruction Derby was held on the racetrack in front of the grandstand on the last day of the fair. Contestants brought their old vehicles to intentionally wreck into each other until only one car and driver were still operable. The 1963 Destruction Derby attracted 5,000 fans. The fair discontinued the Destruction Derby during the 1980s due to track damage.

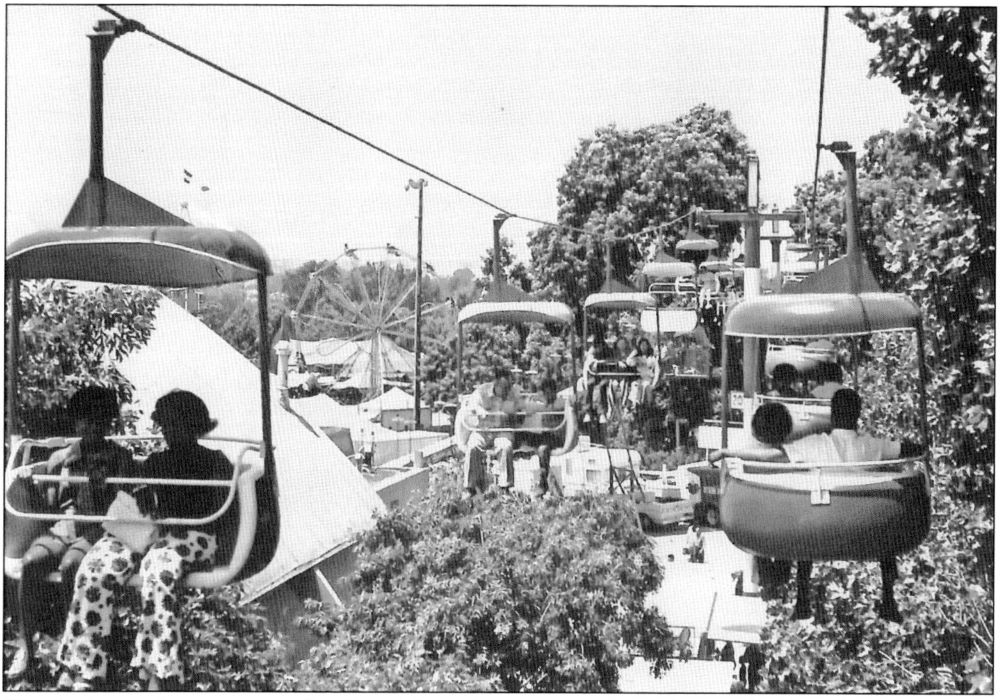

The fair's aerial tram was only offered for a few years in the 1960s, and although it was a very popular ride, it was removed for several reasons: the tram interfered with carnival rides, it was expensive to operate, and it took up space that was need for parking.

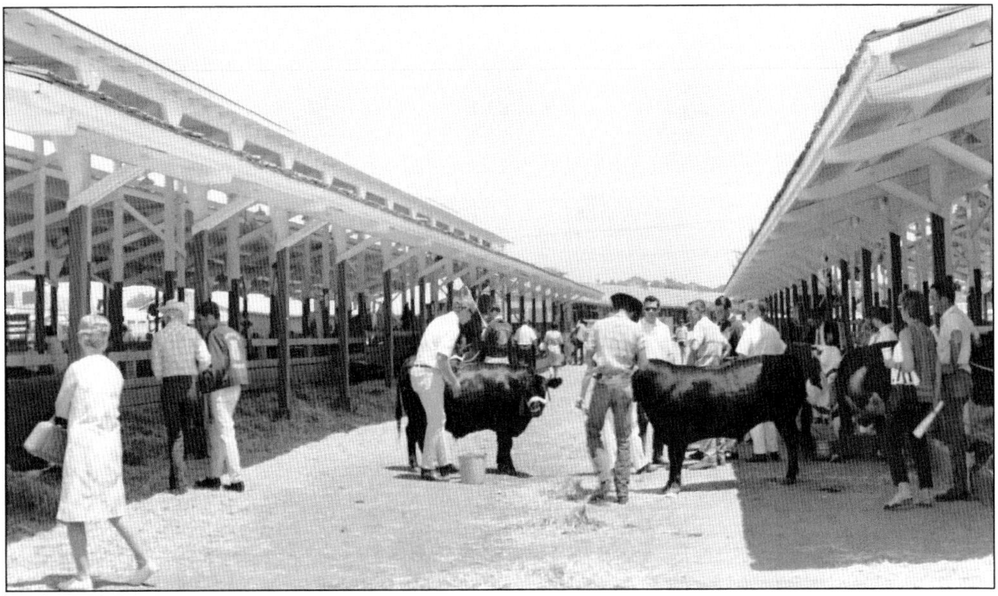

The above picture from the 1960s shows the barns used for housing competing livestock during fair time. After the Amador Pavilion was built, most of these barns were removed except for a few that were artfully turned into a shopping area, as seen in the more recent image below.

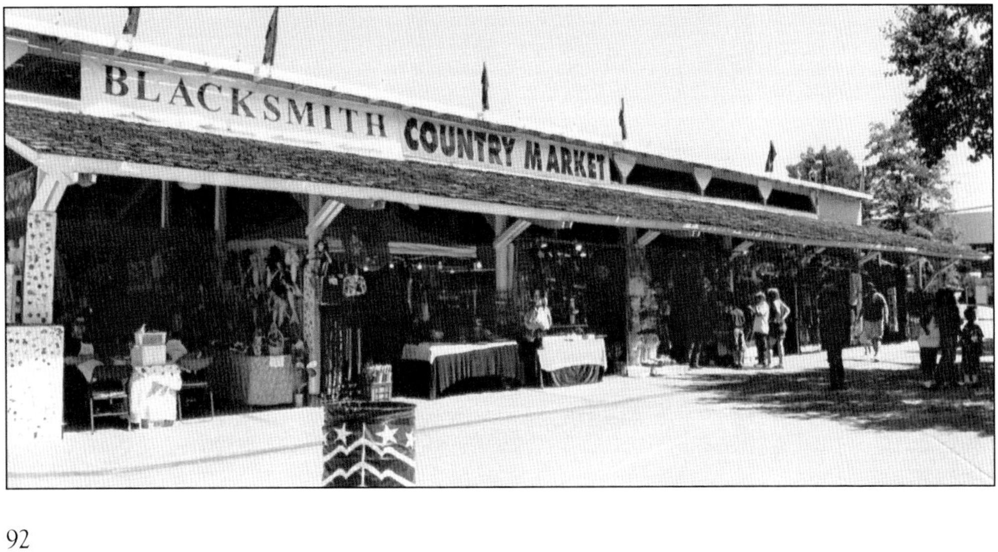

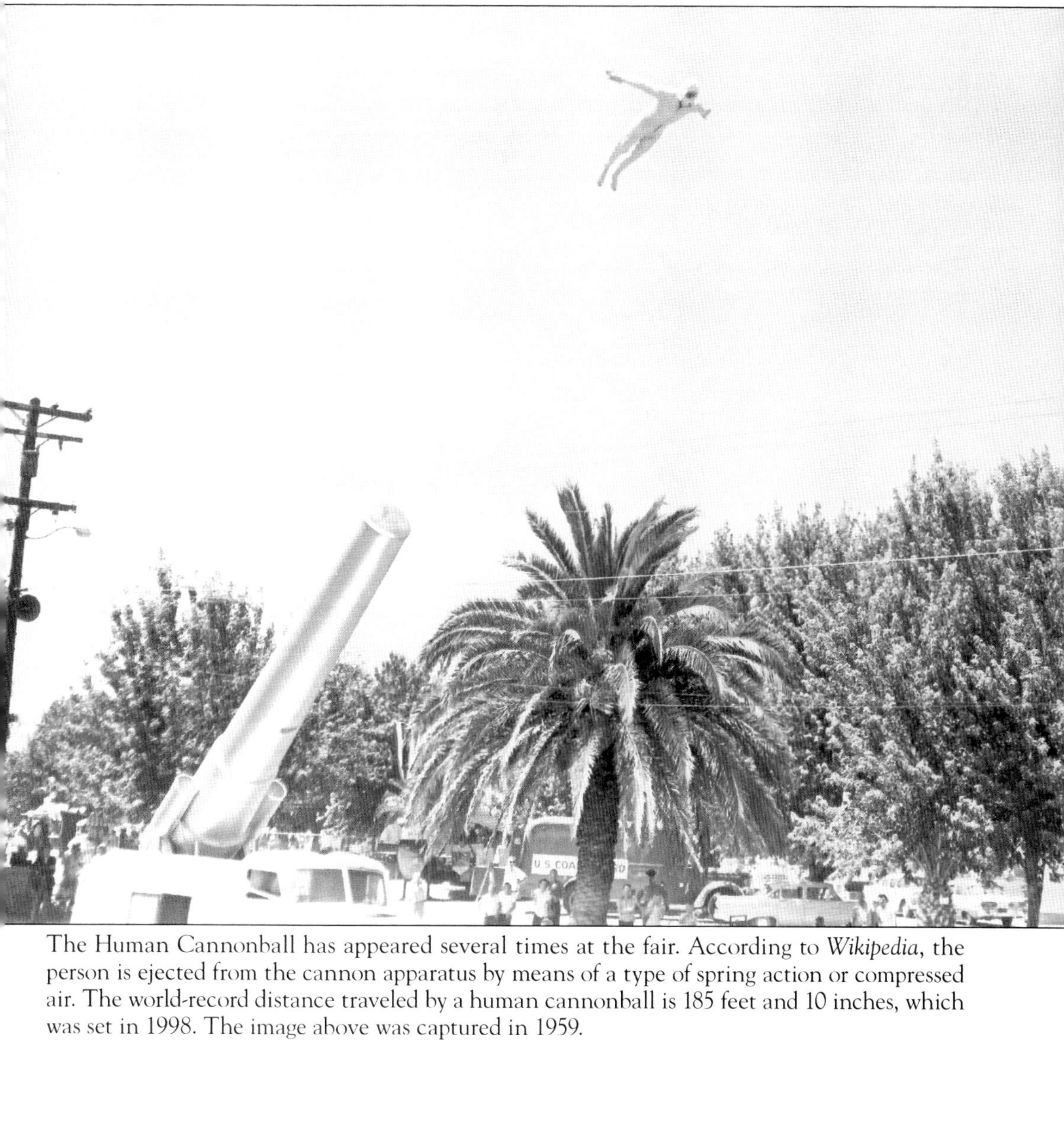

The Human Cannonball has appeared several times at the fair. According to *Wikipedia*, the person is ejected from the cannon apparatus by means of a type of spring action or compressed air. The world-record distance traveled by a human cannonball is 185 feet and 10 inches, which was set in 1998. The image above was captured in 1959.

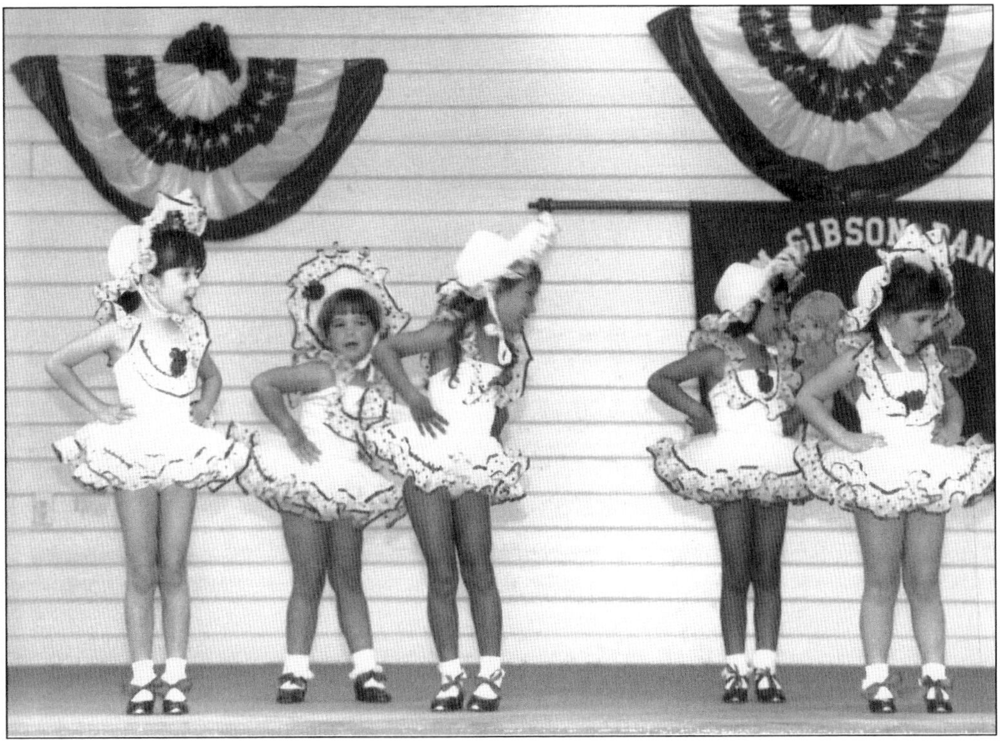

Dance troupes, young and old alike, perform several times a day during the fair. The photograph above is from the Court of Four Seasons stage, and the photograph below was captured on the new amphitheater stage.

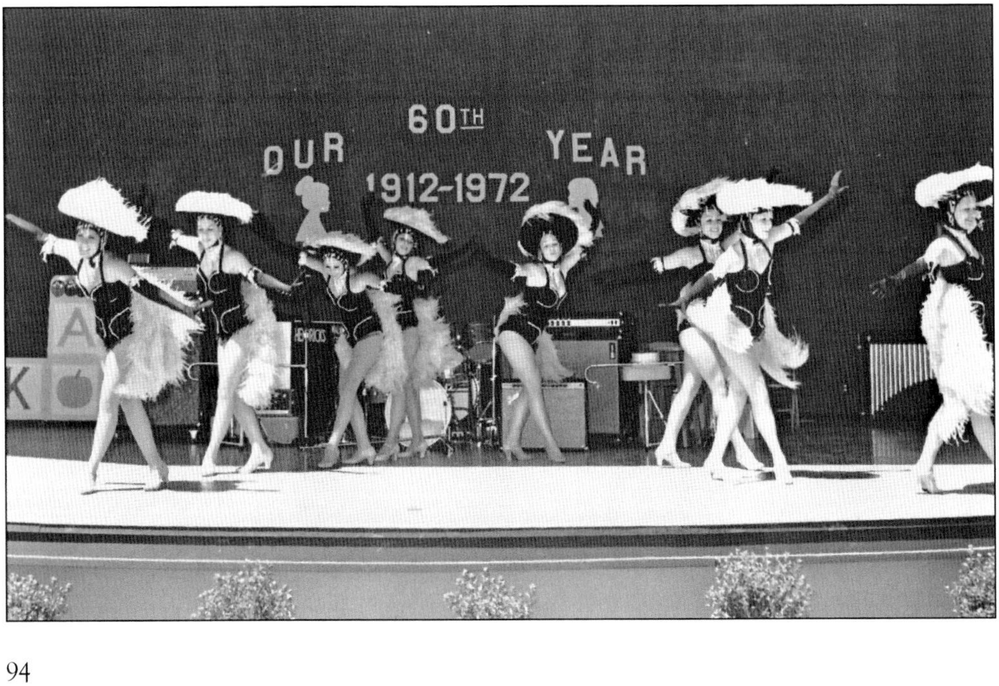

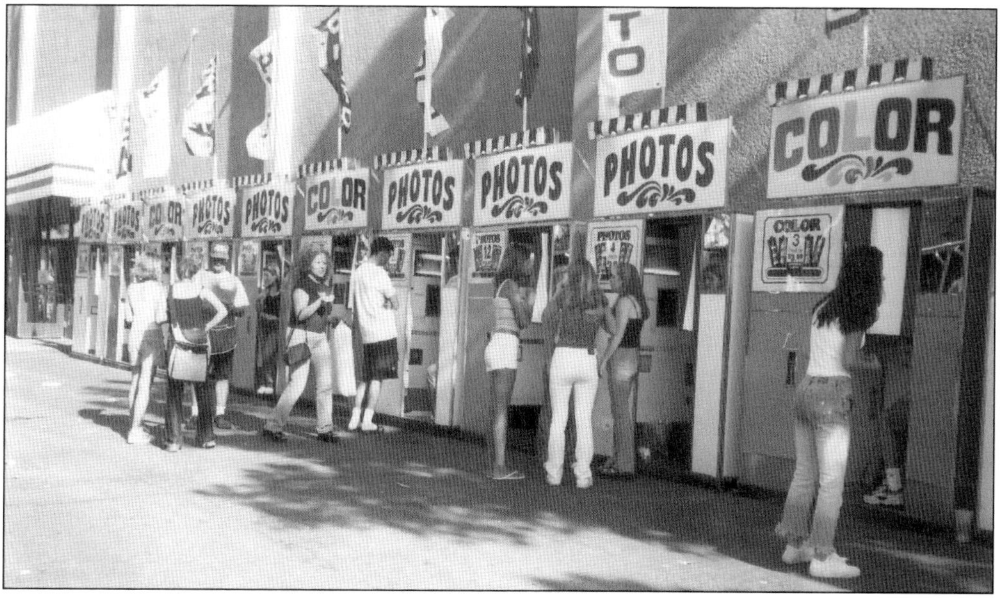

Nostalgic, one-of-a-kind photograph strips from these unique photograph booths capture special moments at the county fair.

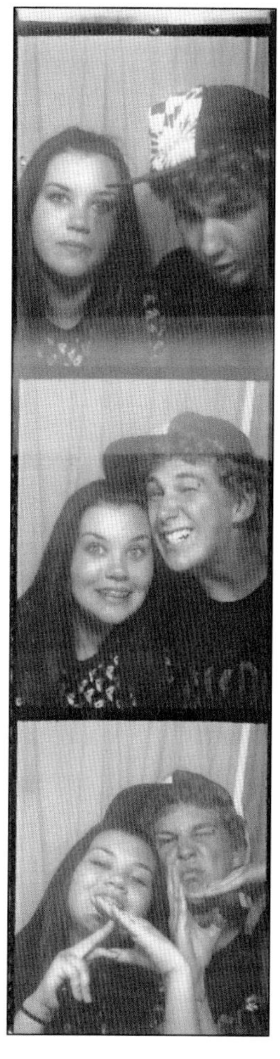

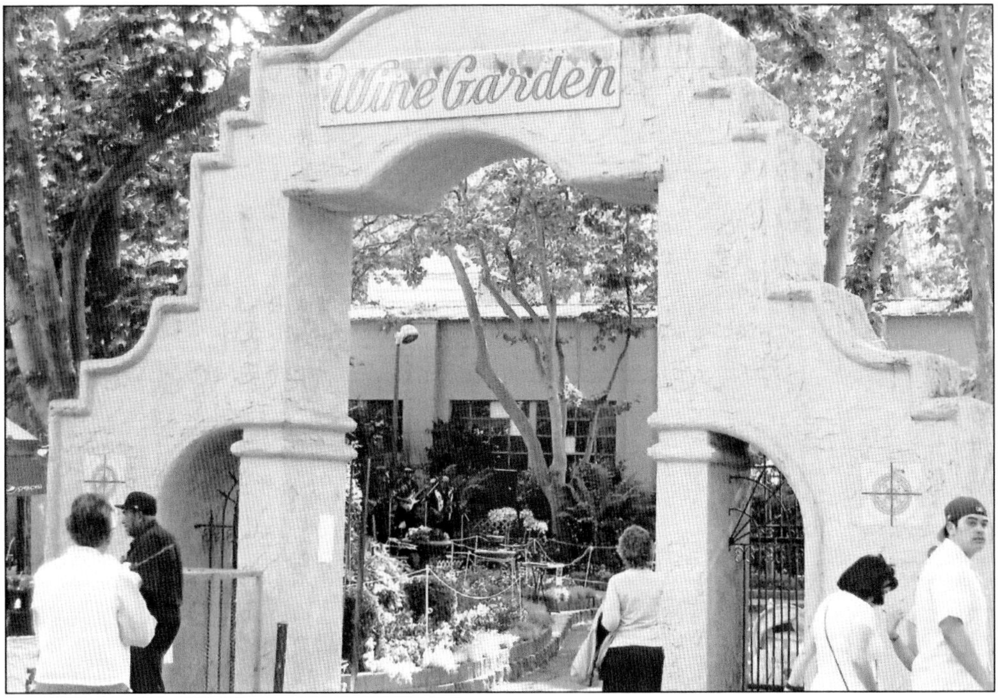

The fair's Jazz Wine Garden, built in 1988, has a Spanish-style stucco entryway. Its beautifully landscaped patio and wine bar provide the perfect atmosphere to relax and enjoy the entertainment.

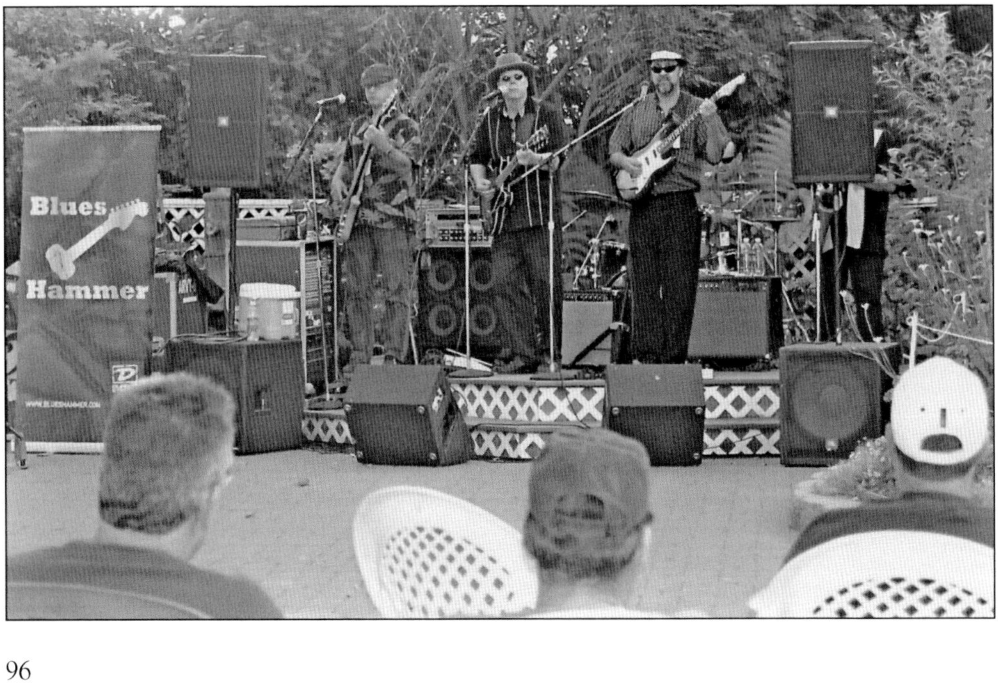

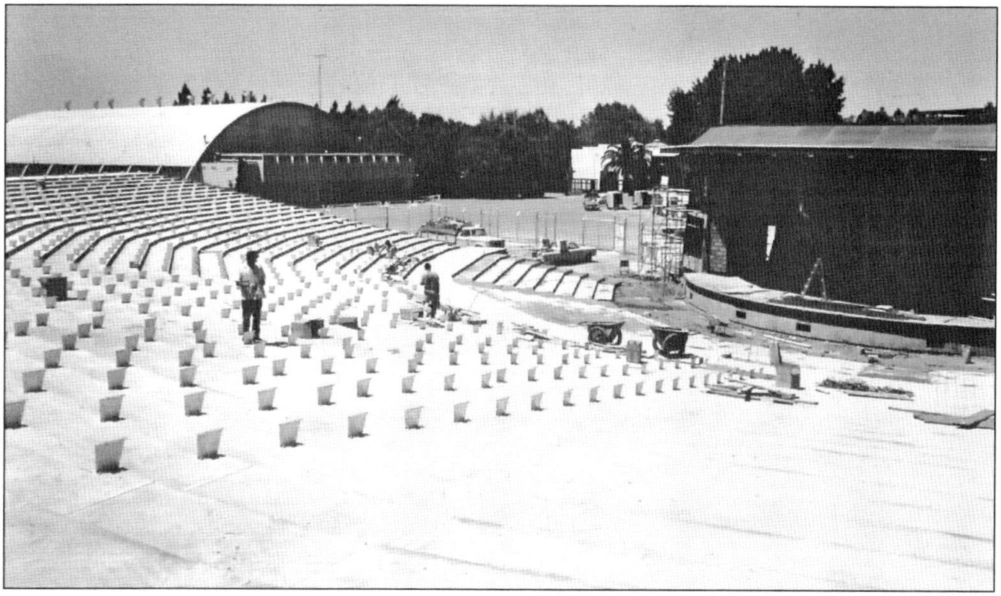

Built in 1972, the amphitheater, seen above, holds 3,000 seats and offers free shows twice nightly. The amphitheater has dressing rooms, star suites, a state-of-the-art sound system, and a backstage technical control room. Big-name acts over the years include Johnny Cash, Tony Bennett, Wayne Newton, Night Ranger, the Osmond Brothers, Faith Hill, the Temptations, the Judds, Rosemary Clooney, George Lopez, Tower of Power, the Jonas Brothers, and hundreds more. (Both courtesy of Peter Bailey.)

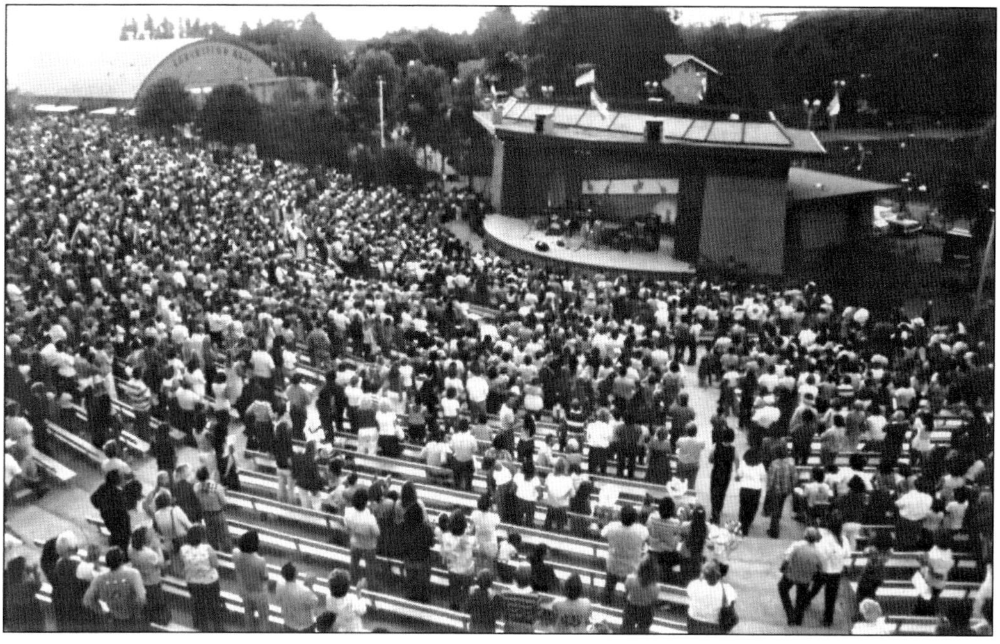

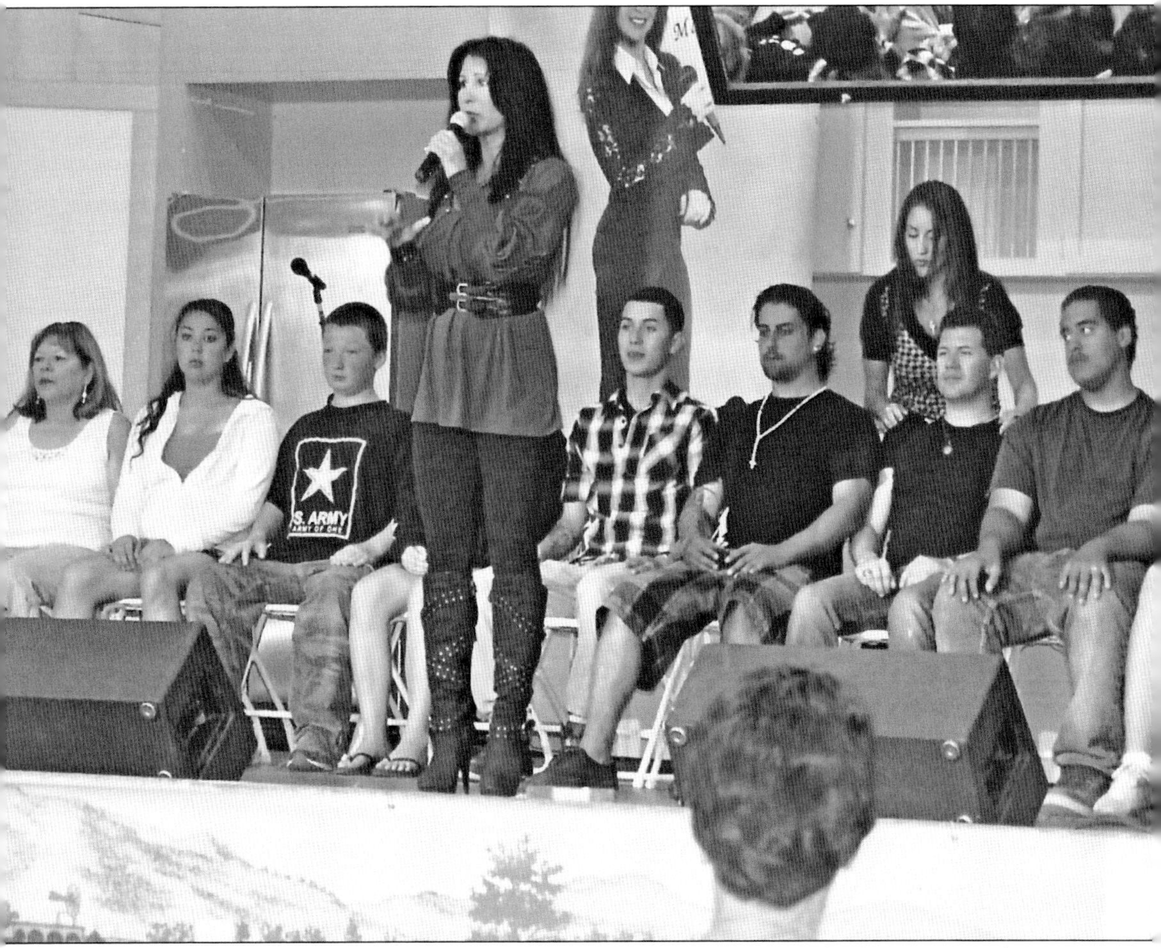

Hypnotist Tina Marie is a yearly favorite at the fair. She draws hundreds of spectators to her twice-daily shows, and dozens of folks line up to volunteer to be hypnotized on stage. Marie coaxes the volunteers into performing a variety of hilarious antics such as playing air guitar, believing they are secret agents, and running around the stage acting like a chicken or a famous entertainer.

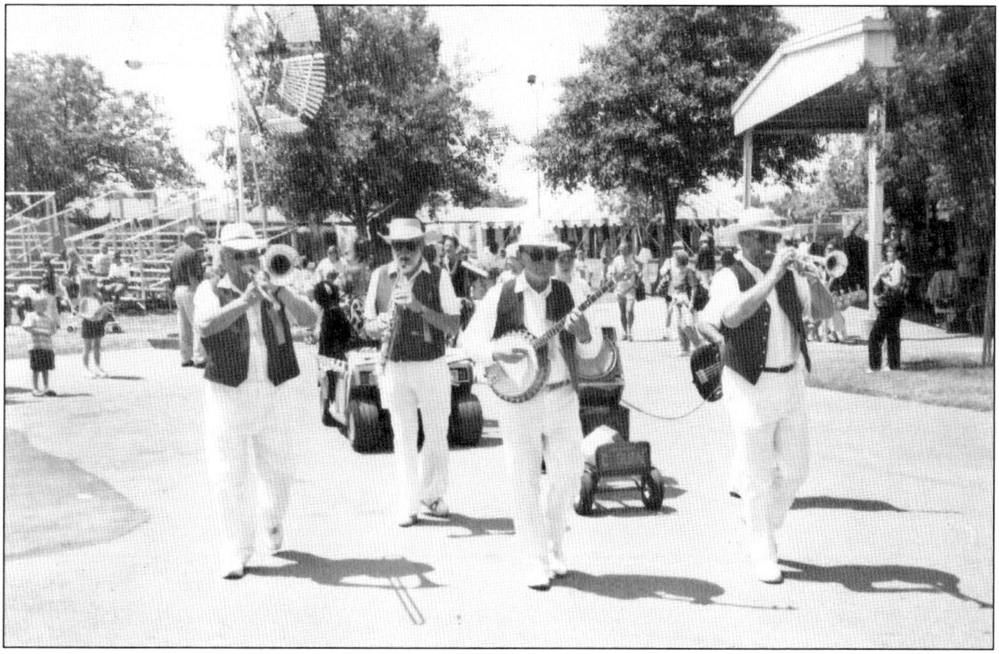

Strolling musicians are frequently seen on the grounds, and live, local entertainment performs on the Bandstand Stage, the Community Stage, the Park Place Stage, and the University of Fun Stage in the Kids Adventure Park.

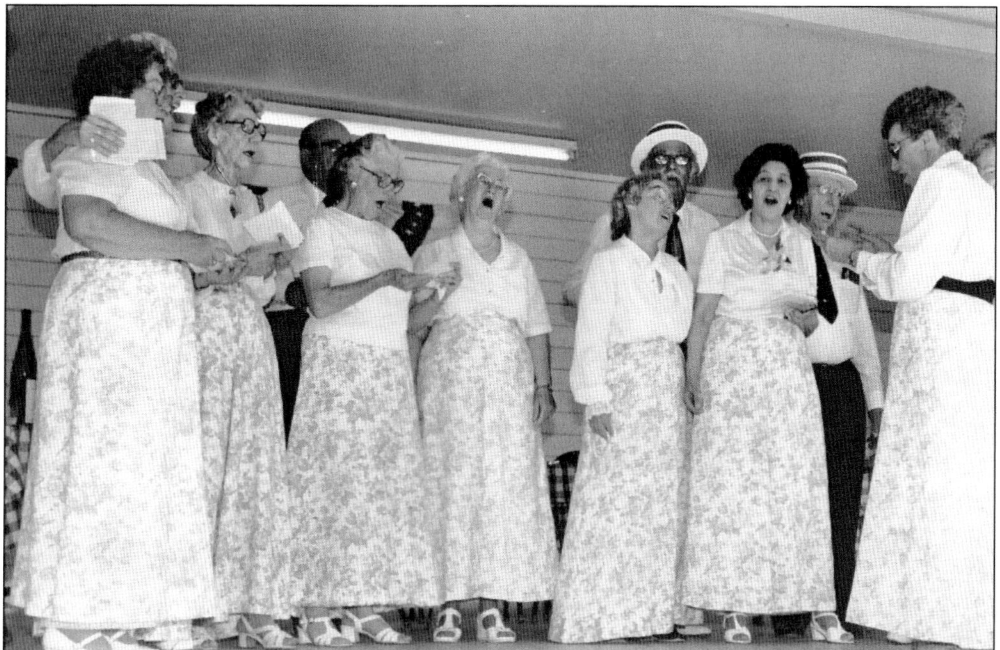

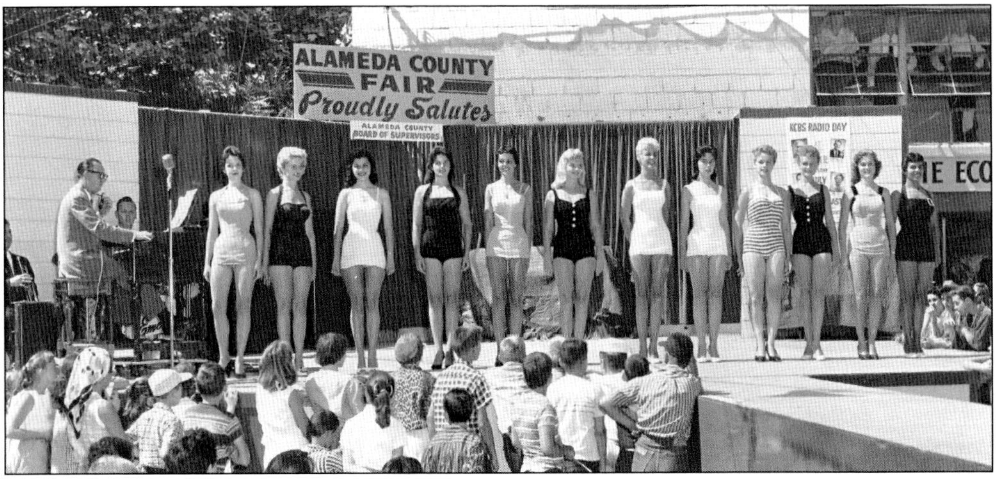

The Maid of Alameda County Pageant began in 1949. Judged on poise, personality, and appearance, the beauty contest was comprised of young ladies that represented 14 communities: Alameda, Albany, Berkeley, Castro Valley, Fremont, Hayward, Livermore, Newark, Oakland, Pleasanton, San Leandro, San Lorenzo, San Ramon, and Union City. The pageant was traditionally held on opening day of the fair. The photograph above was captured in 1958, and the image below was taken in 1968.

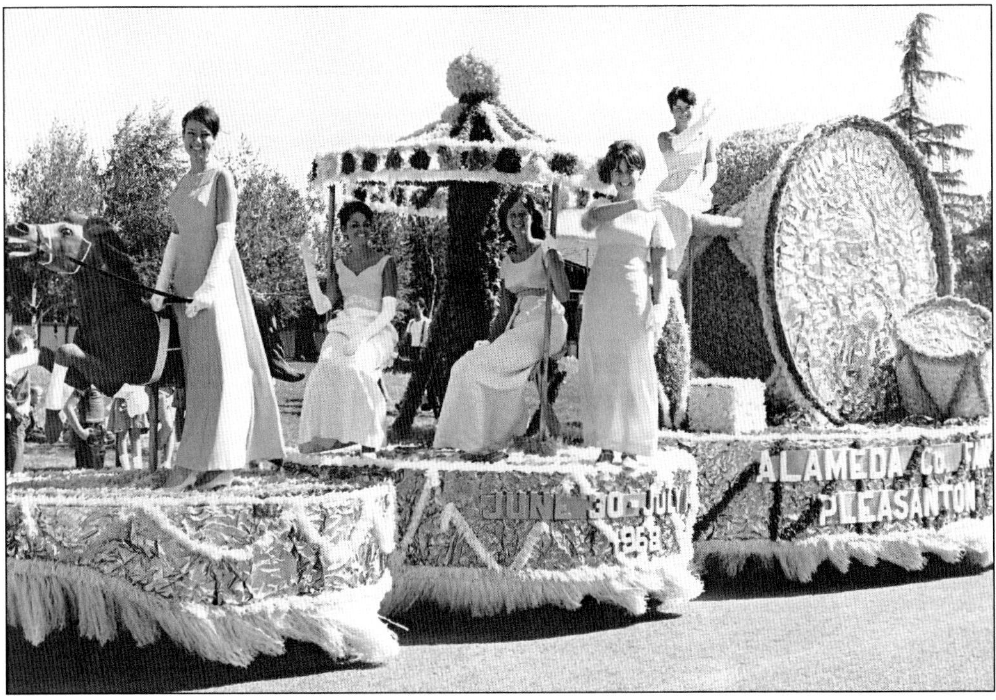

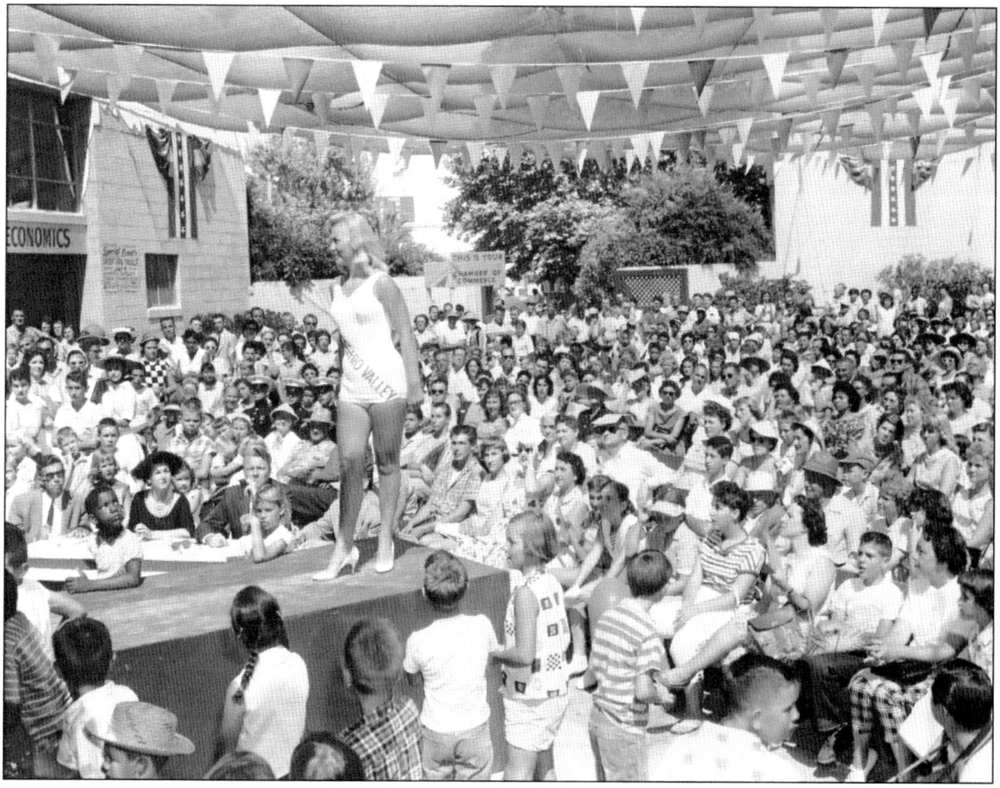

The Maid of Alameda County winner reigns over fair displays, exhibits, contests, and horse racing. In 1963, the winner received a $300 modeling and charm course, a $100 wardrobe gift certificate, $150 in cash, and she served as the official hostess of the fair. The winner advanced to the Maid of California pageant at the state fair in Sacramento. The pageant was cancelled in 1981 after the state fair decided not to continue its beauty contests.

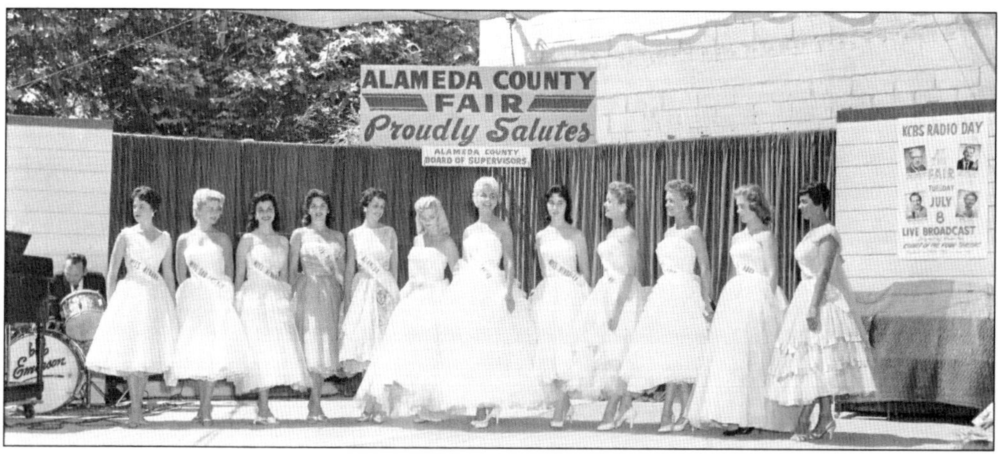

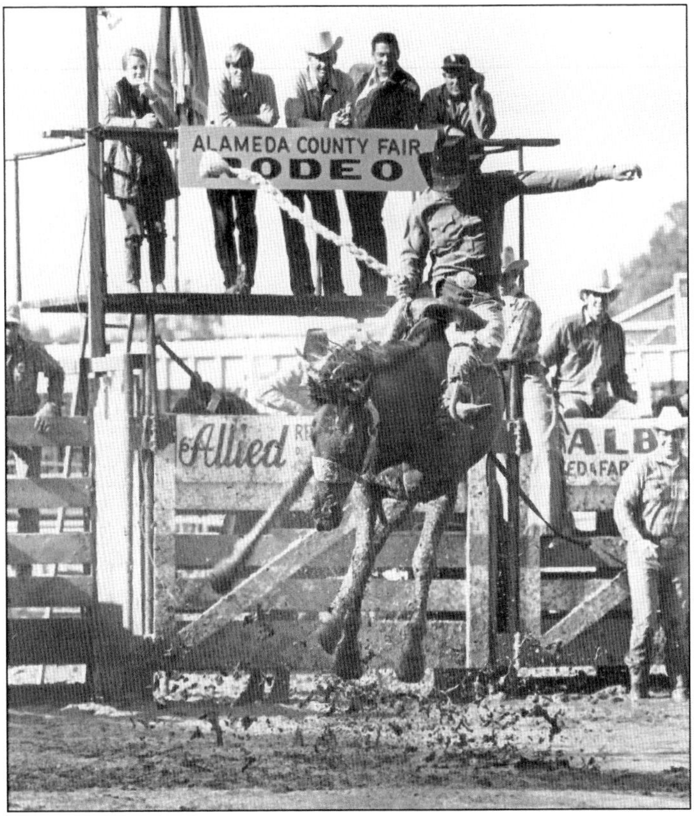

This photograph captures a cowboy and bucking bronco at the fair's only rodeo. It was decided that rodeos should not be held since there are two other rodeos held in nearby cities. (Courtesy of Peter Bailey.)

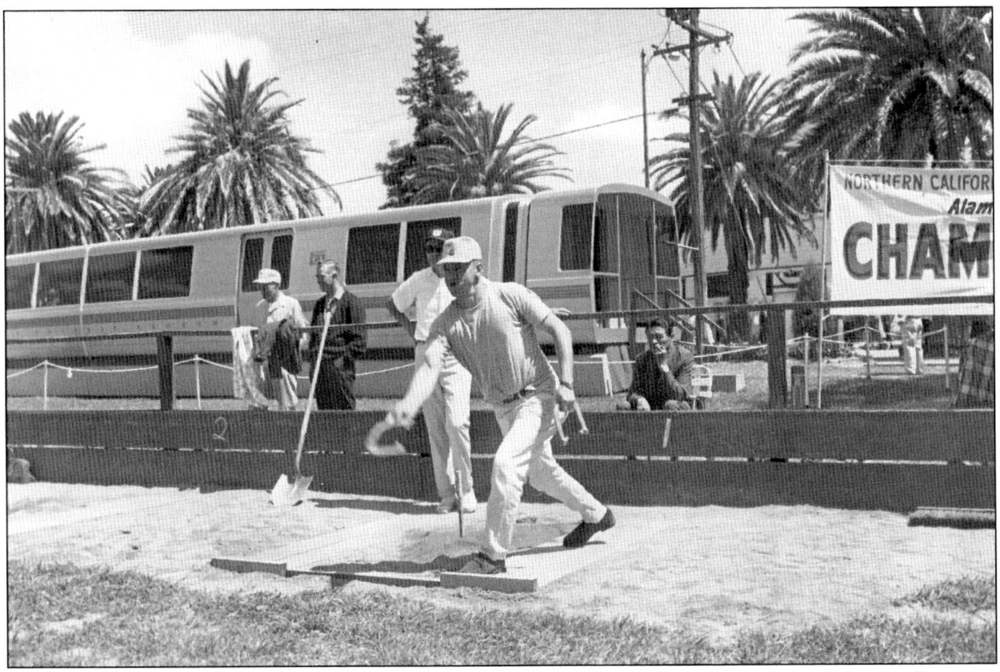

The horseshoe championship was once an annual contest at the fair. Note the exhibit for the first-ever Bay Area Rapid Transit (BART) car in the background in this image from the early 1970s.

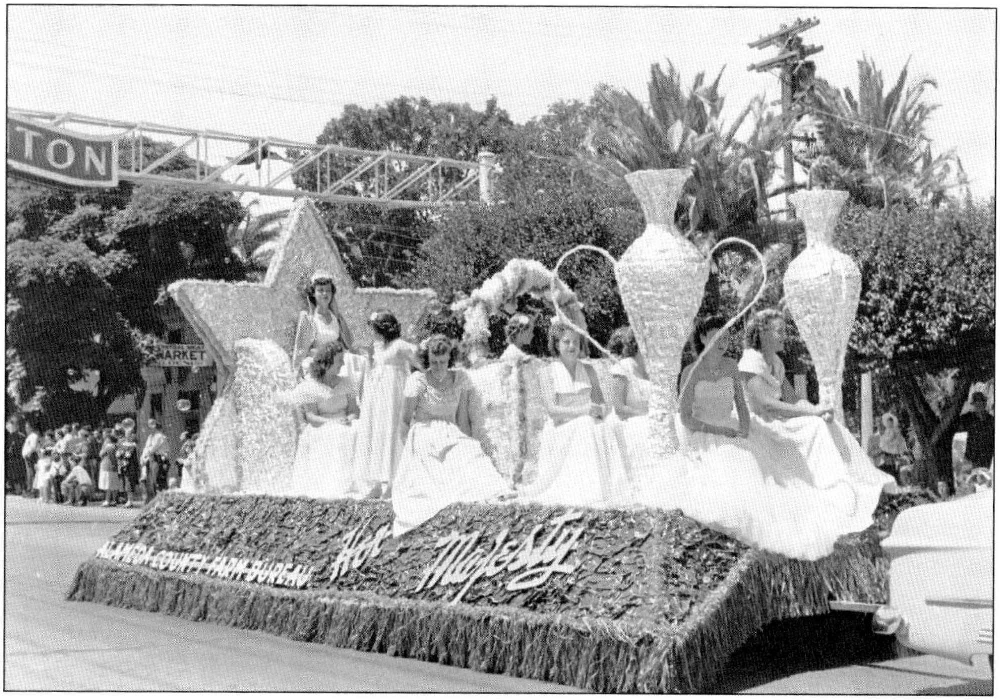

The county fair parades began in 1935 and, with the exception of a few years, are held annually. The 1948 parade included floats, drill teams, uniformed groups, drum and bugle corps, horse-riding groups, antique firefighting equipment, and other civic leaders. (Below, courtesy of Amador Livermore Valley Historical Society.)

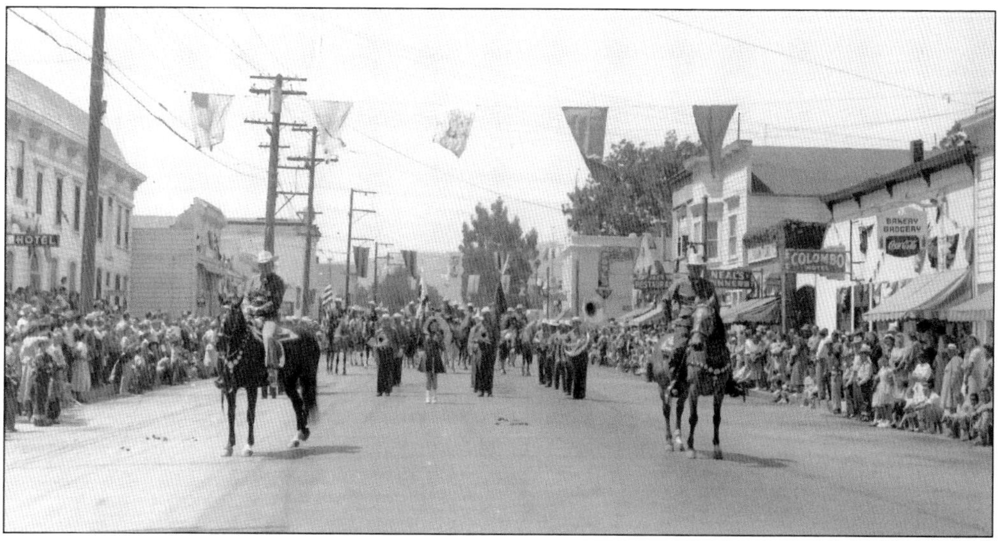

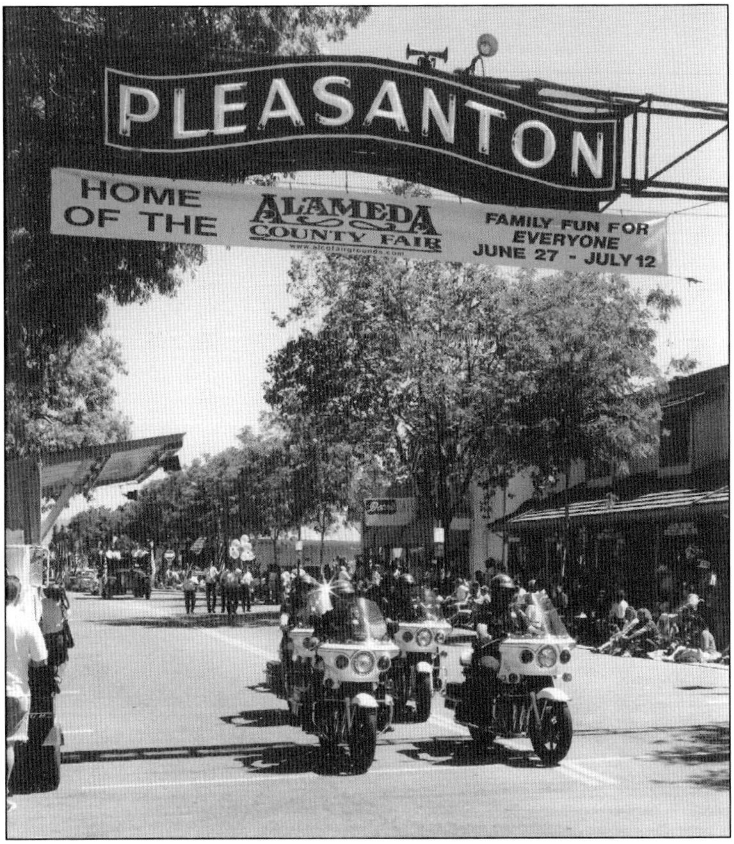

Residents arrive from all over the county and line Main Street in Pleasanton to catch a glimpse of the traditional parade floats, marching bands, community groups, horse riders, and local dignitaries.

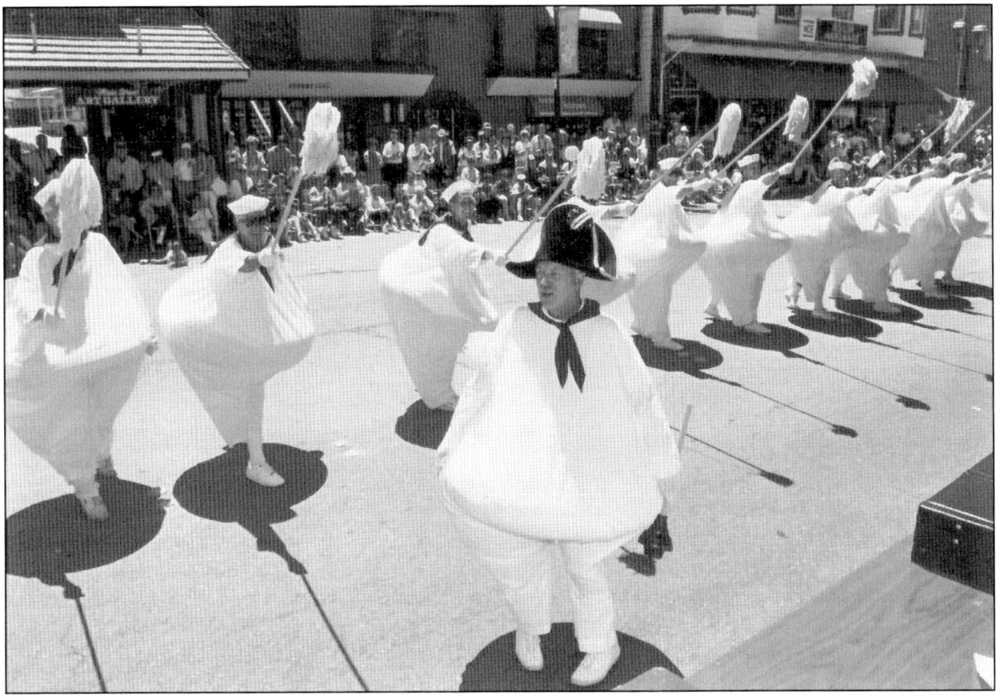

A crowd favorite at the parade is the Centerpointe Presbyterian Church Balloon Platoon. The Pleasanton group has been entertaining spectators during the Main Street parade since 1974.

In 2010, the fair introduced a few new attractions such as mutton bustin.' Similar to bronco riding, a child who is 6 years old or younger and less than 60 pounds attempts to ride a sheep longer than any fellow competitor. Also new that year was the Puppy Party Palooza, a hot dog relay contest for kids, and the dance group Power House, pictured below.

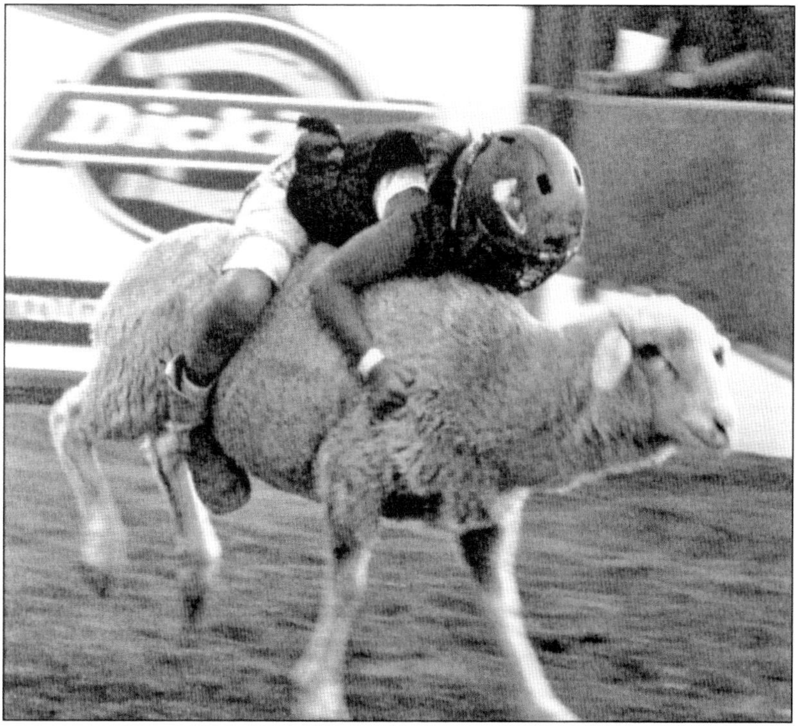

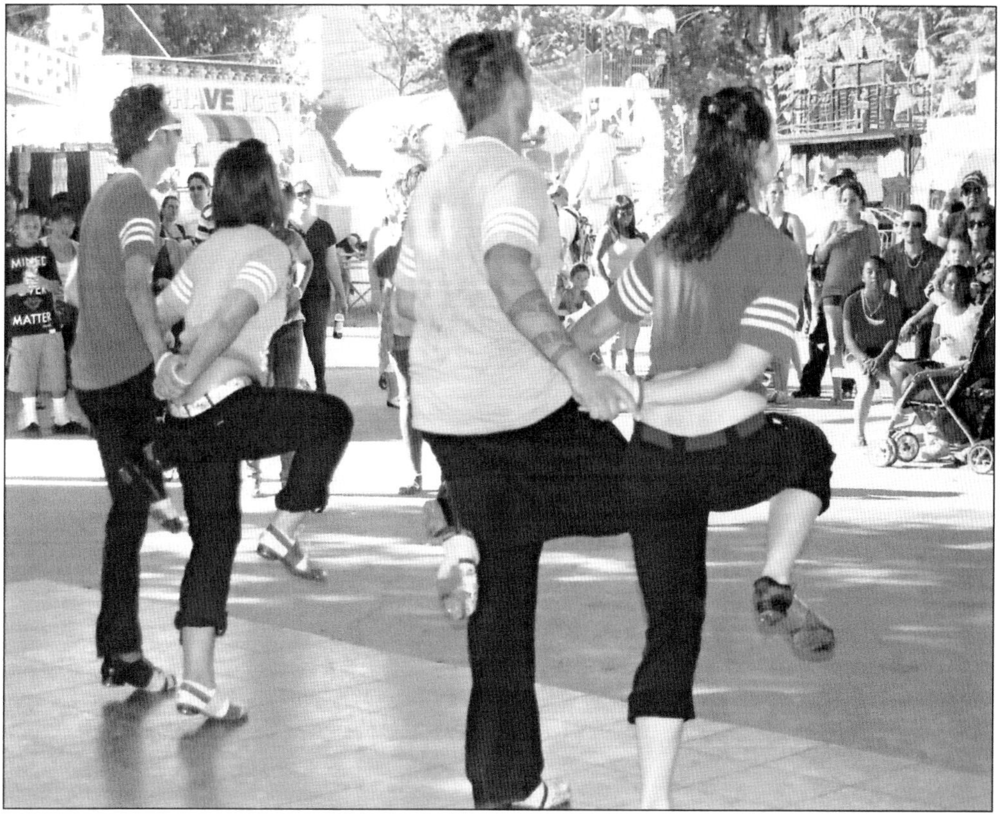

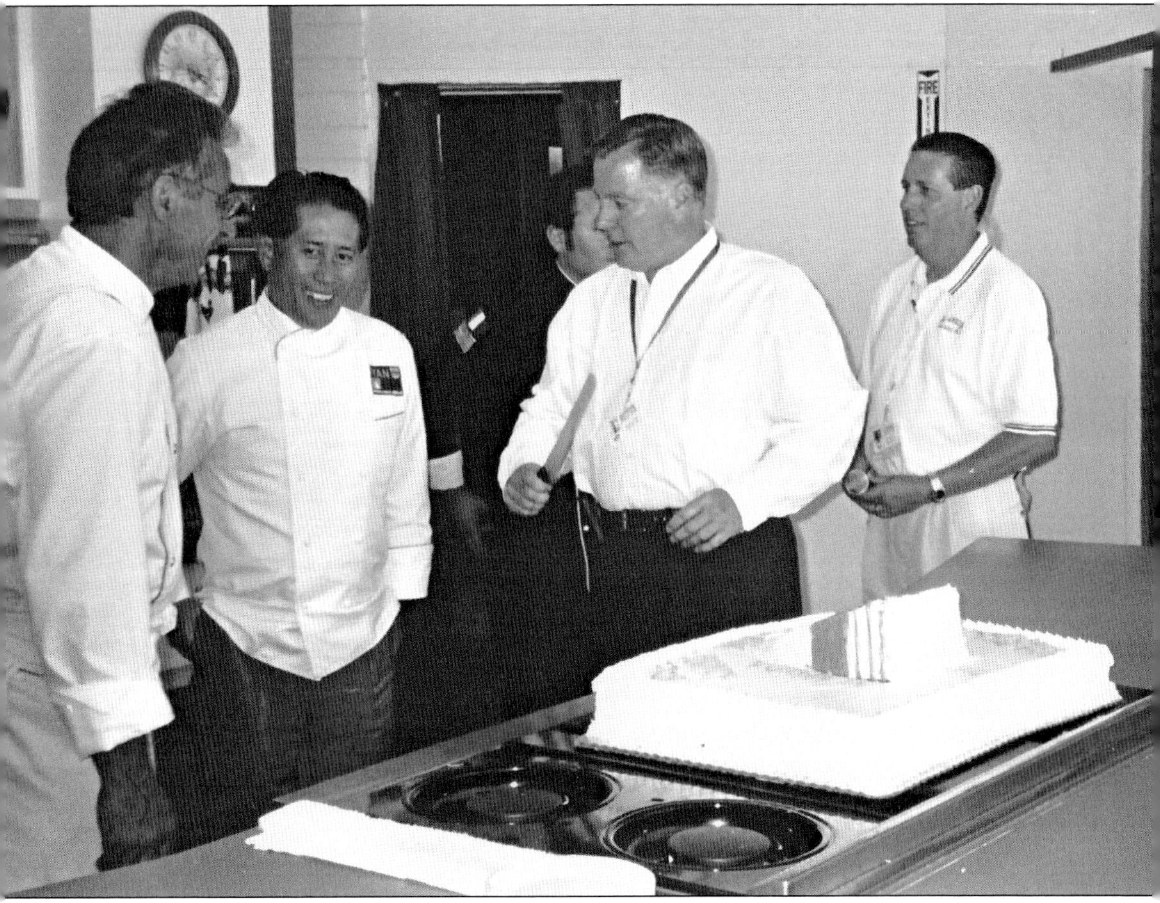

The 2001 cooking competitions included a SPAM recipe contest, a chocolate chip dessert bake-off, the Softasilk Cake Contest, Hormel Chili's Fast and Fabulous Recipe Challenge, the Beef is King Cookout, a best pie challenge, a rib cook-off, and a cheesecake contest. Pictured above, from left to right, are Tony LaRusso, celebrity chef Martin Yan, Alameda County supervisor Scott Haggerty, and Alameda County Fair chief executive officer Rick Pickering.

Seven

Annual Events

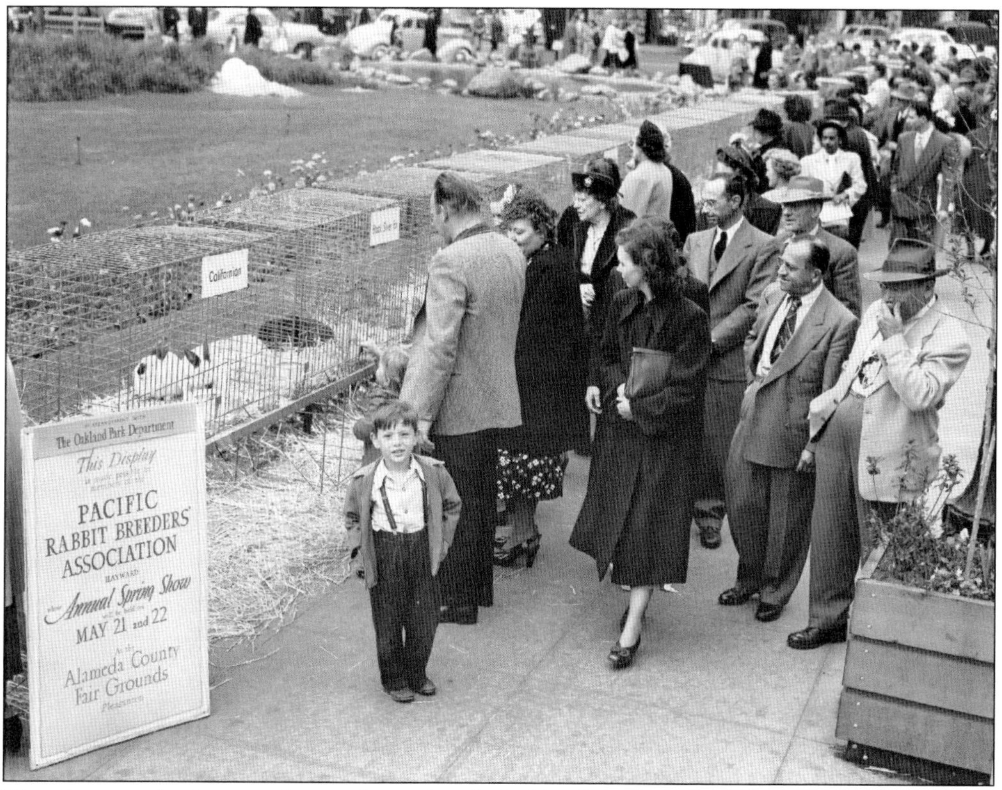

The photograph above is of an early-era Pacific Rabbit Breeders Association competition at the fair. The fair continues to provide the location for several public and private events such as the Orchard Supply How-To Fair Home and Garden Show, American Indians Arts Show, Sewing and Quilting Expo Doll Show, Antiques and Collectables Show, Harvest Festival, Country Folk Art Craft Show, International Cat Show, and the International Sportsmen's Exposition, as well as hiking, hunting, and fishing exhibits, and fly-casting competitions.

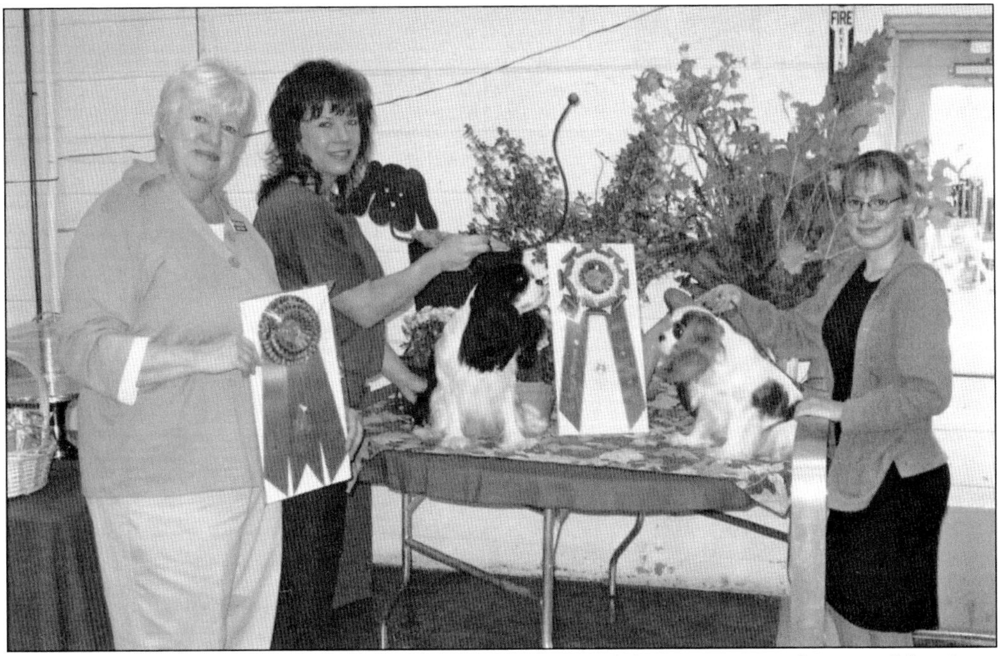

A member of the American Kennel Club, the Del Valle Dog Club participates at the annual dog show. Pictured above, from left to right, are Sandy Olsen, Carla Mathis, and Robyn Christensen.

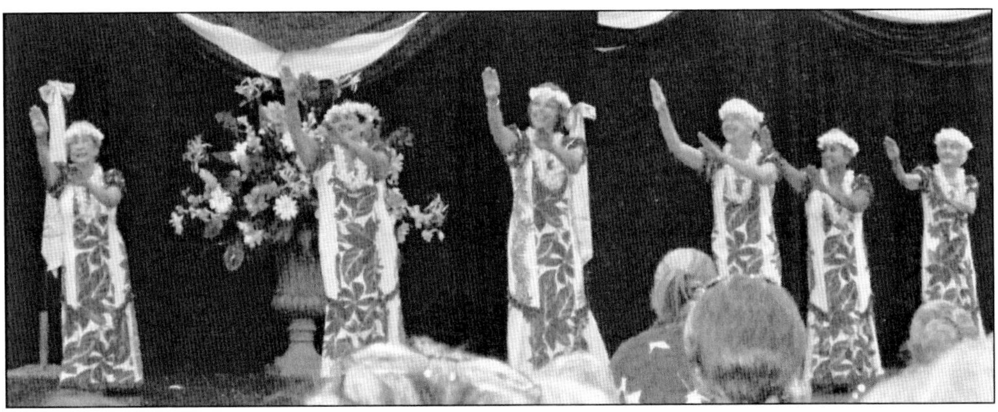

The La 'Oe E Ka La Hula Festival, hosted by the Kumu Hula Association of Northern California, is one of the largest Hawaiian festivals in the state. The gathering includes several competing hula dance groups, music, shopping, and food. The group annually holds two festivals a year, one in May and one in November.

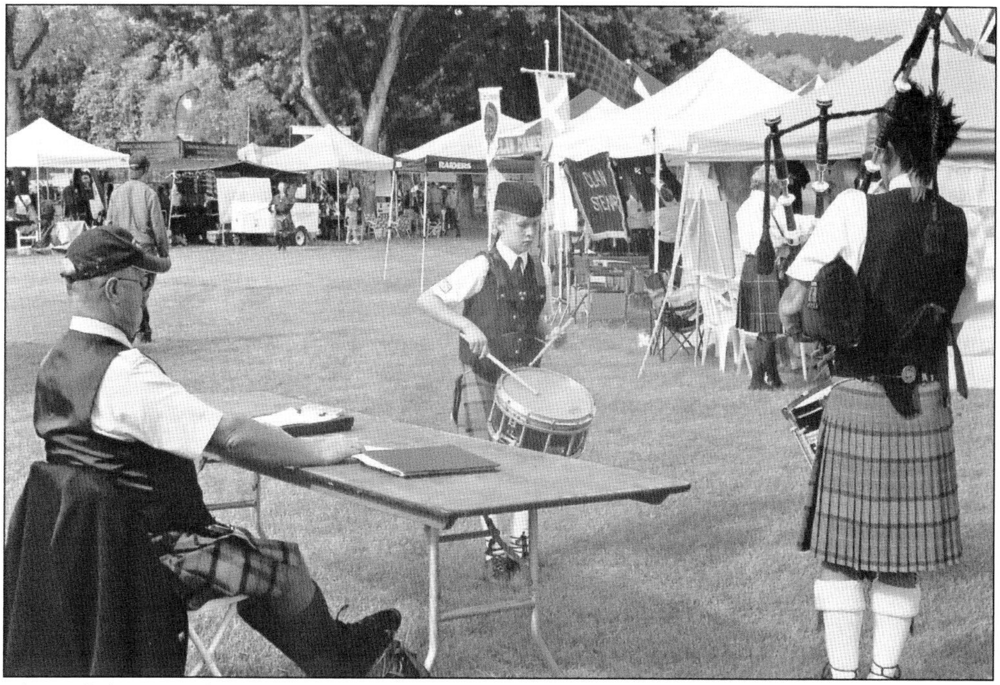

The Caledonian Club of San Francisco annually presents the Scottish Gathering and Games. Traditionally held over the Labor Day weekend, this event is the largest and oldest Scottish event in America. Formed in 1866 and previously held in Santa Rosa, the games have been held at the Alameda County Fairgrounds since 1994.

The Scottish Festival includes bagpipe competitions, the Western US Highland Dancing Championship, Scottish country dancers, folk music, Celtic rock musicians, birds of prey, living history, Scottish fiddlers, a Five-a-Side Soccer Tournament, a clan tent area, a children's glen, and men's and women's athletic world heavyweight events, culminating with the world championship. In the photograph at right, Mayor Jennifer Hosterman of Pleasanton demonstrates her hobby of falconry.

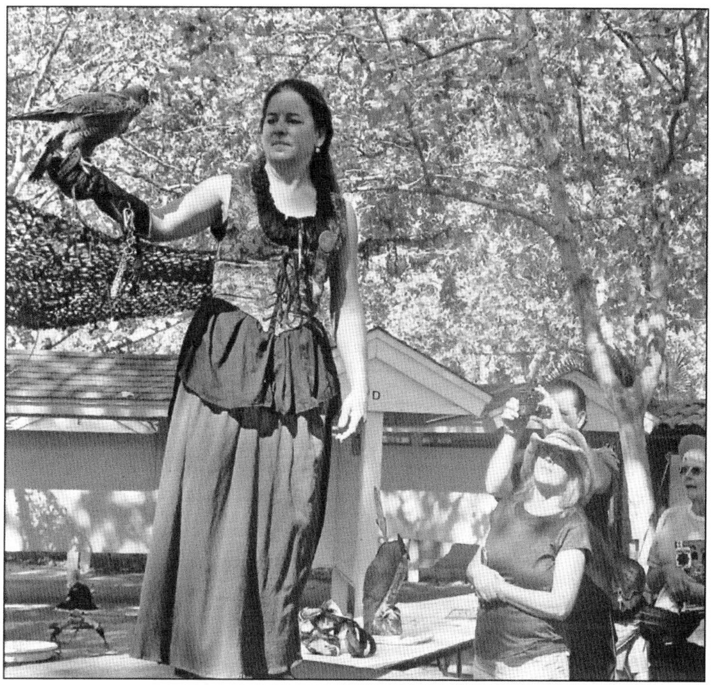

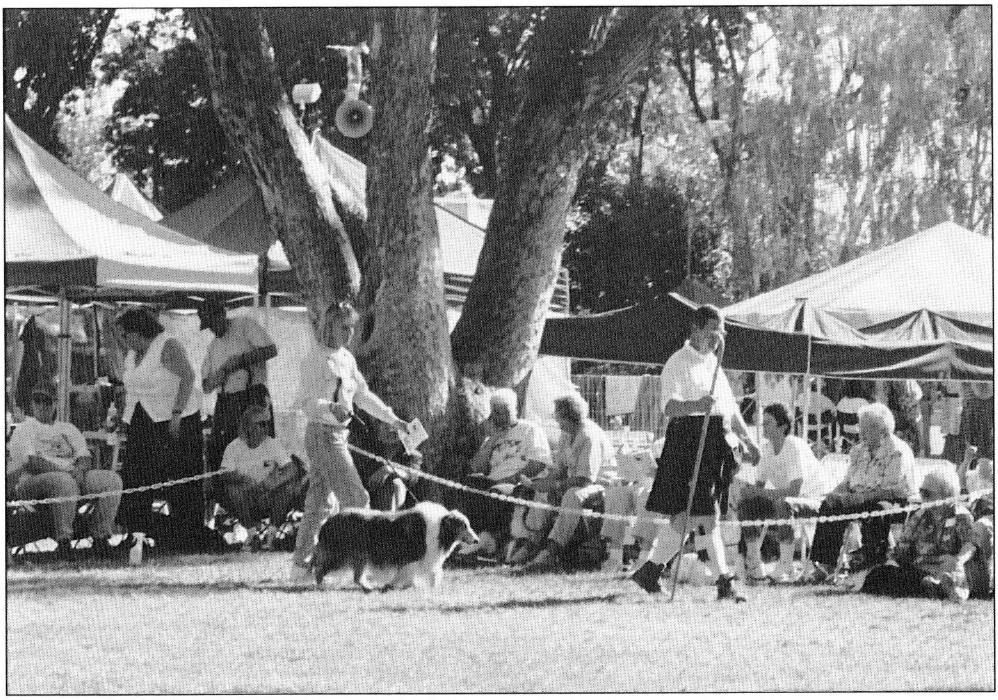

Other festival activities include a March Under the Arch, which is a Main Street parade featuring Scottish bagpipers and bands; a Friday night concert; a ballroom dance; and an appearance by the US Marine Corps band. Closing ceremonies include a massed bands show featuring hundreds of bagpipers in front of the grandstand. Also included is a living history area where groups participate in honoring their Scottish heritage. Pictured below is Richard Brown and members of the Highland Warriors, who reenact battle scenes in the living history area of the Scottish Games. (Above, courtesy of Marge Armosino; below, courtesy of Highland Warriors.)

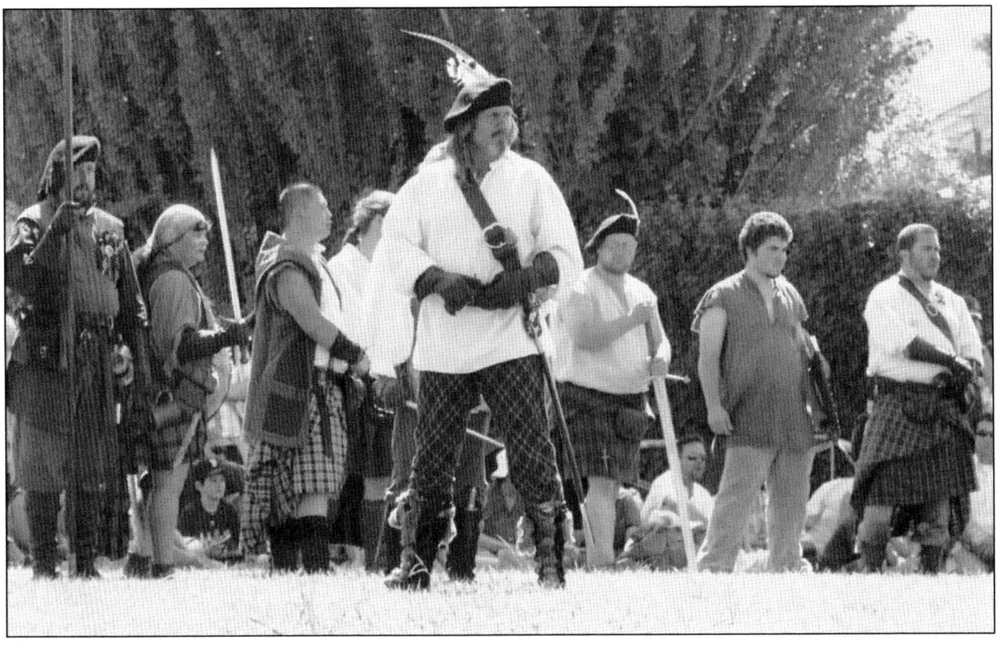

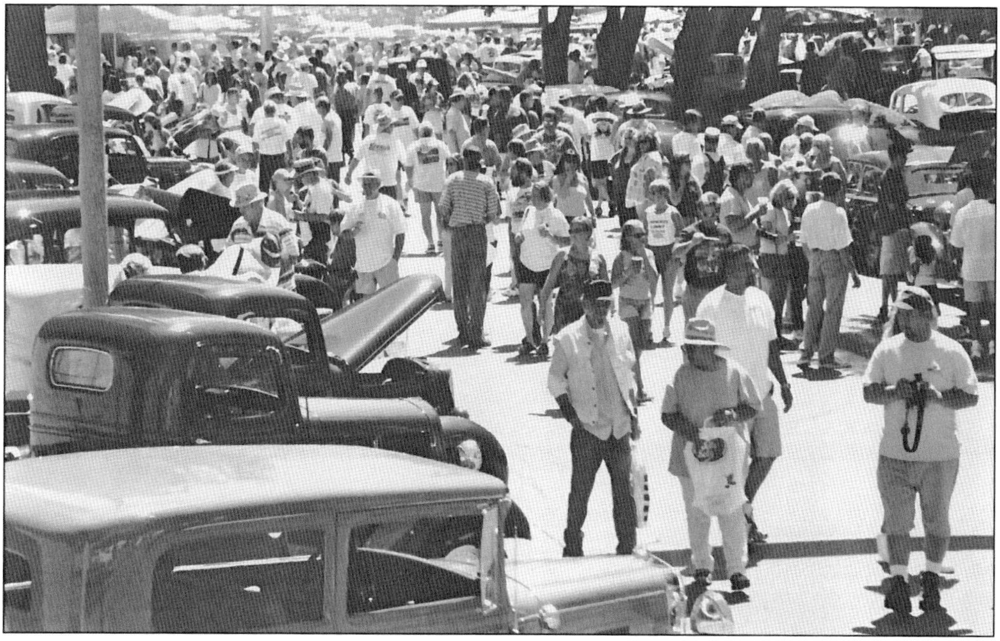

Held for more than 20 years at the fairgrounds, the Good Guys Rod & Custom Association's annual West Coast Nationals features more than 3,000 custom hot rods and custom cars. The event attracts car buffs from all over the state and beyond and offers memorabilia, a car auction, classic cars, unusual cars, a swap meet, and retail vendors.

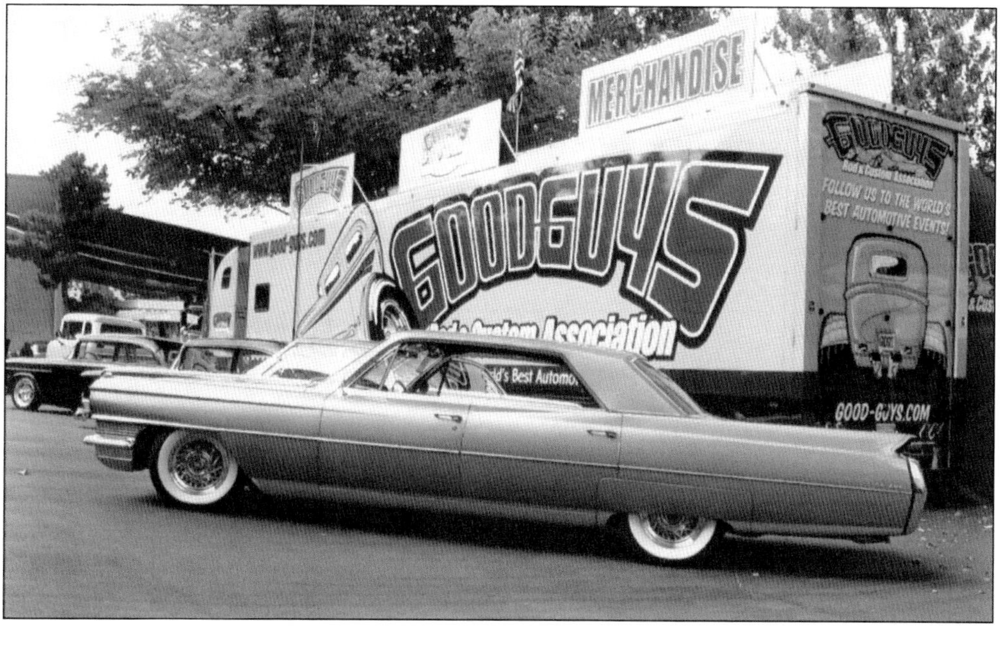

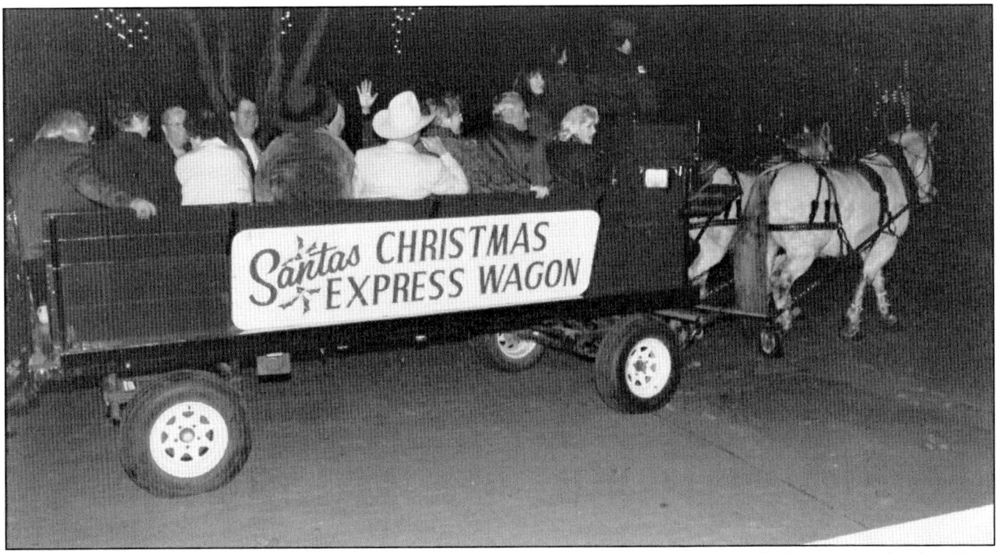

First called the Winter Fair in 1998, it eventually became known as the Holiday Festival of Lights. The 2.5-mile route through a display of Christmas lights around the fairgrounds featured two million lights and drew 16,000 cars during a 45-day period. The event was only held one more year, in 2000.

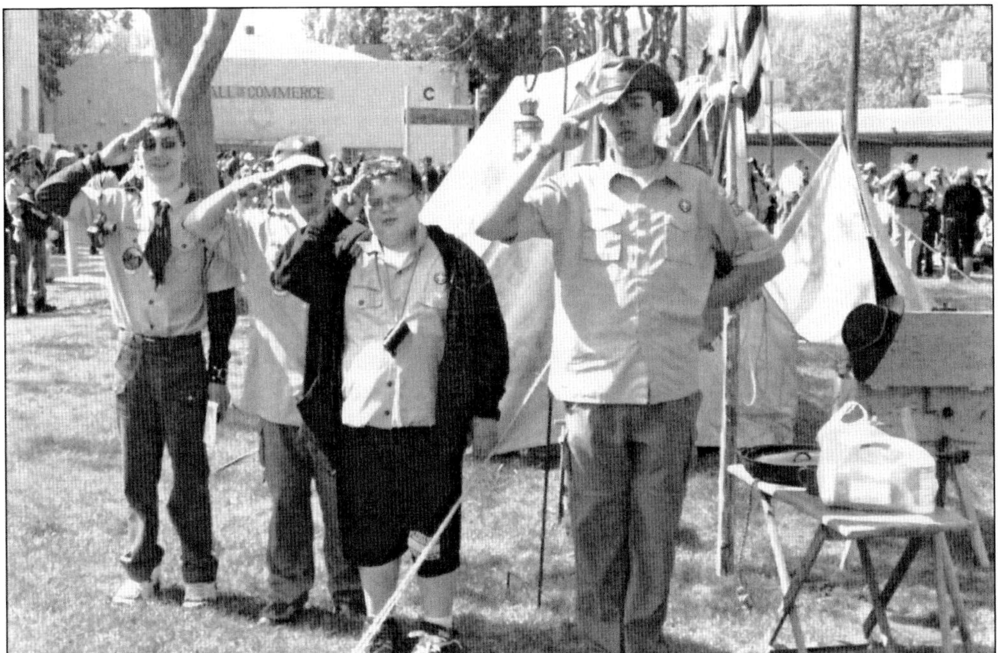

The Boy Scouts celebrated their 100th Anniversary Jamboree at the fair April 16 through April 18, 2010. Attended by more than 20,000 Scouts, the event included science exhibits, astronomy, campfires, movies, rock climbing, team building, and music.

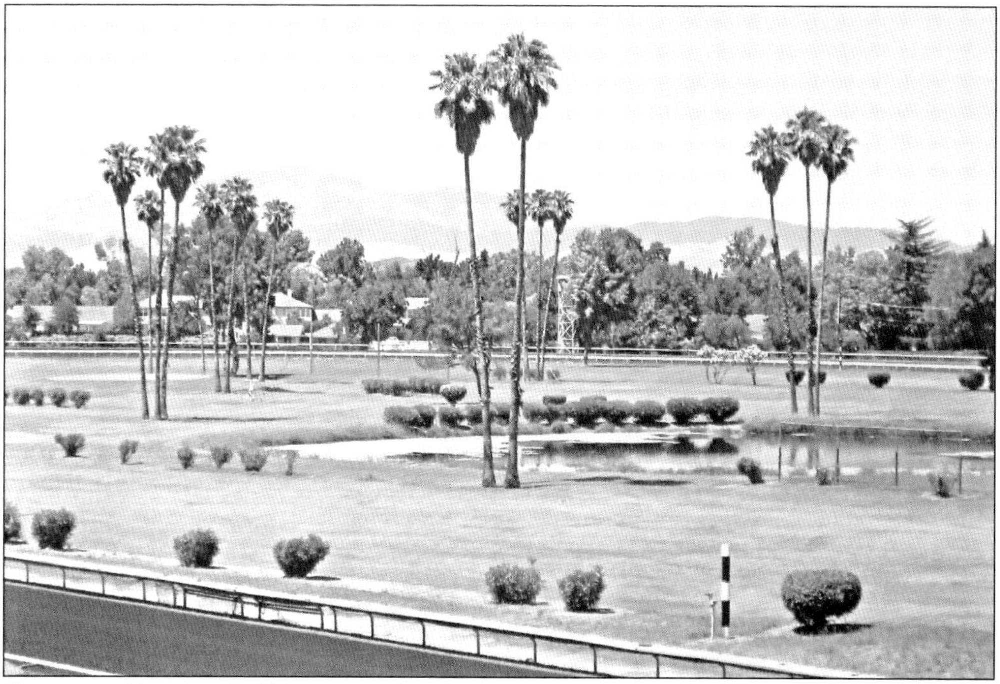

Pleasanton Fairways Golf Course and Golf Center replaced the inner racetrack in 1974. The nine-hole golf course has a par-30 course.

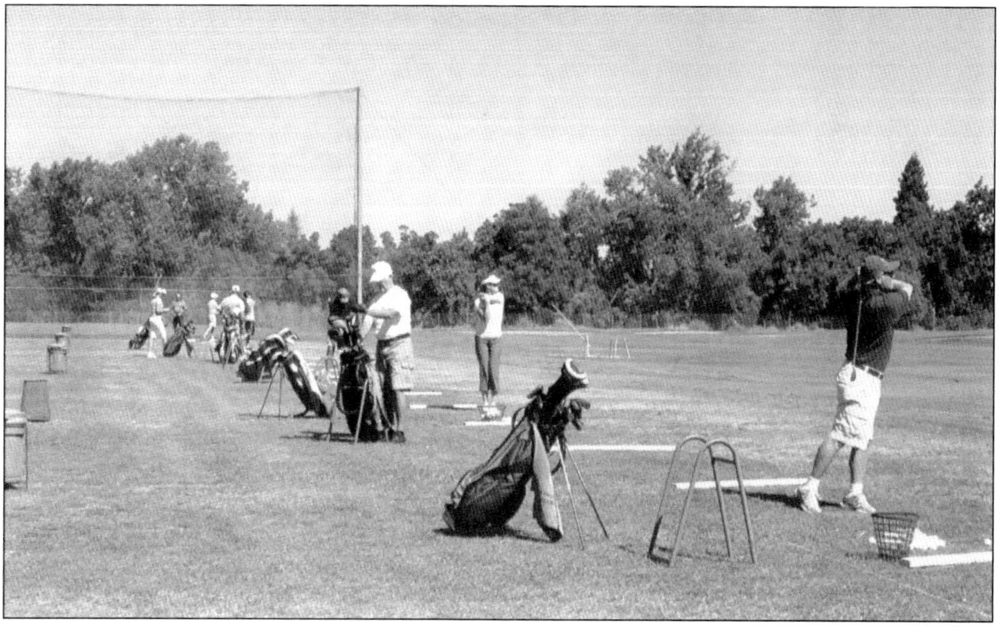

In 1989, Northern California's largest golf driving range opened in the far northwest area of the fairgrounds. Covering nearly 16 acres, the Pleasanton Driving Range also includes a pro shop and a youth golfing program.

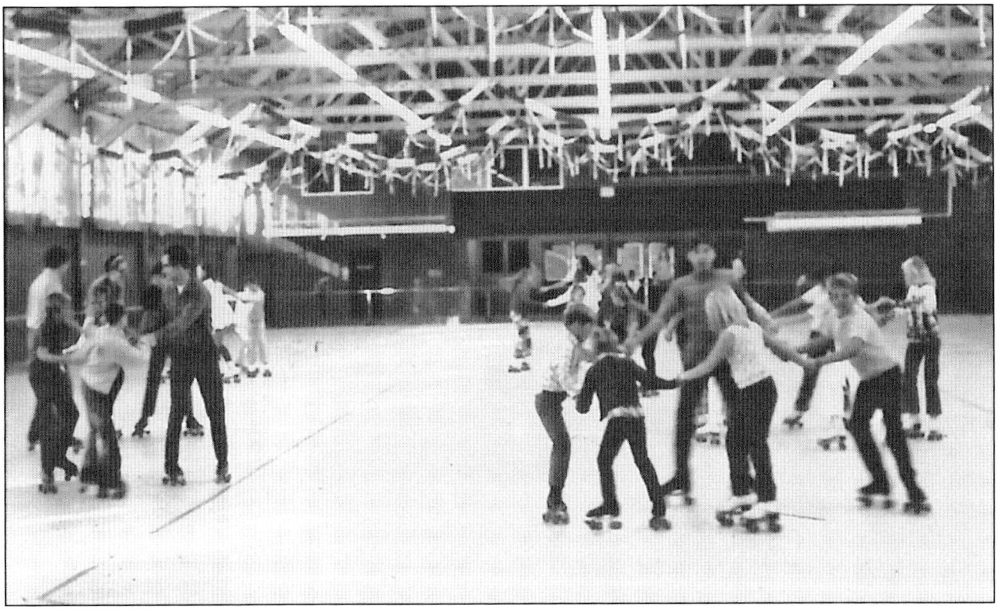

Held in the 12,000-square-foot Hall of Commerce Building during the fair's off-season, Roller Faire was a popular spot for the area's kids and teens for a few years in the late 1960s and early 1970s. The facility also offered concessions, lockers, and skate rentals.

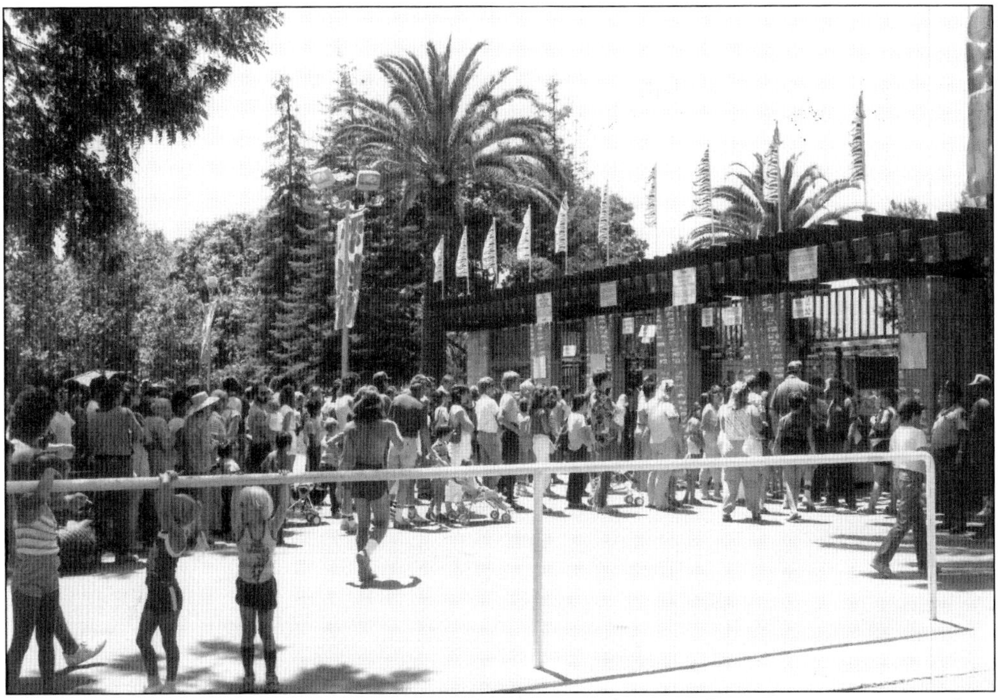

In 2010, the fair continues to provide the perfect location for several community events such as the East Bay Stand Down, high school graduations, youth science fairs, 4-H guide dog training, police dog and motor officer training, ethnic celebrations, an Iraqi national elections polling site, religious events, and organized labor events. There are several picnic and barbecue areas available to rent for family reunions, birthday parties, and other celebrations.

Eight

FUTURE OF THE FAIR

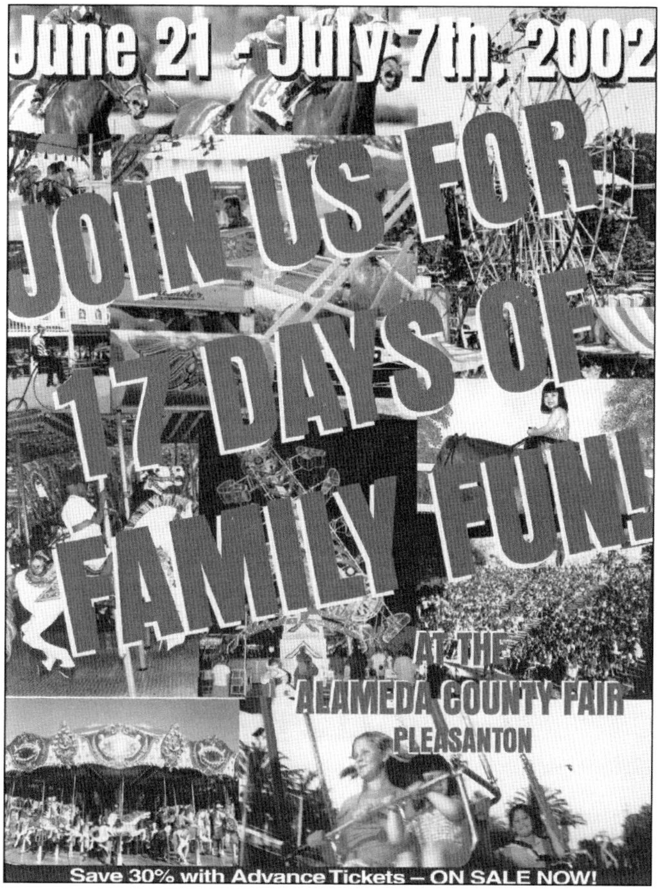

The fair's 90th anniversary celebration in 2002 included a ribbon-cutting ceremony and a parade featuring 90 Livermore Harley-Davidson Association motorcycle riders, including Livermore mayor Marshall Kamena and Superior Court judge Hugh Walker, who led the annual parade on June 22, 2002. The parade also featured Joe Morgan, a Baseball Hall of Fame inductee, as grand marshal. Celebrities included actors Max Gail of *Barney Miller*, Dorothy DeBorba Habereitter of *Little Rascals*, Sonja Christopher of *Survivor*, and Yvonne Bassard and the Books family of *Frontier House*. Ten former Alameda County Fair Maids also attended the festivities, including Elvamae Borghi of Union City, the first Alameda County Fair Queen from 1937. A quilt from the first fair of 1912 was on display as well.

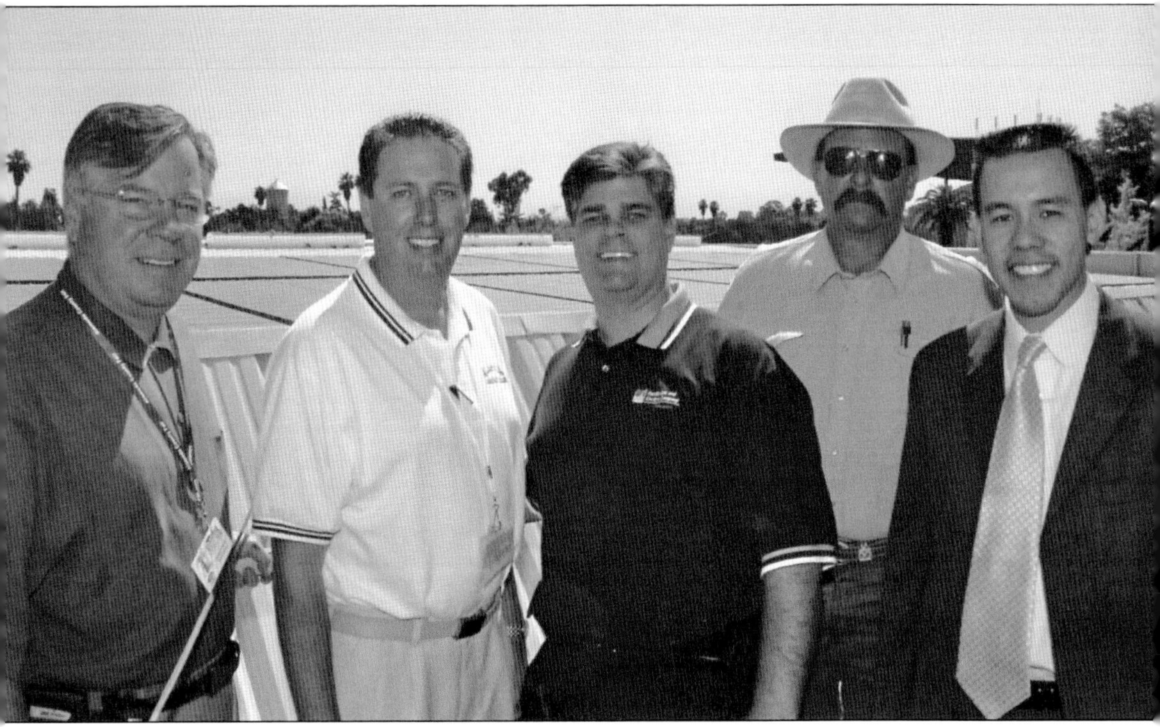

In an era when being green is important to every organization, the fair is doing its part by installing solar panels. In June 2003, roughly 20,000 square feet of solar panels were installed on the tops of 16 horse stables and three buildings, including the massive Amador Pavilion. At a cost of $5.3 million, the panels, which will produce $240,000 worth of electricity every year, have a 50-year life expectancy. The panels contain photovoltaic cells that convert sunlight to electricity. Any electricity produced by the solar panels that is not used by the fair will go back into the power grid, and the fair will be credited. The fair is recognized for being the largest nonprofit organization in the country to generate more than 1,250 megawatts of solar energy per year. Pictured are, from left to right, Alameda County supervisor Scott Haggerty, fair chief executive officer Rick Pickering, PG&E representative Gordon Galvan, former Alameda County Fair board member president Tim Koopman, and Bruce Lim of the California State Division of Fairs and Expositions.

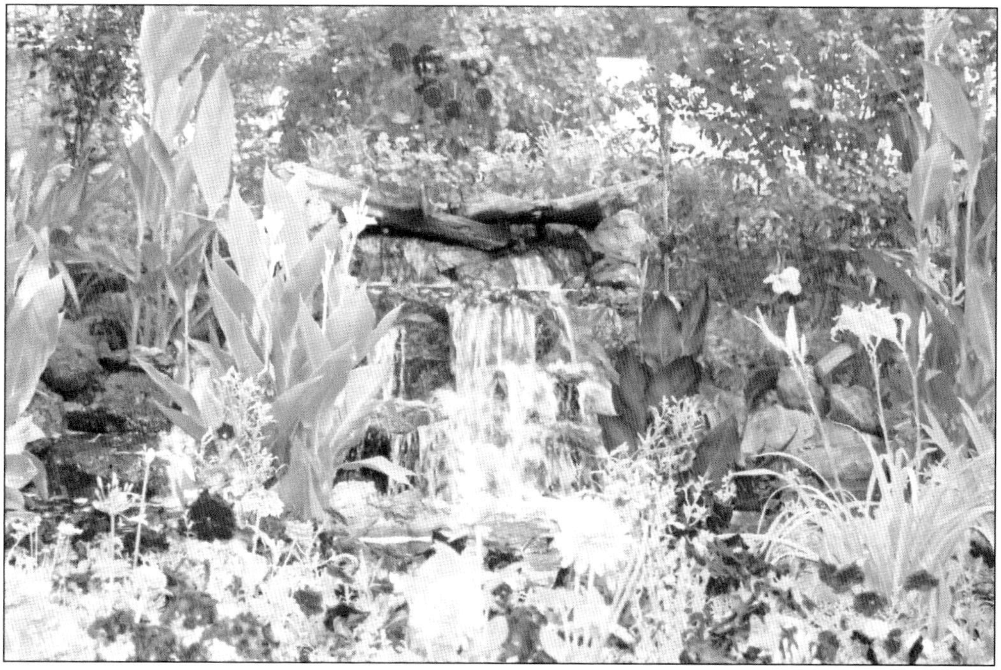

For several years, the Monterey Mushrooms farm has been the lucky daily recipient of two semi-trucks of horse manure from the fair. In 2007, the fair received a $20,000 Educational Advisory Board grant that helped to launch its zero-waste recycling program, and in 2008, it began the EAB DR3 (divert, reuse, recycle, reduce) program. In 2010, the fair was certified by the state as a recycling center, making it eligible to receive California state refund monies.

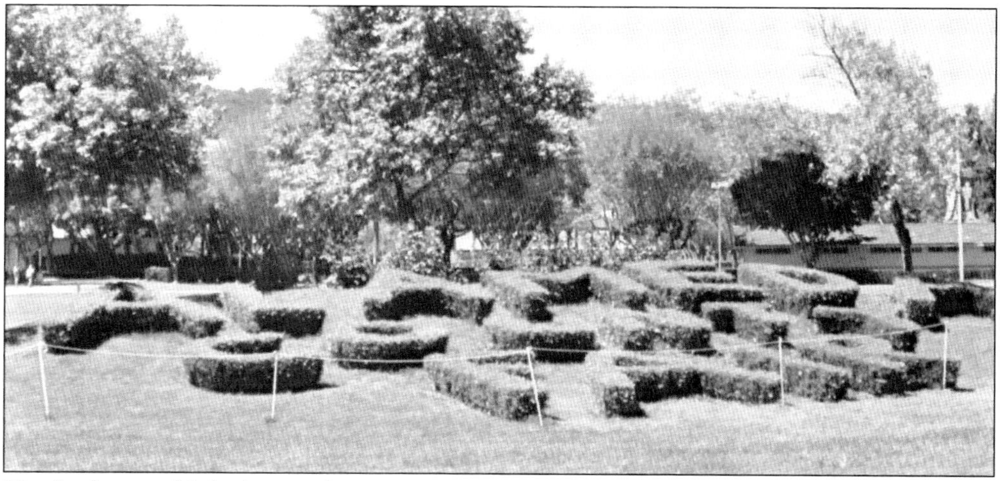

The fair has established a recycling program to conserve and reduce cost. Having approximately 2,000 trees on the its property and 30 acres of manicured lawns, flowers, and shrubs makes for a large amount of compost material. Developed in 2000, the fair's cardboard recycling program allowed for a large trash compactor to be installed. By 2005, more than 61 tons of cardboard were recycled. The fair also uses recycled asphalt chips to line dirt roadways and parking lots. That year, more than 2,500 tons of recycled asphalt chips were donated to the fair by various local agencies.

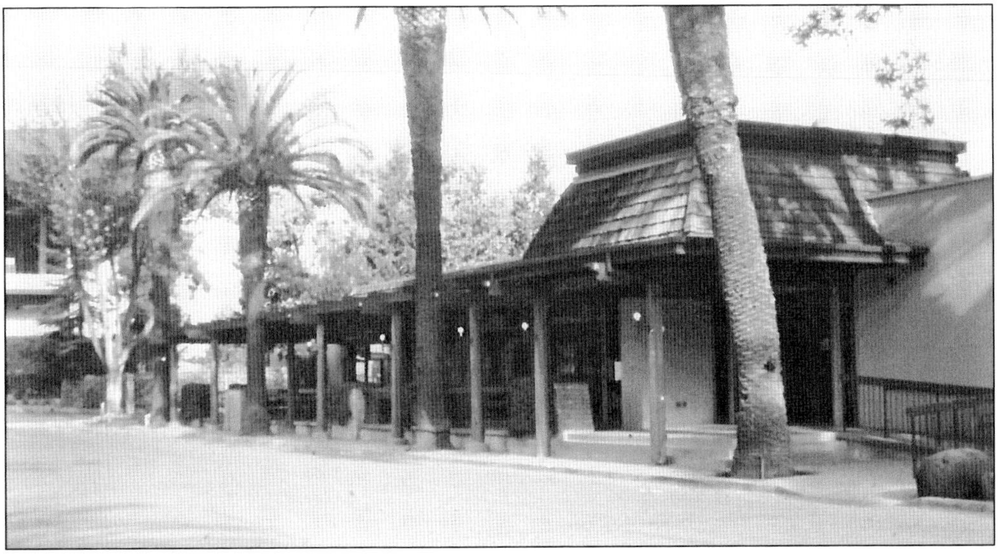

Seen above when it was called "the cafeteria," the building recently received a major renovation into a completely new, modern structure with updated floors, windows, doors, and furniture. Now called the Palm Pavilion, the facility (below) is available to rent for a variety of uses during the fair's off-season, such as business meetings, birthday celebrations, and other events.

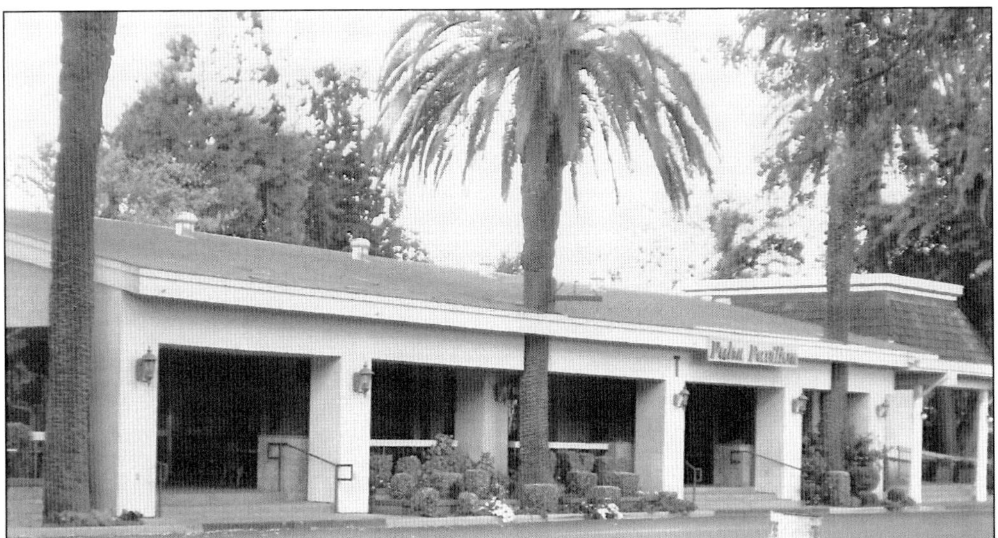

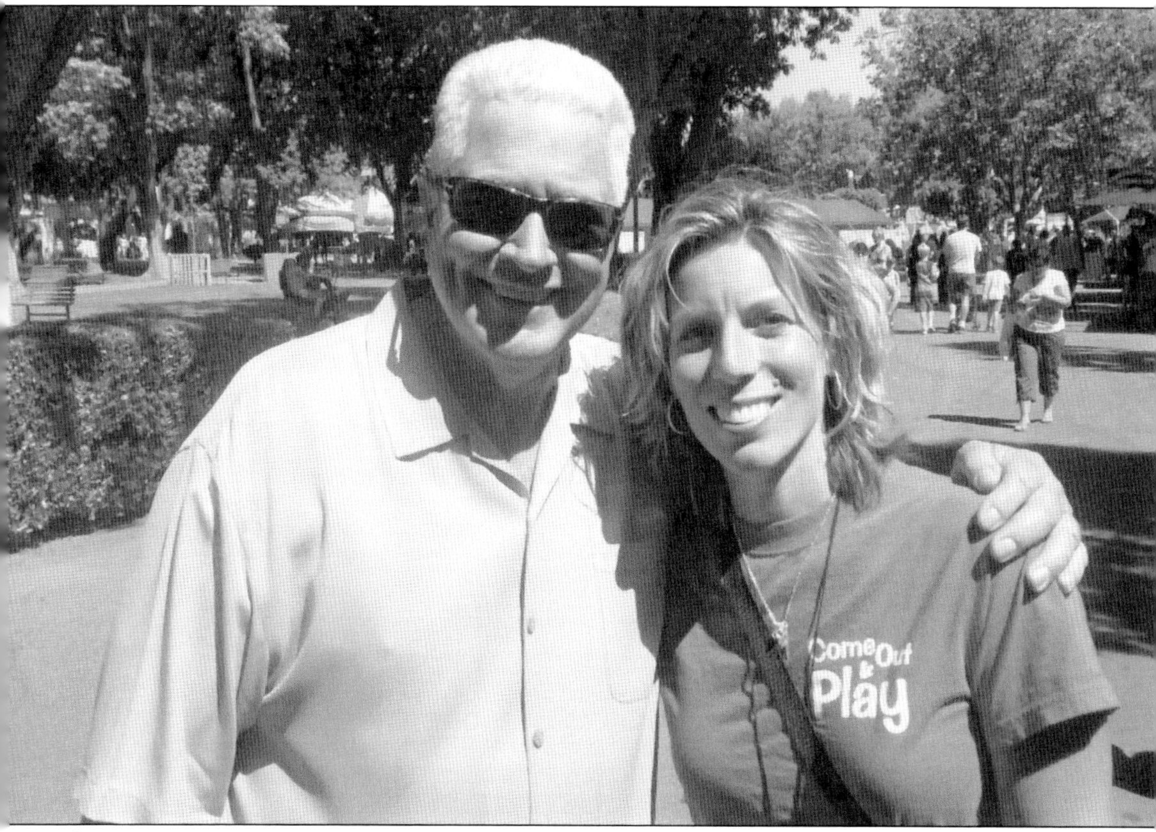

The 2009 fair generated the highest revenue in history. It hosted 434,919 patrons over its 17-day run, and July 3 had a one-day total of approximately 50,000 guests. Pictured above are Huell Howser, television personality and host of the travel show *California's Gold*, and April Mitchell, the fair's marketing manager.

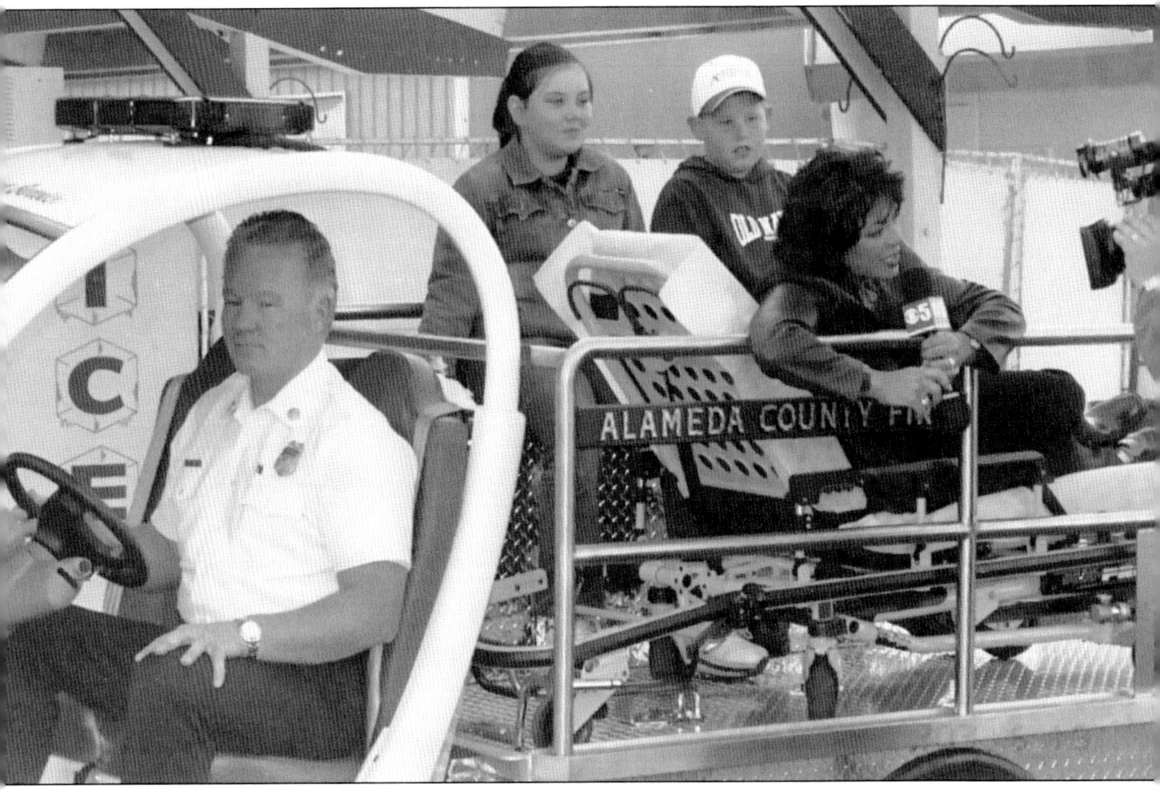

KPIX-TV weather reporter Roberta Gonzales regularly reports from the fair during her early morning segment. The fair is featured often on local San Francisco Bay Area television stations. Pictured from left to right are Rich Brown of the Alameda County Fire Department, Jessica Christian, Josh Pickering, and Gonzales.

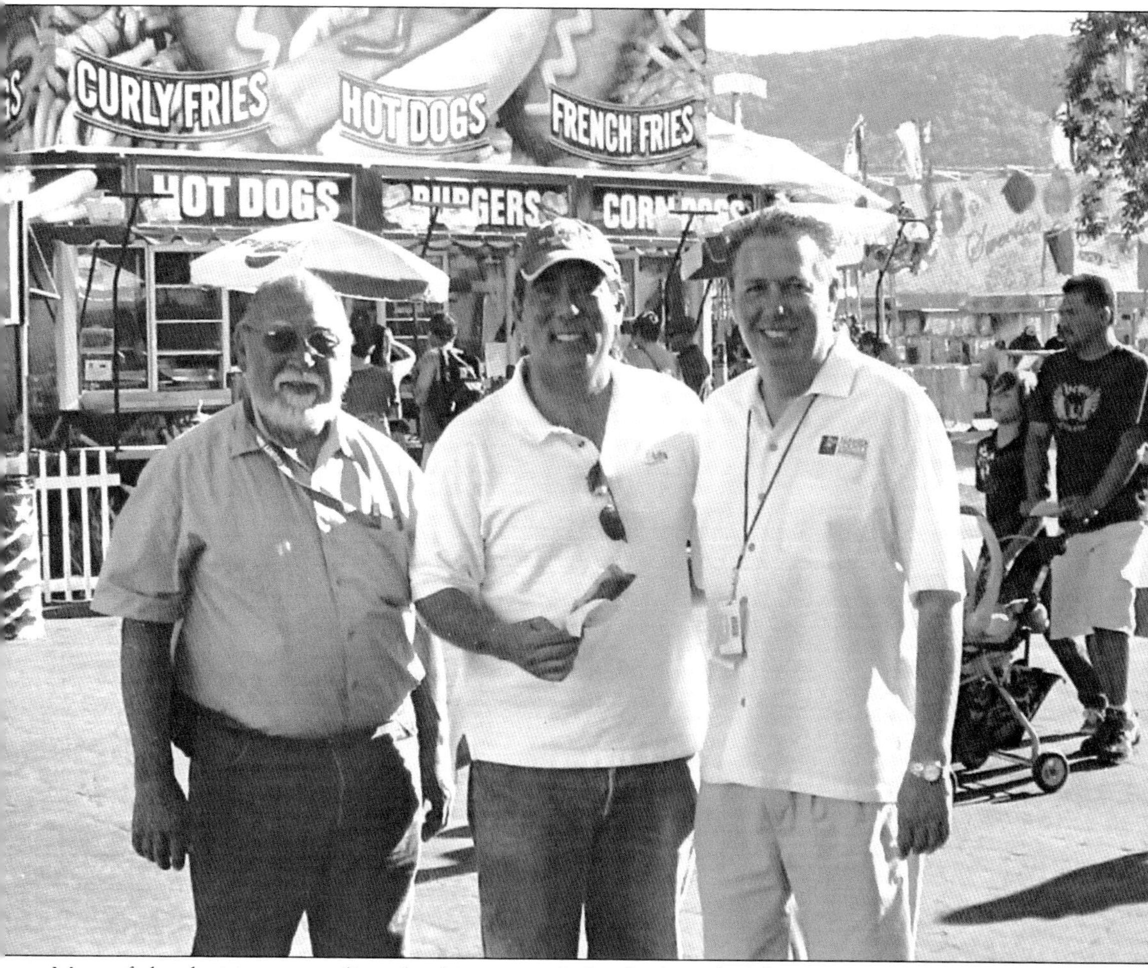

Most of the decisions regarding the fair are made by the board of directors. At one time, the fair board had 82 directors, then it was reduced to 21 in 1963. In 1972, it was decided that an additional five directors be appointed by the Alameda County supervisors for a total of 26. The 2009–2010 Alameda County Fair Board members are Pres. Anthony Pegram, Vice President Patrick O'Brien, Lil Arnerich, Sherman Balch, Paul Banke, Connie Campbell, Jason Chin, Gordon Galvan, Patsy Gilbert, Frank Imhof, Patricia Ising, Jack Kavanagh, Jim Knudsen, Janet Lockhart, Tony Macchiano, Bill McCammon, Charlie Plummer, Pete Ruggeri, Bonnie Sabraw, Dean Schenone, Arthur Scott, Richard Sealana, Harvey Smith, Anthony Varni, Naomi Wallace, and Ario Ysit. Pictured above are, from left to right, director Ario Ysit; California Department of Food and Agriculture secretary A.G. Kawamura; and fair chief executive officer Rick Pickering. (Courtesy of Jeffrey Ysit Jr.)

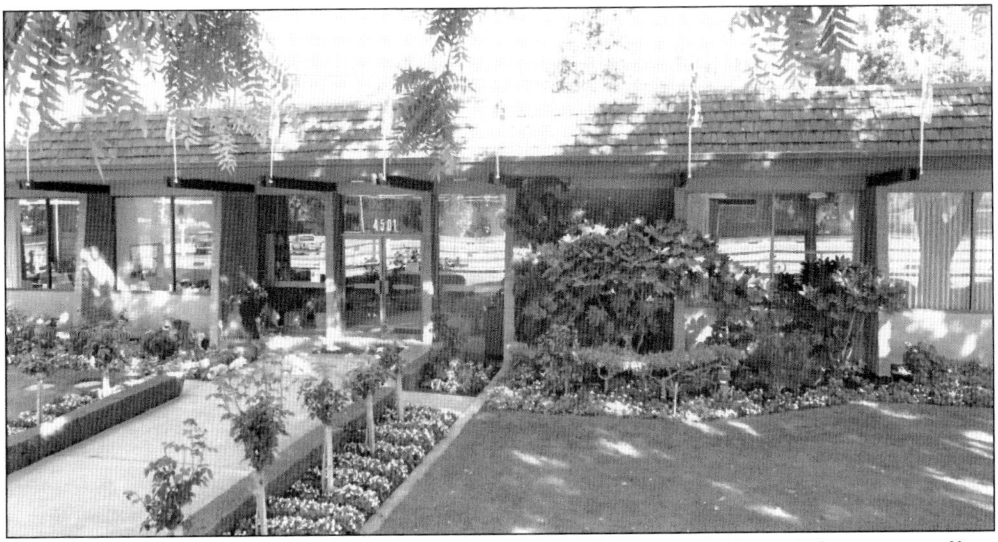

The fair's administrative office was previously located in the Heritage House. The current office, built in 1967, is a hub of activity on a daily basis where staff and board members make all sorts of important decisions regarding the fairgrounds.

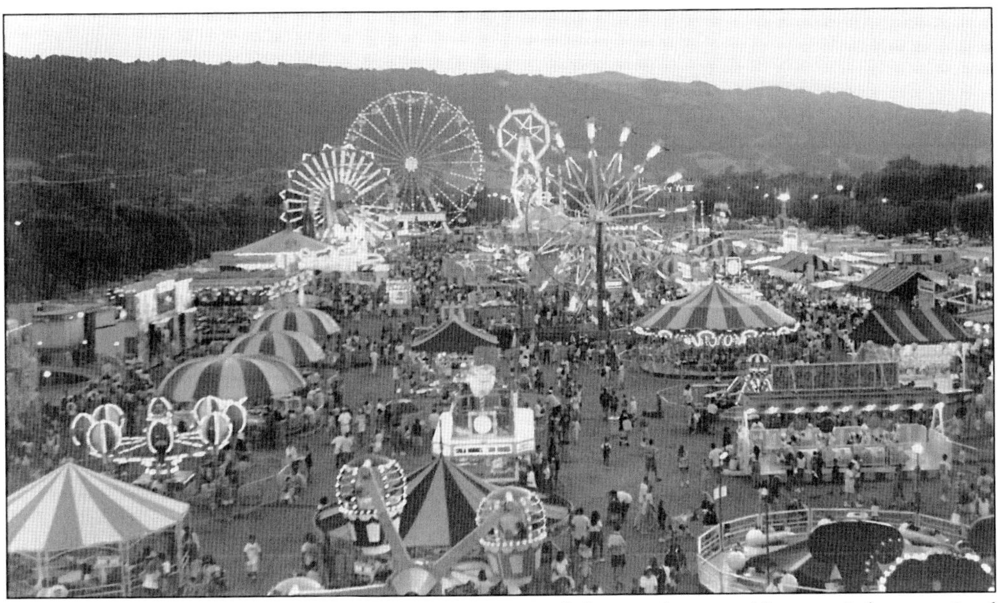

The fair belongs to the Western Fair Association, and during the past 10 years, it has received more awards than any other fair in the United States and Canada. At the 2009 WFA Conference, the fair won 23 first-place awards for its Community Outreach Program, Emergency Preparation, Conservation Program, Customer Service Training Program, and Children's Programs. The fair continues to be recognized as one of the top 50 fairs in North America.

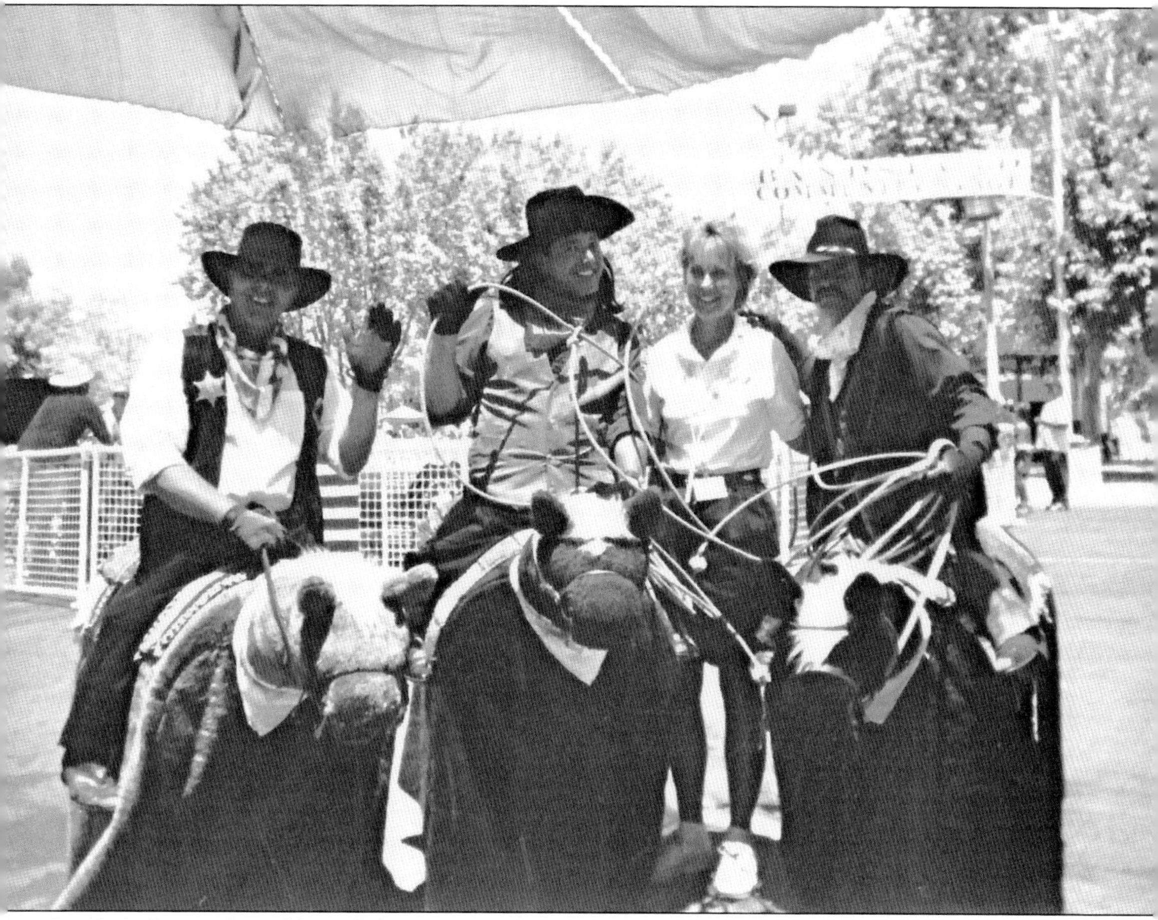

In 2010, the number of fair exhibits rose to 16,185. At the time of publication, there are 76 county fairs in California, and they all provide a positive economic impact on their communities. Pictured above are the Doo-Wah Riders Comedy Act and fair employee Bonnie Bruton.

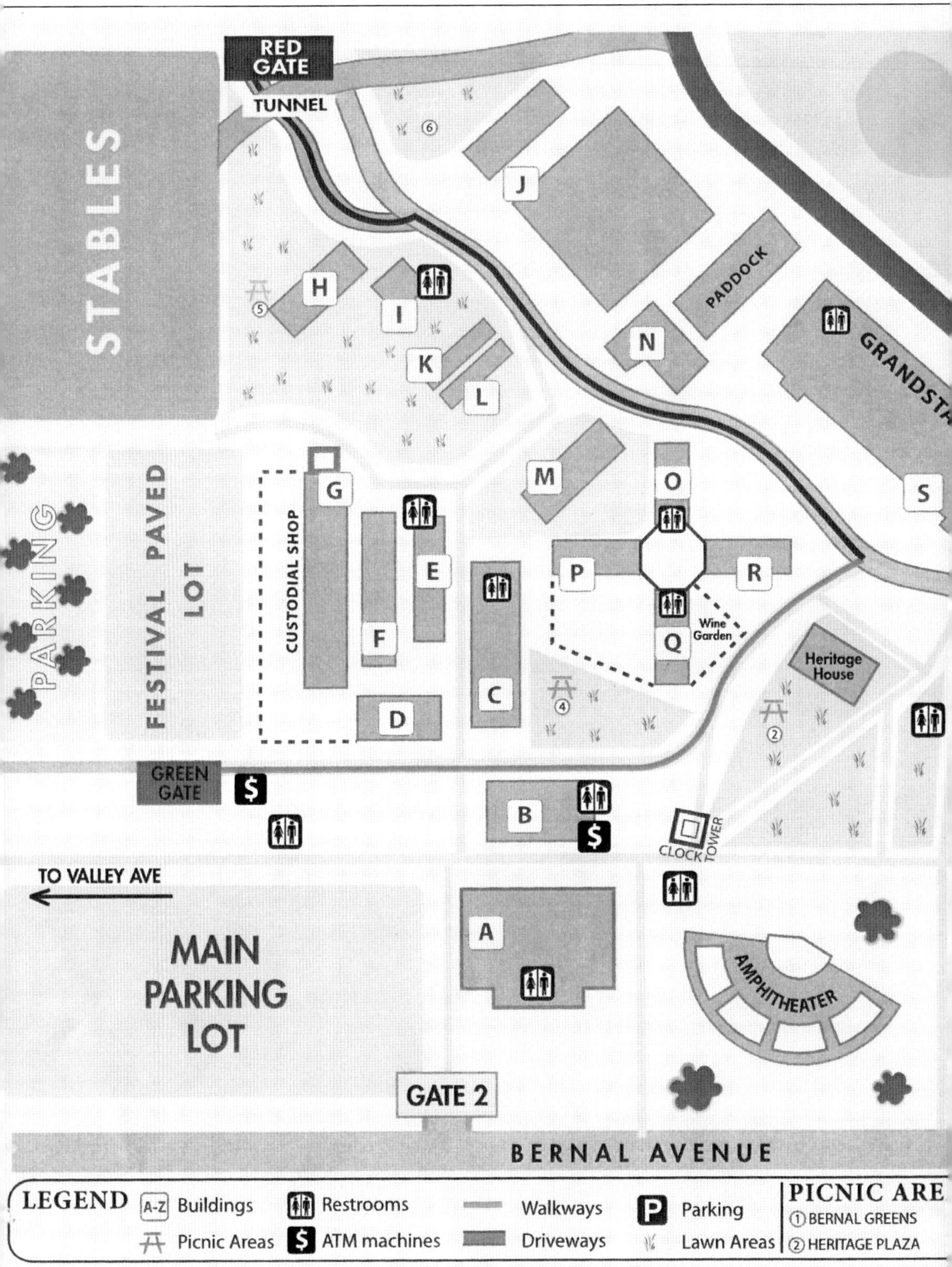
RED GATE
TUNNEL
STABLES
J
PADDOCK
H
I
K
L
N
GRANDSTA
PARKING
FESTIVAL PAVED LOT
CUSTODIAL SHOP
G
M
O
S
E
P
R
F
Wine Garden
Q
Heritage House
C
D
GREEN GATE
B
CLOCK TOWER
TO VALLEY AVE
MAIN PARKING LOT
A
AMPHITHEATER
GATE 2
BERNAL AVENUE
LEGEND
A-Z Buildings
Restrooms
Walkways
Parking
Picnic Areas
ATM machines
Driveways
Lawn Areas
PICNIC ARE
① BERNAL GREENS
② HERITAGE PLAZA

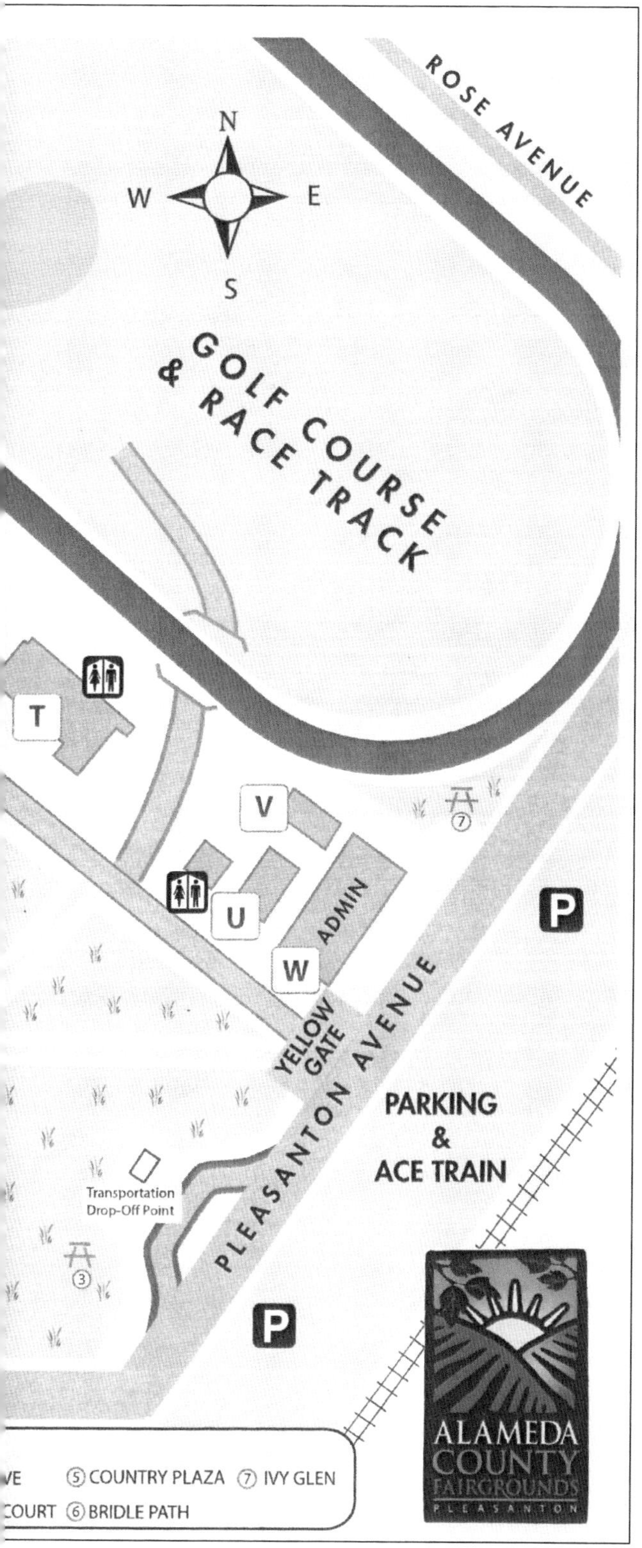

This map represents the layout of the fair in 2010. Building A is the Young California Building; B is the Main Exhibit Hall; C is an exhibit hall; D is the Science and Technology Exhibit; E is the Small Animal Exhibit; F is the Model Railroad Exhibit; G is the Antique Farm Equipment Exhibit; J is the Amador Pavilion and Livestock Exhibit; K and L is the Country Market; M is the security building; O is the Minerals, Gems, and Hobbies Exhibit; P is the Agriculture Exhibit; Q is the Floriculture and Wine Exhibit; R is the Commercial Shopping Building; S is the Racetrack Grandstand; T is the Palm Pavilion; and U, V, and W are administrative offices. The carnival is in the main parking lot. The lawn area adjacent to the amphitheater is where the children's rides are located.

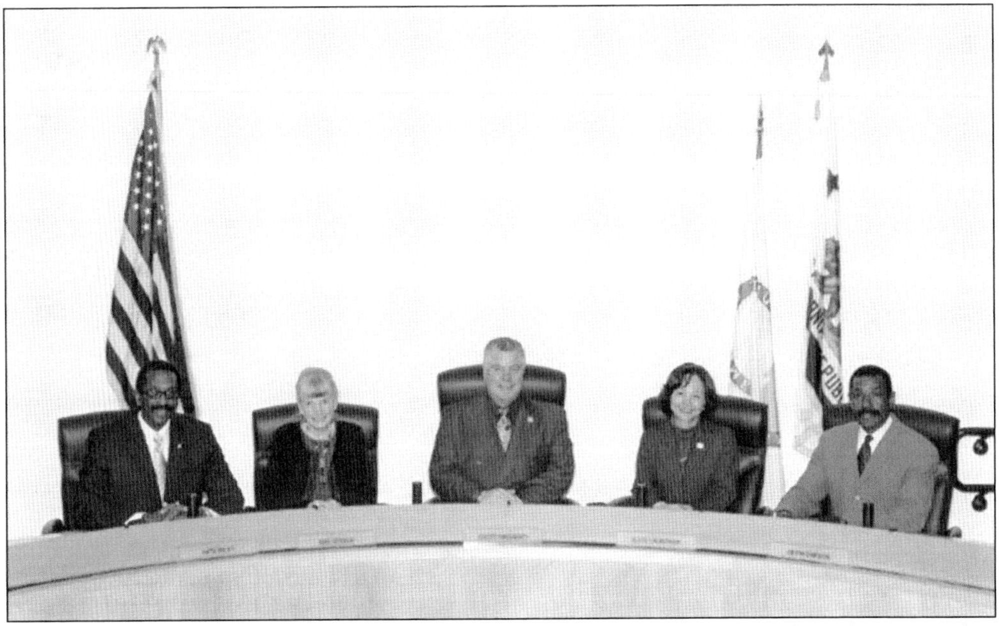

According to a 1910 census, there were approximately 250,000 residents in Alameda County that year. The US Census Bureau reported in 2009 there are nearly 1.5 million residents in the county, making Alameda the third largest county in California. Pictured above are the 2010 Alameda County supervisors. They are, from left to right, Keith Carson (District 5), Gail Steele (District 2), Scott Haggerty (District 1), Alice Lai-Bitker (District 3), and Nate Miley (District 4). Pictured below are Alameda County's newly elected 2011 county supervisors, Wilma Chan (left, District 3) and Nadia Lockyer (District 2). (Both courtesy of Alameda County Supervisor's Office.)

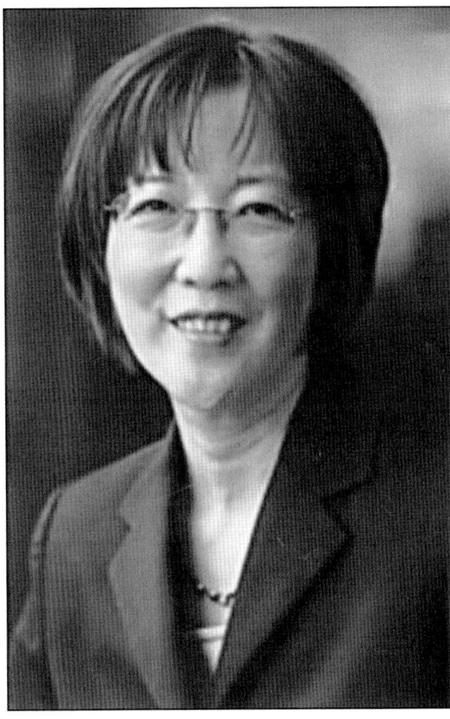

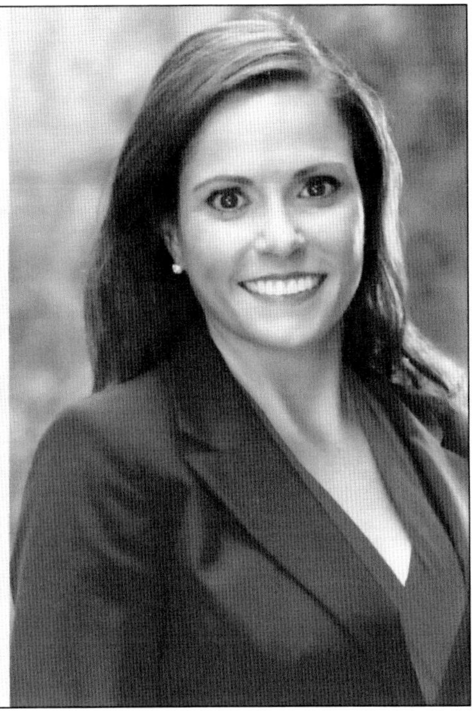

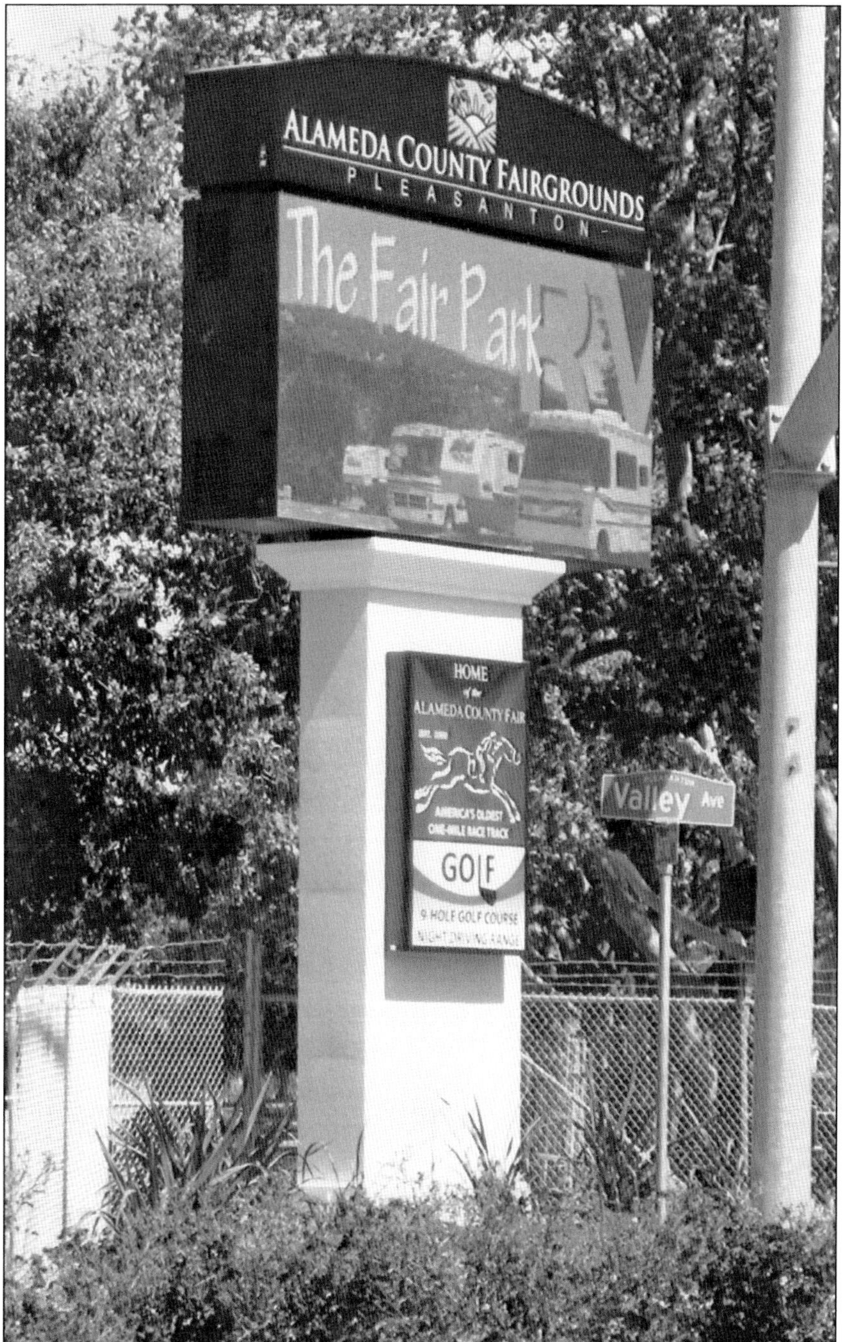

The new electronic sign at the southeast corner of the fair greets guests as they make their way to the Alameda County Fair. When it ran from June 23 through July 9, 2010, it was the second time the fair offered 16 days of horse racing. This time also marked a record second-highest attendance in 20 years with 418,000 fair guests. The fair, which is the single largest event in Alameda County, has also been named the "Fastest Growing Fair in America" due to its record attendance numbers over the past few years.

Find Your Place in History.

www.arcadiapublishing.com

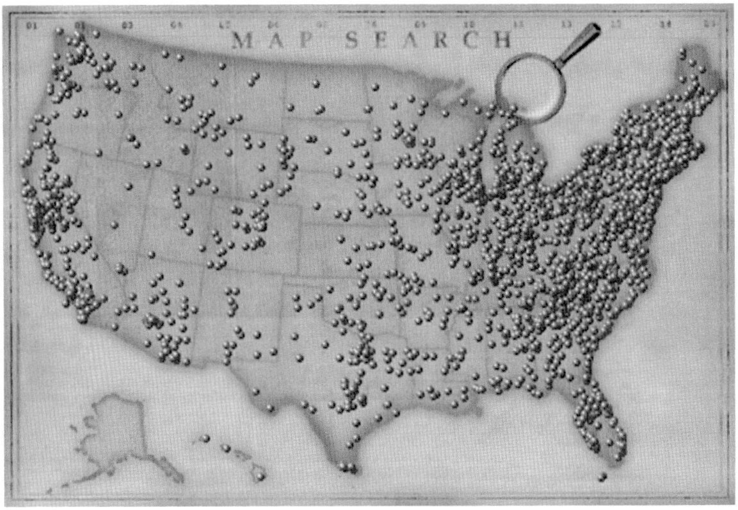

Discover books about the town where you grew up, the cities where your friends and families live, the town where your parents met, or even that retirement spot you've been dreaming about. Our Web site provides history lovers with exclusive deals, advanced notification about new titles, e-mail alerts of author events, and much more.

MADE IN THE USA

Arcadia Publishing, the leading local history publisher in the United States, is committed to making history accessible and meaningful through publishing books that celebrate and preserve the heritage of America's people and places. Consistent with our mission to preserve history on a local level, this book was printed in South Carolina on American-made paper and manufactured entirely in the United States.

This book carries the accredited Forest Stewardship Council (FSC) label and is printed on 100 percent FSC-certified paper. Products carrying the FSC label are independently certified to assure consumers that they come from forests that are managed to meet the social, economic, and ecological needs of present and future generations.

FSC
Mixed Sources
Product group from well-managed forests and other controlled sources

Cert no. SW-COC-001530
www.fsc.org